W9-BDG-183

TUSCANY & UMBRIA'S BEST-LOVED DRIVING TOURS

Wiley Publishing, Inc.

Touring Club Italiano
Chairman: Roberto Ruozi
Touring Editore
Managing director: Armando Peres
General manager: Marco Ausenda
Assistant general manager: Renato Salvetti
Editorial director: Michele D'Innella
Head of guidebooks: Anna Ferrari-Bravo
Editing: Cinzia Rando
Editorial production and layout: Studio editoriale Selmi
Written by: Stefano Baldi
Translated by: Barbara Fisher
Picture research : Rossella Barresi
Cover: *Federica Neeff* con *Mara Rold*
Maps: Graffito-Cusano Milanino
Revised maps: Sergio Seveso

Revised second edition published 2004
First published 2002

© 2002, 2004 Touring Editore
Management and editorial offices: Corso Italia 10, Milano

© Concept and design The Automobile Association Developments Limited

This Best Drives guidebook was produced by Touring Club Italiano in agreement with The Automobile Association Developments Limited, owner of the 'Best Drives' series

© English translation: The Automobile Association Developments Limited 2002, 2004

Published by AA Publishing

Published in the United States by
John Wiley & Sons, Inc.
111 River Street, Hoboken, NJ 07030

Find us online at Frommers.com

ISBN 0-7645-4329-6
ISSN 1536-9005

Photolitho and photocomposition: Emmegi Multimedia, Milan
Printed and bound by : G. Canale & C. S.p.a., Torino, Italy

A01744

CONTENTS

ABOUT THIS BOOK

This book is not only a practical touring guide for the independent traveller, but is also invaluable for those who would like to know more about Tuscany and Umbria.

It is divided into 5 geographical regions, with town visits and itineraries included for each one. Specific city tours are featured for Lucca, Florence, Siena and Perugia.

Each tour has details of the most interesting places to visit en route. Boxes catering for special interests follow some of the main entries – for those whose interest is in history or walking or those who have children. There are also boxes which highlight scenic stretches of road and which give details of the natural environment, local traditions and gastronomy. Special features cover the Tuscan islands and coastline, oil and wine, spas and places associated with St Francis.

The simple route directions are accompanied by an easy-to-use map at the beginning of each tour, along with a chart showing how far it is from one town to the next in kilometres and miles. This can help you decide where to take a break and stop overnight. (All distances quoted are approximate.) Before setting off it is advisable to check with the information centre listed at the start of the tour for recommendations on where to break your journey, and for additional information on what to see and do, and when best to visit.

Tour Information
See pages 163–73 for the addresses, telephone numbers and opening times of the attractions mentioned in the tours, including the telephone numbers of tourist information centres. General information on boat services on the lakes and in Venice is on pages 158–9.

Accommodation and restaurants
Pages 158–62 list hotels, farm holiday centres and camping sites situated at the point of departure or along the route of each tour. Also listed are restaurants where you may like to stop for a meal. There are, of course, other possibilities to be found along the way.

Credit Cards
All principal credit cards are accepted by most establishments, but not petrol stations.

Currency
Italy is one of the 12 European Union countries to start using a single currency, the Euro (€). Euro notes and coins were introduced on 1 January 2002 and the lira was phased out at the end of February 2002. Euro bank notes are in denominations of €5, €10, €20, €50, €100, €200 and €500; coins are in denominations of 1, 2, 5, 10, 20 and 50 cents, and €1 and €2.

Customs Regulations
Items for personal or professional use may be brought into Italy free of charge, but take receipts for valuable articles to avoid paying duty on them. Travellers' allowances for Italy are the same as other EU countries. Check current guidelines.

Electricity
The current is 220 volts AC, 50 cycles, with two round-pin plugs. UK and North American visitors should check whether 110/120-volt appliances require a voltage transformer.

Emergency Telephone Numbers
Police and ambulance tel: 113. Fire tel: 115.

Entry Regulations
The only document necessary for UK, Commonwealth and US citizens is a valid passport for any stay of up to three months. Visitors from EU countries need only a visitor's card.

Health
Health insurance is recommended, but visitors from EU countries are entitled to health services available to Italians. This means obtaining, prior to departure, Form E111 or equivalent from the post office. The high cost of treatment makes insurance essential if you are a non-EU citizen. Keep all bills for medical treatment and medicines to claim back later.

Post Offices
Post offices are generally open 8–1.30/2 Mon–Fri and to 11.45 on Sat. On the last day of the month offices close at noon. Times vary from place to place.

Public Holidays
1 January – New Year's Day
6 January – Epiphany
Easter Monday
25 April – Liberation Day (1945)
1 May – Labour Day
2 June – Proclamation of Republic (celebrated on following Saturday)
15 August – Ferragosto (Assumption)
1 November – All Saints
8 December – Immaculate Conception
25–6 December – Christmas.

Roads
Tuscany and Umbria are served by a basic motorway network: the A12 from the border with Liguria to Rossignano Marittimo; the A11 from Florence to Pistoia, Lucca, Pisa and Versilia; the A1 from the Apennine border with Emilia to Florence, Arezzo and Orvieto, with the

Florence–Siena and Bettolle–Perugia motorway link roads. The major state roads are: the SS1 Aurelia along the Tyrrhenian coast; the SS2 Cassia from Siena to the border with Lazio; the SS3 Flaminia from the border with Marche to Foligno, Spoleto and Terni; the SS3bis–E45 between Città di Castello, Perugia, Todi and Terni.

Motorways can always be used to cover certain sections of the tours quickly or for rapid returns, but tours generally use A roads and sometimes secondary roads. The few difficult routes (coastal roads, for instance) are indicated so that you can choose whether or not to take them.

In Florence, Lucca, Siena, and Perugia the main problems

Typical Tuscan landscape

are road congestion and parking. Some suggestions are given in the text; others can be obtained from tourist information offices.

Route Directions
The following abbreviations are used in the book for Italian roads:
A – Autostrada (motorway)
SS – Strada Statale (state road)
bis – suffix to state roads (SS) relating to links and extensions of major roads.

Speed Limits
Motorways (*autostrade*): 130kph (80mph)
Main roads: 110kph (68mph)
Secondary roads: 90kph (55mph)
Built-up areas: 50kph (31mph).

Telephones
Most phone booths on streets and in bars, tobacco shops and restaurants take coins or a phone

card (*una scheda telefonica*), bought from post offices, stores or bars.

To call abroad, dial 00, then the country code, followed by the city code and number. The prefix for the UK is 0044; for Eire 00353; for the US and Canada 001; for Australia 0061.

Tourist Offices
The Italian State Tourist Office (ENIT) is represented in the following:
Australia: Level 26, 44 Market Street, Sydney NSW 2000 (tel: (02) 9262 1666).
Canada: Suite 907, 175 Bloor Street East, Toronto M4W 3R8 (tel: 416/925-4882).
UK: 1 Princes Street, London W1R 8AY (tel: 020 7408 1254).
US: Suite 1565, 630 Fifth Avenue, New York NY 10111 (tel: 212/245-4822).

NORTHWEST TUSCANY

Spread over the provinces of Massa Carrara, Lucca, Pistoia and Prato, the northwestern part of Tuscany comprises territories with widely varying attractions. This is Apennine country, historically a place of travellers – peaceful or otherwise – as shown by its castles, fortified villages and wayfarers' hospices. Its air of remote transience couldn't be further from the seaside and society life of Versilia, a straight, sandy beach that contrasts spectacularly with the Apuan Alps.

From the mouth of the Magra river in the north to the Serchio in the south, tourism has invaded the formerly unhealthy marsh areas, bypassed by the roads. On the other side, the rugged Apuan Alps, streaked with marble mines, form a dramatic backdrop to the wooded Garfagnana – the Serchio valley to the north of Lucca – bordered to the west of the river by the green and undulating Apennines. Monte Pisano is a geological extension of the Apuan Alps, a solitary peak that separates Lucca and the Serchio valley from the Pisa plain. In the 6th century BC Pisa overlooked the sea; now it lies 12km (8 miles) away. Woods and more woods are the prime feature of the Pistoia mountain landscape. This part of Tuscany contains a number of valleys that were once hotly fought over by Lucca and Florence. Last comes Prato, a town of industry and art, 'dangerously' close to Florence, from which it was separated in 1992 to become a province, taking with it the Florentine Bisenzio valley, the former route taken by travellers crossing the Apennines to Bologna.

As is always the case in Tuscany, tourism is divided between nature – the glorious Tuscan landscapes – and art. Natural beauty draws the crowds to the seaside at Viareggio, Forte dei Marmi and other towns in Versilia; it offers the quieter pleasures of the *maquis*, dunes and Tyrrhenian flora and fauna at San Rossore and Migliarino; and it provides striking mountain views in the Apuan Alps and wooded hills and chestnut groves of Garfagnana and Lunigiana.

The Leaning Tower of Pisa, the town's most famous view

Tour 1

Marble quarries provide the theme for the initial stages of this tour, which passes through the blinding-white reflections of quarry debris and crystalline rock faces cut perpendicularly with wire. A brief detour into Liguria takes in the lovely town of Sarzana and deserted Luni, giving a glimpse of the present and past of Lunigiana. This land is wedged in the Apennine ridge, on the border with Emilia and Liguria, and linking the Po plain to central Italy. Then it's time to relax and drive through the temples of summer seaside tourism along the beaches of Versilia.

Tour 2

Ancient Lucca 'of a hundred churches' is enclosed within its ring of walls and bastions – the monumental defences of an independence that lasted almost a thousand years. However, Lucca is a far from stern and forbidding fortress-town. Tree fronds grow from the tower-houses, the church fronts are softened by elegant loggias, and the entire urban layout bears the gracious mark of two forceful women – Elisa Baciocchi, a member of Napoleon's family, and the enlightened restorer Duchess Marie Louise of Bourbon.

Tour 3

From the villas, parks and spas that provided relaxation for Lucca's nobility and wealthy citizens, this tour climbs the upper Serchio valley between the steep mountain slopes and dense woods of Garfagnana, to enter the lunar scenery of marbled Monte Altissimo. After leaving behind the dazzling landscape of the Apuan Alps, you return to the coast to visit a quiet lakeside spot of subtle old-fashioned charm.

Tour 4

Marking the division between the lands of Lucca and Pisa, Monte Pisano was for centuries at the centre of disputes and parochial feuds that constantly erupted between the small states of Italy. Between spats, these were the societies that created, among other things, such gems as the Romanesque bell tower of San Piero a Grado, and the baroque Charterhouse of Calci. The itinerary starts with a journey along the Pisan coastline, where the San Rossore estate has preserved intact the blanket of foliage that covers the mouths of the Serchio and Arno rivers.

Tour 5

This tranquil tour takes you up mountains and down into valleys, through forests and

chestnut groves, taking in wonderful scenery as well as the legacies of generations of peasants, woodcutters and shepherds, displayed in the Pistoia mountains' ecomuseum. After passing through the lush, green Valdinièvole, with its Swiss-style charm, take a break at the Montecatini spa before heading back towards the increasingly built-up zones of the Arno plain to discover the artistic treasures of Prato.

Above: trekking in Lunigiana
Below: Forte dei Marmi beach

Lunigiana
& Versilia

It's a short journey from the Apuan Alps to the golden sands – or, in summer, the multicoloured expanse of parasols – of Versilia. This itinerary never loses sight of either. The starting point is Massa: here, the palace of the Cybo Malaspina family, the family tombs in the vaults of the Duomo (cathedral) and the Renaissance palace they added to the 14th-century scenic stronghold are all reminders of a supremacy that lasted from 1442 to 1741.

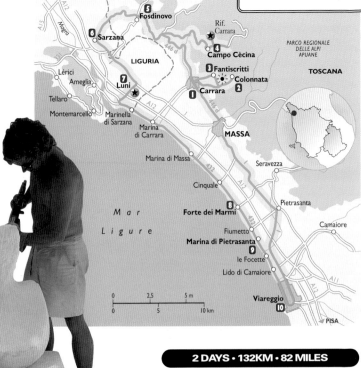

2 DAYS · 132KM · 82 MILES

The grey-and-white striped façade of the Duomo of Carrara

i *Lungomare Vespucci 25, Marina di Massa*

▶ *Follow the signs to Carrara.*

❶ Carrara

In its past, Carrara suffered a stormy succession of rulers; in the first half of the 14th century alone it was controlled by Pisa, Lucca, Genoa, Parma and the Della Scala and Visconti families. Finally, in 1442, it came under the governance of the Malaspina and Cybo Malaspina families, who reigned for 300 years. From their residence, now home to the Academy of Fine Arts, the medieval Via di Santa Maria leads to the Duomo (cathedral). Its marble façade, Romanesque at the bottom and Gothic at the top, is a reminder of its long building process (from the 11th to the 14th century). In this 'marble capital', a look at the Marble Museum is the best prelude to a visit to the quarries.

i *Via del Plebiscito, Carrara*

SCENIC ROUTES

Before venturing into the massive quarry of the Colonnata 'canal' (always giving way to marble lorries!), you can enjoy a fine view of the Apuan Alps from the hilltop Bedizzano (276m/905 feet). The stretch of road leading to Fantiscritti is beautiful, and excellent views of Versilia are offered by the road that climbs to Campo Cècina with a panorama of quarries as far as the eye can see.

▶ *Travel northeast, following the signs to Colonnata.*

❷ Colonnata

Accompanied by breathtaking views of the 22km (13-mile) railway line, a masterpiece of engineering that between 1886 and 1964 linked the quarries to the port of Marina di Carrara, you reach the centre of the quarrying area for the famous black Colonnata marble. Since the times of the Roman slave colony that gave Colonnata its name, life has been harsh for the

quarrymen of this rural village – as is particularly evident in the tablets on the walls of houses here, which proclaim the workers' anarchist ideals.

▶ *Descend from the Colonnata hill and take the road to Fantiscritti.*

❸ Fantiscritti

This part of the route follows the viaducts of the 19th-century railway (the stunning 'Vara bridges'). To the right of a gallery cut through the marble slopes you'll find an immense fairy-tale hall carved into the polished marble. Further on, the Fantiscritti gorge (450m/1,476 feet) takes its name from a 3rd-century AD bas-relief found here in 1863 and now in the Accademia in Carrara. The *fanti*, or young men, are Jupiter, Hercules and Bacchus. Flemish sculptor Jean de Boulogne, better known as Giambologna, carved his name somewhat disrespectfully here in 1590, and in 1800 his example was followed by Antonio Canova. At the base of the gorge, tunnels

Curing *lardo* (fatty bacon) in the cellars of Colonnata

Walton quarries, named after the English entrepreneur who introduced new marble-processing technology in the first half of the 19th century.

▶ *Descend from Campo Cècina, following the signs to Fosdinovo.*

5 Fosdinovo

The 14th-century castle of Fosdinovo was built for Spinetta Malaspina, whose family ruled Lunigiana from 1306 to 1797. This served both as a military bastion and as an elegant residence. Redesigned during the Renaissance, it is one of the loveliest castles in this part of Tuscany. Italian poet Dante Alighieri is said to have stayed in one of the rooms in 1306.

▶ *North of the village, take the road to the left that leads via Giucano to Sarzana.*

6 Sarzana

Geographically a part of Tuscany, the Ligurian town of Sarzana lies in the basin of the Magra river, inhabited since the

3rd millennium BC. The earliest residents were the Palaeo-Ligurians, who sculpted the enigmatic stelae-statues kept in the Piagnaro castle museum at Pontrèmoli (38km/24 miles north of Sarzana). Its position, at the point where the Cisa Pass road joins the Aurelia road made Sarzana a strategic base for the control of lower Lunigiana. Under Castruccio Castracani's rule, the people of Lucca built the splendid Sarzanello fortress here (1322); the Florentines, in Lorenzo d' Medici's era, erected the Cittadella (1488); and the Genoans gave it walls in the 1500s. A notable feature of Sarzana's rich artistic and monumental heritage is the splendid cathedral. Inside, the great cross painted in 1138 by Master Guglielmo is considered the

SPECIAL TO...

Now a fad among foodies all over Italy, tasty Colonnata *lardo* (fatty bacon) was once the staple meal of the quarrymen, who seasoned and spiced it before leaving it to cure for ten months in marble basins in their cellars. A visit to Colonnata is the best opportunity to taste the genuine article, which is on sale in incredible quantities.

---

branch out to the Ravaccione and Colonnata quarries and a splendid private open-air museum shows the marble excavation, processing and transport techniques used from the Roman era to the present day, as well as a reconstruction of the everyday lives of quarrymen of the past.

▶ *Return to Carrara and take the SS446d; after 9km (6 miles) turn right on to the road for Campo Cècina.*

4 Campo Cècina

The vast, open space of Campo Cècina (1,357m/4,452 feet) was already popular with the Romans during the golden age of the port of Luni (1st–2nd century AD). Today it is home to the Belvedere and Carrara refuge huts, used by hikers. Extending all around are the

---

RECOMMENDED WALK

An easy path leads from Campo Cècina to an ancient *via di lizza* – a formidable chute created in the sheer rock face, down which the blocks of marble were sent, tied to a sledge (*lizza*) made of sturdy planks bolted together. This was secured at the top by the workers' ropes. If the huge load broke loose, there was no escape for those who soaped the runners and inserted the rollers along the way. Now that the lethal sledge has disappeared, lorries zigzag up and down the white mounds of waste. Often there is no room to turn the bends and the lorries advance by alternating forward and reverse gears.

---

archetype of all similar Tuscan and Umbrian works.

▶ *Take the SS1 southbound to the Via San Pero turning, which to the right leads to Luni.*

7 Luni

Remains of the forum and the 'house of frescoes', sections of wall and an amphitheatre are among the few remains that tell of the rise and fall of Luni, which was founded as a seaport in 177 BC and subsequently exported marble all over the Roman empire. After centuries of prosperity, the floods of the Magra river filled in the port, gradually distancing the coastline (which is today about 2km/1 mile away). Floods, malaria and feudal conflicts led to its final decline in the early 1200s. Both Dante and writer Petrarch used Luni to symbolise the precarious state of human fortunes. At the centre of what is now an archaeological site is a national museum housing relics and documents.

▶ *After reaching the coast road, proceed southeast to Forte dei Marmi.*

8 Forte dei Marmi

In the 16th century there was a quay here, where marble from the quarries was loaded on to ships. Then, in 1788, Grand Duke Leopold I ordered the construction of the fort that still stands in the middle of the square. Today, elegant hotels and town houses – and famous entertainment nightspots such as the

Cutting marble in the Apuan Alps

SPECIAL TO...

The Romans quarried marble by prising open the fissures with their chisels and inserting iron or wooden wedges. The advent of gunpowder brought more powerful but wasteful mining methods. But the real revolution came in 1895, with three interwoven steel wires that could 'cut' between 2 and 15cm (1 and 6 inches) per hour. (In fact it was the mixture of water and abrasive sand drawn by the helical wire that did the cutting.) This method has been replaced by 'diamond' wire. Effective but dangerous, it vibrates halfway between the pulleys and the marble banks. If it should break, any quarrymen caught by the lash are in real trouble.

Views of Viareggio: the seafront
(left) and the carnival (above)

Pietrasanta in the Middle Ages
after which the town was
named). Leading from the canal
are the Supercinema, the Duilio
'48 store, the Galleria del Libro
bookshop, Gran Caffè
Margherita and the Balena baths.
A few steps from the sea, in a
square named after him, is a bust
of Percy Bysshe Shelley. The
English poet drowned at the age
of 30 off the Versilia coast and
was cremated, in the presence
of Byron, on the beach of
Viareggio (1822). Happier scenes
are conjured up by the famous
local carnival, with its parade
of comic and satirical papier
mâché floats.

Capannina – make Forte dei
Marmi a seaside and holiday
legend. Set on the fine sand of
the Versilian beach, it is backed
by pine woods, Mediterranean
maquis and, beyond, by the
Apuan Alps.

ℹ️ *Via A Franceschi 8*

▶ *Continue along the coast road
to the Capannina, then on the
parallel Viale Morin to
Fiumetto, in the comune of
Marina di Pietrasanta.*

9 Marina di Pietrasanta
Inland lies the Principe bridge,
built by Leopold I in 1776, and
to the left, before you reach the
Fiumetto channel, stretch 80
hectares (198 acres) of the coastal
forest that originally extended
from the River Magra to the
Livorno hills. Today, this makes
up the lovely Versiliana Park,
owned by the town authorities.
In summer, exhibitions and

meetings are held here, continuing the tradition of Versilia's
lively literary café society.

ℹ️ *Via Donizetti 14*

▶ *Back on the coast road,
continue south to Viareggio.*

10 Viareggio
The main axis of the town, one
of Italy's pioneers of seaside holidays, is the beautiful flowered
avenue on the seafront, lined
with eclectic art deco and art
nouveau hotels, town houses,
cafés, restaurants, pavilions and
shops. The first 'seaside homes'
– segregating men and women –
were built in 1828. Of the
numerous wooden constructions,
however, only Chalet Martini
survived a disastrous fire in 1917.
Above the Burlamacca canal rises
the Matilda tower (1544),
erected by the people of Lucca
near the Via Regia (the road
which ran from Migliarino and

ℹ️ *Viale Carducci 10*

▶ *Return to Massa on the SS1
northbound.*

Lucca

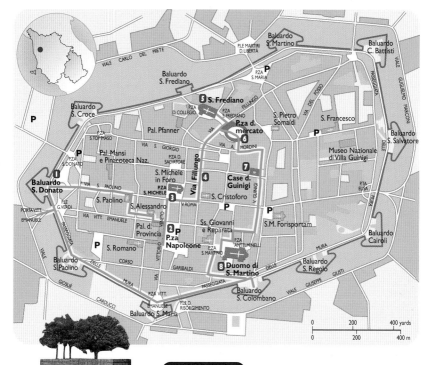

1 DAY

Lucca has been the headquarters of many a political master: it was the capital of Lombard Etruria, then of the Carolingian marquisate of Tuscany, before becoming an autonomous *comune* in 1119. But between 1369 and 1799, this small model-state retained its independence, and established a quality of life that can still be seen in its brick and marble buildings, and in the streets and squares around the town.

Above: riding the ring of walls
Below: San Michele in Foro

ℹ️ *Piazza Guidiccioni 2*

▶ *Enter the town through Porta Vittorio Emanuele and turn left on to Baluardo San Donato.*

❶ Baluardo San Donato
Only pedestrians and bicycles are allowed on the 4,200m-long (13,779-foot) ring of walls that still surrounds Lucca. Designed to resist heavy artillery, they stand 12m (39 feet) high, with large ramparts linking the 11 arrowhead bastions; but they remained unused until Marie Louise of Bourbon transformed them into a splendid tree-lined promenade during her stay between 1815 and 1824.

▶ *Follow Via San Paolino east-wards to the church of the same name.*

The narrow street on the left leads beyond Via Burlamacchi to the church of Sant' Alessandro. A turning to the right of the church takes you to Via Vittorio Emanuele; the left leads to Piazza Napoleone.

❷ Piazza Napoleone
Vast and shaded by plane trees, the square was opened in 1806; the site had already been established as the centre of municipal power under the rule of Castruccio da Castracani (1320–8) and Paolo Giunigi (1400–30). In 1578, Bartolomeo Ammannati designed the impressive Palazzo della Signoria, now home of the provincial offices (the right-hand wing was added in 1728) for the local authorities. It was later adapted for Elisa Baciocchi, Bonaparte's sister. The Duchess Marie Louise of Bourbon also lived there, and the monument in the centre of the square is dedicated to her. To the south is the Corte del Pesce, a delightful little medieval spot, leading to Via Pescheria.

▶ *Follow Via Vittorio Veneto north-wards to Piazza San Michele.*

❸ Piazza San Michele
The former site of the Roman forum continued as the hub of medieval town life. Between 1070 and the 14th century, workmen from Pisa and Lucca constructed the fine church of San Michele in Foro in the centre of the square; the ornamental arches on columns and rows of loggias on the façade are their trademarks. In the 15th century, after the seat of secular power was transferred to what is now the Piazza Napoleone, the ancient forum became the meeting place for bankers and silk merchants.

▶ *Take Via Roma eastwards and turn left into Via Fillungo.*

❹ Via Fillungo
On the site of the main juncture of Roman Lucca, this street remains the favourite local promenade, marked since 1471 by a mechanical clock installed on the Torre delle Ore. Many of the shops between the palaces and towers still have their old signs and furnishings.

▶ *Pass Via dell'Anfiteatro on the right and turn left for Piazza San Frediano.*

❺ San Frediano
A large 13th-century mosaic adorns the façade of San Frediano, built between 1112 and 1147 so close to the walls that its crenellated bell tower was

Lucca's elliptical Piazza del Mercato

used for military purposes. Inside is an unusual holy fountain (12th-century), with a column in the form of a flame and imps, and a rich marble polyptych (1422) by Jacopo della Quercia. It also houses the tomb of Santa Zita (1218–78), venerated by the people of Lucca.

▶ *Return to Via dell'Anfiteatro and take one of the passages to Piazza del Mercato.*

6 Piazza del Mercato

This surprising elliptical square, enclosed between tall medieval houses, has its origin in the 2nd century AD, when an amphitheatre for 10,000 spectators stood here: sections of the two rows of arches that supported the auditorium are still visible along Via dell'Anfiteatro. Engulfed by houses and used for various purposes – over the centuries it has been a prison, salt warehouse and abattoir – it was cleared of its central buildings in 1830 and became a public space once more. Today, it's enlivened by meeting places and small shops.

▶ *Leave the square to the south and take one of the streets leading to Via Mordini. Follow this to the left, then turn right*

into Via Guinigi until you come to Via Sant'Andrea.

7 Casa dei Guinigi

Via Giunigi was where the palaces and towers belonging to this wealthy merchant family were concentrated, and they still form a fascinating ensemble of 14th-century Gothic architecture. At the corner with Via Sant'Andrea, climb to the top of the high tower with its tiny garden of ilex trees. The view of the town rewards the effort.

▶ *Continue along Via Giunigi and Via dell'Arcivescovado, then turn right into Via del Battistero and left across Piazza Antelminelli to Piazza San Martino.*

8 Duomo di San Martino

Pilgrims marching along the Via Francigena would come to San Martino to venerate the famous Volto Santo, a crucifix sculpted in wood by the Pharisee Nicodemus (today's crucifix is a 13th-century copy of a Syrian original, perhaps dating from the 8th century). Now most visitors are attracted to the church, which was rebuilt in the 13th century, to see the tomb of Ilaria del Carretto, the second wife of Paolo Giunigi, who died in 1405. Jacopo della Quercia even

sculpted her little dog lying on the sarcophagus at her feet – a symbol of faithfulness. Victory is symbolised by the 'Vizir's horse's tail', a bizarre trophy from a battle against the Turks, kept in a glass case.

▶ *Leave the square to the south to reach Corso Garibaldi, which to the left leads to Baluardo San Colombano. From here follow the walls east along Baluardo Santa Maria and Baluardo San Paolino to Porta Vittorio Emanuele.*

SPECIAL TO...

A few steps from Via San Paolino, the Palazzo Mansi National Picture Gallery exhibits paintings from the Renaissance to the first half of the 18th century with works by Beccafumi, Bronzino, Pontormo, Andrea del Sarto, Paolo Veronese, Tintoretto, Salvator Rosa and Guido Reni. These were donated to the town by the Grand Duke Leopold II as compensation for the loss of the palace collection of paintings, sold by Charles Louis Bourbon, last Duke of Lucca (1824–47). The palace features a splendid 17th-century wedding chamber.

Garfagnana &
the Apuan Alps

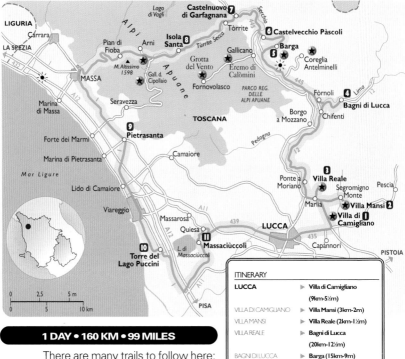

1 DAY • 160 KM • 99 MILES

There are many trails to follow here: those taken by the rich of Lucca to the gardens of their villas, or by Europe's nobility to the warm marble spa baths; the footsteps of pilgrims and craftsmen across the mountains; the escape routes of poets and musicians into a world of nature; and, of course, the trail of workers carrying crystalline rocks from the Apuan Alps to ports for transportation.

i *Piazza Guidiccioni 2, Lucca*

▷ *Leave Lucca to the east on the **SS435** to Pescia; just outside Borgonuovo turn left for Segromigno in Monte then right to Villa di Camigliano.*

❶ Villa di Camigliano
In the second half of the 17th century, this was the villa of Nicolao Santini, ambassador of Lucca at the court of Louis XIV. The baroque façade was inspired by Versailles, as were the gardens – the work of André le Nôtre, who created the gardens of the Sun King in Paris. As well as the villa you can visit the spectacular Giardino di Flora, with grottoes, temples and water features. The rest of the park has been landscaped in keeping with romantic early 19th-century tastes.

▷ *Continue towards Segromino in Monte to Villa Mansi.*

❷ Villa Mansi
The Italian Renaissance gardens of Villa Mansi were redesigned in the 18th century by Filippo Juvarra, complete with a star-shaped wood, fishpond and theatre. Nowadays, there is also an English-style garden to visit. The grand house was originally built in the late 16th-century but was transformed in the first half of the 17th century, and is rich in frescoes and fine furnishings.

▷ *Proceed towards Marlia to Villa Reale.*

❸ Villa Reale
In 1811 Elisa Baciocchi – the sister of Napoleon – bought a 16th- to 17th-century villa to convert into her country residence. Fortunately, the restructuring work left untouched the monumental yew and box hedges that form an amazing 'vegetable theatre', as well as the lemon grove, the fountain and the water-grotto. The woods, streams and lake of the romantic park were created in the first half of the 20th century. Past guests of Villa Reale (not open to visitors) include the great violinist and composer Paganini.

▷ *After reaching the Abetone-Brenner **SS12**, turn right for*

Villa di Camigliano, near Lucca

▷ *Ponte a Moriano and follow the road on the left of the Serchio and then the Lima rivers to Bagni di Lucca.*

❹ Bagni di Lucca
At Borgo a Mozzano, the River Serchio is spanned by a staggering 14th-century hump-backed bridge known as the Maddalena. A shrine here once either contained a statue of the saint (now in the local parish church), or of the Devil. A little further on, the iron Ponte alle

---

SPECIAL TO...

Essayist Michel de Montaigne tried many spas in his attempts to relieve the pain of kidney stones, but (he wrote in 1581) only Bagni di Corsena (Lucca) helped. However, he took a sceptical view of the 'miraculous' waters. His advice to a friend worried about his wife's infertility was: 'If you want your wife pregnant, send her to Bagni and don't go yourself!'

Catene crosses the Lima river, linking Chifenti with Fòrnoli.

Made up of several hamlets, Bagni di Lucca was once the cosmopolitan haunt of Lucca's aristocracy, and a magnet to artists and scholars (including Byron, Shelley, Dumas, Rossini, Liszt, Verdi and Puccini). The Bagni Caldi spa, on Corsena hill, is still open; neo-classical architecture and the remains of abandoned spas can be seen at Ponte a Serraglio and La Villa.

[i] *Via Umberto I 103*

▶ *Return to the* **SS12** *and turn right on to the* **SS445** *for Barga.*

5 Barga
Barga was a Florentine outpost on Garfagnana territory from 1341. Today, its Giardino district is a flat expanse of modern industry, but from here the town's steep, narrow streets

The spa town of Bagni di Lucca

climb to the Arringo, a grassy clearing at the top of the hill. The contours of the Apuan Alps and the Apennines frame the Romanesque sculptures of the façade of the Duomo (cathedral). Altered many times between the 9th and the 16th century, the building contains a splendid 12th-century *ambo* (oblong pulpit) resting on red marble columns.

> RECOMMENDED
> EXCURSION
>
> From Gallicano (opposite
> Barga, across the River
> Serchio), climb westwards
> along the Tùrrite river to the
> turning for the Calòmini
> hermitage, a spectacular 11th-
> century sanctuary partially
> excavated in the sheer rock.
> Further on, near Fornovolasco,
> is the Grotta del Vento –
> 4km (2½ miles) of halls, tunnels,
> wells, lakes, siphons and
> subterranean rivers which
> can be visited along a
> marked route.

ℹ️ *Piazza Angelio 3*

▶ *Follow the provincial road that leads via Ponte di Catagnana to Castelvecchio Pàscoli.*

6 Castelvecchio Pàscoli
In a secluded spot just before you reach the village is the small house bought by poet Giovanni Pascoli (1855–1912) in 1895 with the proceeds from the medals won at a Latin poetry competition in Amsterdam. Local life is reflected in the pages of his *Songs of Castelvecchio*, published in 1903. The house is now a museum, preserved exactly as it was when Pascoli spent his holidays here in the company of his sister 'Mariù'. Both are buried in the annexed chapel.

▶ *Continue along the road and turn right on to the SS445 for Castelnuovo di Garfagnana.*

Bas-reliefs in Barga's Duomo

7 Castelnuovo di Garfagnana
'Land of wolves and brigands' – this was how poet Ludovico Ariosto described wooded Garfagnana. Between the early 15th century and Italy's 19th-century unification, this area belonged (apart from a few brief intervals) to the Este family. Ariosto was obliged to act as governor, in service to the lords of Ferrara, and lived from 1522 to 1525 in the Rocca (stronghold), which still has a loggia overlooking the square of Castelnuovo.

In the 17th century another poet, Fulvio Testi of Ferrara, is said to have stayed there – again acting as governor (between 1640 and 1642) for the Este family of Modena. Today, the building houses a permanent exhibition on the ancient Ligurian civilisation of the Upper Serchio Valley.

ℹ️ *Piazza delle Erbe 10*

> SPECIAL TO...
>
> The rich marble deposits on
> the north side of Monte
> Altissimo were first exploited in
> the 1800s, after the opening of
> the Cipollaio tunnel. Among
> them, the disused Henraux
> quarry (reached by a high
> fissure at the exit from a tunnel
> just past Arni) stands as a
> beautiful amphitheatre of
> polished geometrical shapes
> cut into the marble.

Canoeing in the marshy waters of
Lake Massaciùccoli

▶ *Follow signs for Tòrrite
through a harsh landscape to
Isola Santa, in the heart of
the central Apuan Alps.*

8 Isola Santa

Isola Santa's dilapidated, stone-
roofed houses are usually the
only visible part of this village,
which grew up around a 13th-
century hospice serving travellers between Garfagnana and
Versilia. The rest of the crum-
bling community reappears
every ten years (next in 2004),
when the waters are drained
from the lake-reservoir that has,
since 1949, supplied the Tòrrite
hydroelectric station.

▶ *Continue (passing the turning
for the Cipollaio tunnel on the
left) via Arni and Pian della
Fioba to Massa; here take the
SS1 south to Pietrasanta.*

9 Pietrasanta

In 1255, Guiscardo Pietrasanta
founded a village to strengthen
Lucca's control of Versilia. From
its rectangular nucleus, this
settlement grew across the Via
Francigena, linked to the
forbidding Rocca di Sala (a
Lombard fort) by two wings of
crenellated walls. Today, the
village is renowned among

sculptors, mosaic-workers and
art lovers. At its entrance is the
Rocchetta, built in the 14th
century by Castruccio
Castracani and rebuilt in
1486–7. A little further on is the
cathedral (13th–14th century)
and, before it, the Marzocco
column (1514) and the lion,
symbol of Florence. In the
background are the Apuan Alps.

☐ *Piazza Duomo 11*

▶ *After reaching Viareggio
on the SS1, continue along
Viale dei Tigli to the turning
on the left for Torre del
Lago Puccini.*

10 Torre del Lago Puccini

A faded holiday atmosphere
hangs around this peaceful
village, which was chosen in
1891 by Luccan composer
Giacomo Puccini (1858–1924) as
the site for his lakeside villa.
Puccini spent long periods of
time writing several works in
the village, and is buried here.
His period furniture and curios
are still on display. Every year,
the open-air theatre on the
shores of the lake hosts a highly
regarded Puccini festival.

▶ *Return to the SS1 and follow it
southbound; immediately
before the Pisa Nord slip road
of the A12, a secondary road*

*to the left leads to
Massaciùccoli.*

11 Massaciùccoli

Swampy Lake Massaciùccoli is
the last remnant of an ancient
lagoon formed by the Arno and
Serchio rivers, and provides the
ideal habitat for more than 250
species of migratory and non-
migratory birds. On the eastern
shore is the small village of
Massaciùccoli, where the
Romans built a villa and, higher
up, the spa known as Bagno di
Nerone (1st–2nd century AD).
At the foot of the village, long
footbridges lead over the water
to birdwatchers' hides.

▶ *Continue northwards to
Quiesa and then turn right on
to the SS439 to Lucca.*

SCENIC ROUTES

Staggering views of mountains
half-eaten by quarries mark the
beginning of the descent to
Massa. The route leads to a
chapel with a stone commem-
orating the dramatic events of
World War II, when the
Germans fortified the 'Gothic
line' here. The best view of
Monte Altissimo is enjoyed
from the Cipollaio road, just
after passing through the
tunnel of the same name.

The Sea
& Monte Pisano

Tucked into a corner of Pisa's walls are the glories of the Piazza del Duomo (popularly known as Campo dei Miracoli). Tourists come to see the marble wonders of the Duomo (cathedral, 1064), baptistery (1152) and cemetery (1277), and, of course, the famous leaning bell tower (1173).

1/2 DAYS • 110 KM • 69 MILES

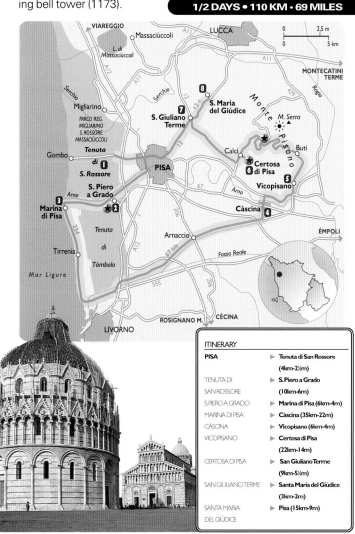

ITINERARY

PISA	▶ **Tenuta di San Rossore** (4km-2½m)
TENUTA DI SAN ROSSORE	▶ **S. Piero a Grado** (10km-6m)
S. PIERO A GRADO	▶ **Marina di Pisa (6km-4m)**
MARINA DI PISA	▶ **Càscina (35km-22m)**
CÀSCINA	▶ **Vicopisano (6km-4m)**
VICOPISANO	▶ **Certosa di Pisa** (22km-14m)
CERTOSA DI PISA	▶ **San Giuliano Terme** (9km-5½m)
SAN GIULIANO TERME	▶ **Santa Maria del Giùdice** (3km-2m)
SANTA MARIA DEL GIÙDICE	▶ **Pisa (15km-9m)**

i *Via Pietro Nenni 24; Piazza della Stazione 13; c/o airport, Pisa*

▶ *Leave Pisa to the west on Viale delle Cascine to the Trombe bridge and the entrance to San Rossore.*

❶ Tenuta di San Rossore

During Roman colonisation the entire 'plain of Pisa', from Viareggio to Livorno, was a succession of sea straits, dunes, woods and marshes. The Medici family continued the centuries-old struggle to regulate the Serchio and Arno delta, and at the same time large hunting reserves were developed, which were later passed on to the Lorraine and Savoy families, and – as in the case of San Rossore – to the Republic. The estate's history of leisure use has prevented its development; today, only short sections of the drives can be visited. In this way, one of the most unspoilt and precious plant landscapes on the Tyrrhenian coast has been safeguarded against reclamation.

Dense pinewood on the San Rossore estate

▶ *Return towards Pisa, cross the Arno and follow its left bank towards Marina di Pisa to the turning on the left for San Piero a Grado.*

❷ San Piero a Grado

St Peter himself is said to have disembarked here in AD 44, during his voyage from Antakya to Rome. Today, it has a fine Romanesque church, built in Livorno tufa and black and white San Giuliano marble, a solitary landmark in open countryside. There was once a port at the mouth of the Arno and, in the 4th century, a Christian basilica drew pilgrims here. The present church was built over the basilica in the 10th and 11th centuries. An important cycle of frescoes in the nave was commissioned for the Jubilee of 1300, and a Gothic ciborium, or shrine, marks the spot where the apostle is said to have preached to the faithful. The church's design is extremely unusual: three eastern apses and a western apse replacing the original façade, which was destroyed when the River Arno flooded in the late 12th century.

▶ *Return to the bank of the Arno and follow it to Marina di Pisa.*

❸ Marina di Pisa

After passing the picturesque Bocca dell'Arno, dotted with

Basilica of San Piero a Grado

stilted huts and the characteristic *retoni* (fishing nets), you come to Marina di Pisa, the oldest of Pisa's seaside resorts, with its gracious art nouveau buildings. More late 19th-century architecture can be seen further south, at Tirrenia. Behind it stretches the flat Tòmbolo estate, which was established as a 23,000-hectare (56,832-acre) nature park in 1979, along with Migliarino, San Rossore and Massaciùccoli (see Tour 3). After centuries of neglect by its ecclesiastical owners, the Tòmbolo area was finally reclaimed by the Lorraine family in the early 19th century. They planted the pinewoods where, at the end of World War II, the Americans set up a military base.

▶ *Continue along the SS224 southbound, then eastwards to the slip roads leading to the SS67 bis for Càscina.*

4 Càscina
The turreted walls and square layout of the village, arranged around a long, porticoed street, mark Càscina as one of the 'new lands' designed in the Middle Ages as a Pisan outpost against Florence, which still managed to capture it in 1406. Càscina is now given over to the manufacture of furniture, knitwear and bricks; to the west, the grandiose Romanesque parish church of San Casciano has doorways carved in 1180.

▶ *Follow signs for Vicopisano.*

5 Vicopisano
The Florentines called on architect Filippo Brunelleschi (1435–9) to restore Vicopisano's towers and fortifications, having captured the village from the Pisans in 1407. The towers are dotted along the walls near Palazzo Comunale, and on the keep that dominates the rings of narrow village streets, providing Vicopisano with its distinctive

skyline. The defences were originally developed in the Middle Ages to control the River Arno, which, in those days, passed close to its walls.

FOR HISTORY BUFFS

One day in 1364, a group of Florentine soldiers taking a swim in the Arno near Càscina was ambushed by Pisans. They quickly retrieved their arms, however, and emerged victorious from the ensuing clash. In 1504, Republican Florence, led by Piero Soderini, commissioned Michelangelo to create a fresco depicting this episode in Palazzo Vecchio, beside a representation of the victory of Anghiari against the Milanese in 1440, which was assigned to Leonardo da Vinci. But the two works were never finished: only the cartoons (initial drawings) appeared, which were received enthusiastically by contemporaries.

FOR CHILDREN

The museum housed in the Certosa (Charterhouse) di Pisa will fascinate children, with its skeletons of whales, dolphins and porpoises. This is the most important cetacean collection in Italy.

Alternatively, the classic attractions of Fantasilandia amusement park are set amid the pine trees and *maquis* vegetation of the Migliarino-Massaciùccoli Park, just 700m (770 yards) from the main square of Tirrenia, and give direct access to the free beach.

i Via del Pretorio 1

▶ *Proceed northwards to Buti, then follow the signs for Calci and the Certosa di Pisa.*

6 Certosa di Pisa

Rich in marble, frescoes, paintings and stucco work, this huge charterhouse, founded in 1366, is a triumph of 16th- to 17th-century baroque style. The church, cloisters, gardens, fountains, priory and guest rooms used by grand dukes were abandoned by the Carthusian monks as recently as 1969. Today the charterhouse is also home to the Museum of Natural and Territorial History, whose collection of relics was first begun by the University of Pisa in 1591, at the behest of Grand Duke Ferdinand I.

i Piazza Garibaldi 1, Calci

▶ *Follow the signs for San Giuliano Terme.*

7 San Giuliano Terme

Dominating the village square, on the lower slopes of Monte Pisano, is the 18th-century Palazzo delle Terme and its extensive park. The wide avenues of the village, lined with plane trees, are a reminder of the 18th- and 19th-century golden age, when the hot springs of San Giuliano were renowned throughout Europe and drew visitors such as Byron, Shelley, Gustav III of Sweden, George IV of England, Luigi Bonaparte, Paolina Borghese and Charles Albert of Savoy.

i Largo Shelley 18

▶ *Take the **SS12c** northbound to the turning on the left for Santa Maria del Giùdice.*

8 Santa Maria del Giùdice

This charming little mountainside village has two churches of note. The Pieve Vecchia (11th–12th century), just outside the village, has a façade in the Romanesque style of Lucca and a bell tower with two rows of double-mullioned windows. The parish church of Santa Maria Assunta, built in or around 1166 in Pisan-Romanesque style, features an unusual octagonal bell tower set on a semicircular apse.

SCENIC ROUTES

The best views of Monte Pisano are between Buti and Calci. Turn right at the Passo Prato Ceragiola and you will come to Monte Serra, at 917m (3,008 feet), the highest in the range. From the top, the view sweeps across from the Apuan and Apennine ridges to the settlements on the plain and the sea. The descent from Santa Maria del Giùdice to San Giuliano Terme is stunning.

▶ *Go back along the **SS12c**, then take the **SS12** to*

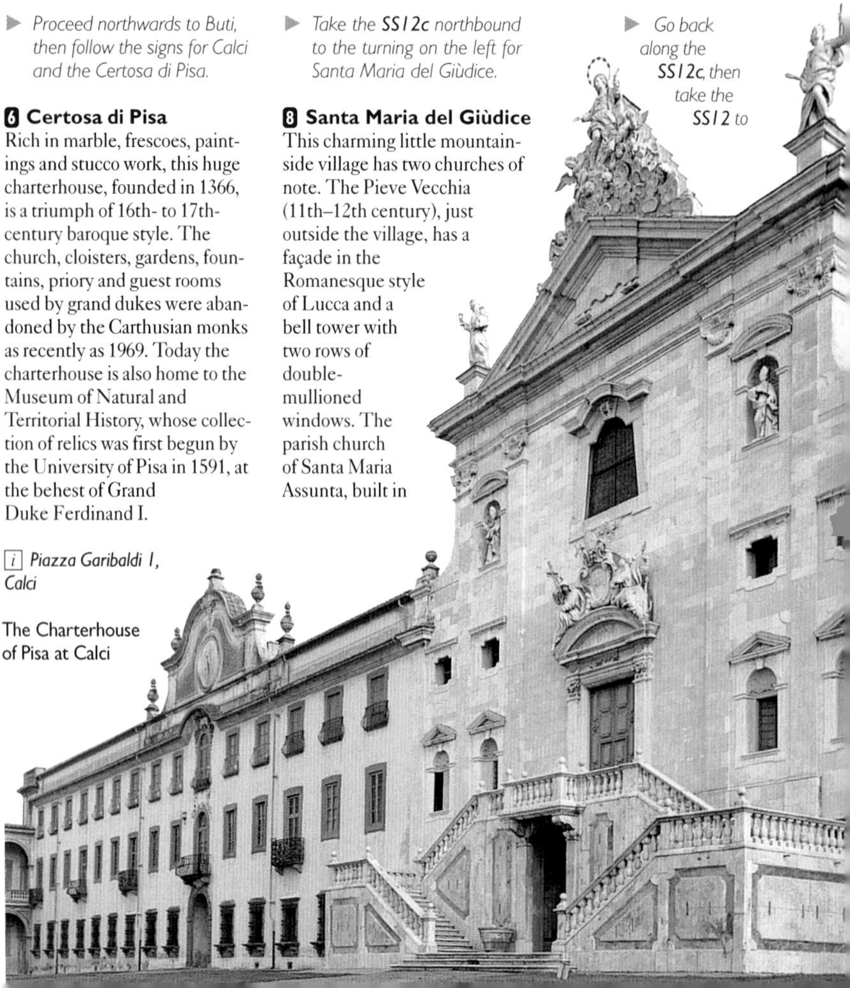

The Charterhouse of Pisa at Calci

The Pistoia
Mountains & Prato

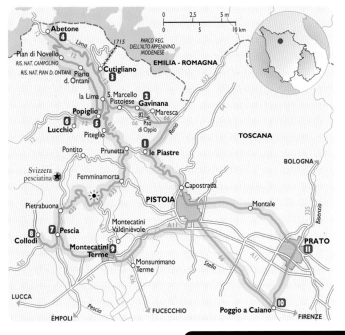

Before surrendering to Florence in **2 DAYS • 216KM • 134 MILES** 1401, Pistoia was a free and wealthy *comune*; its statute of 1117 is one of the earliest recorded in Italy. During this era its main monuments were built in the distinctive zebra stripes of the Pisan Romanesque style, alternating white marble with intense green – executed to perfection in the church of San Giovanni Fuoricivitas.

Above: the Acquerino forest
Right: an orchid in the Campolino
Nature Reserve

i *Piazza Duomo 4, Pistoia*

▶ *Take the* **SS66** *Abetone road
to Le Piastre.*

❶ Le Piastre

Along the Reno river, just past
the village of Le Piastre, a
thatched and tiled roof on the
right covers a truncated, cone-
shaped structure. This is the
Madonnina ice-house, where
the ice that formed during
winter in the nearby canals and
lakes was preserved until spring
(hence the area's title of 'cold
valley'). Once the weather had
changed, the ice was retrieved
to be sold in the towns on the
plain.

▶ *Continue along the* **SS66** *to
the Passo di Oppio; turn right
for Gavinana-Maresca, then
left for Gavinana.*

❷ Gavinana

A 20th-century equestrian
monument in the square of
Gavinana commemorates

Francesco Ferrucci, who led the
Florentines here in 1530 against
the Duke of Orange and his
imperialist forces. Ferrucci was
wounded, captured and publicly
killed by Fabrizio Maramaldo of
Calabria. His defeat marked the
end of the republic and the
return of the Medici family to
Florence. A small museum is
dedicated to the battle.

i *Via Marconi 28, San Marcello
Pistoiese*

▶ *Descend towards San
Marcello Pistoiese, then turn
right on to the* **SS66** *to La
Lima. Turn right again on to
the* **SS12** *to the turning on
the right for Cutigliano.*

❸ Cutigliano

Set in dense woods, this is the
best-preserved village in the
Pistoia Apennines. In 1368,
Cutigliano was the seat of the
mountain commanders of the
local militia (*Capitani del Popolo*)
under Pistoian rule. The coats of
arms of the seven governed
comunes, together with many
others, adorn the façade of
Palazzo Pretorio. Opposite is an

elegant 15th-century loggia, where the commander administered justice from a stone bench.

i *Via Nazionale 42*

▶ *Back on the SS12 continue your ascent to the Passo dell'Abetone.*

4 Passo dell'Abetone
This renowned ski resort has been active since the early 20th century, when winter sports became popular. The 1,388m (4,554-foot) pass is named after a large fir tree which was felled to make way for the road built

The Castruccio bridge at Popiglio

for the Grand Duke of Lorraine Peter Leopold (1767). Francesco III d'Este, who was also involved with the project, wanted a proper triumphal arch to celebrate the undertaking, but had to make do with two stone pyramids bearing the coats of arms of Este (to the right of the summit) and Lorraine (to the left). The posthouse, inn and customs post on the Grand Duke's road, together with a small church (1784), were built just before the pass, at Boscolungo.

i *Via Brennero, Abetone*

▶ *Return along the SS12 and turn right for Popiglio, bearing right after Pian degli Ontani at the asphalted junction with a sign for two farm B&Bs (agriturismo).*

5 Popiglio
About 21km (13 miles) after leaving the SS12, a few minutes' walk in the woods leads to the Torri di Popiglio (signposted), impressive and scenic ruins of Roman fortifications. The route then reaches Popiglio, apparently named after a commander of the Roman garrison, and the lovely 13th-century parish church of Santa Maria Assunta. The nearby Museum of Holy Art

and Popular Devotion contains furnishings, sculptures and hangings from mountain churches.

▶ *Continue to the right on the SS12 to the road signposted on the left that climbs to Lucchio.*

6 Lucchio
Clinging to the side of a breathtaking spur, the village is so steep that women are said to have secured their children with ropes when they were playing on the street outside. The climb culminates in the remains of a medieval stronghold, a fantastic eyrie with sweeping views over the winding Lima river valley.

▶ *Back on the SS12, return to La Lima and turn right on to the SS66. After a short*

stretch, turn right for Piteglio and Prunetta, then right again on to the SS633 and follow the signs to Pescia.

⑦ Pescia

Five districts called *quinti* – four on the right and one on the left of the river – form this little town, the capital of Valdinièvole. Pescia's reputation as a trading and manufacturing centre first began to spread in the 14th century. Arriving from the north, you can still see the old paper mills, recognisable by the countless openings of the top-floor drying-rooms. The 'long market' was held in Piazza Mazzini, between Palazzo dei Vicari (13th to 14th century) and the church of the Madonna di Piè di Piazza (1447). A huge flower market has been held here since the 1970s. Carnations are a local speciality.

i Piazza Castello 118, Pietrabuona

▶ *Follow the signs for Collodi.*

⑧ Collodi

Towering at the foot of this picturesque hilltop village is the large, baroque Villa Garzoni. In the 18th century, its gardens, embellished with steps, terraces, statues and water features, were considered among the finest in Italy. Lower down is the Pinocchio Park and annexed Toyland, an original marriage of artworks and natural environment created by major artists between 1956 and 1987. The author of *Pinocchio's Adventures: Story of a Puppet* (1880), Carlo Lorenzini of Florence, spent his childhood at Collodi, from which he took his pen name.

Villa Garzoni (above) and Toyland (below) at Collodi

▶ *Back at Pescia, follow the signs for Montecatini Terme.*

FOR CHILDREN

Children will find that the exciting crossing of the metal bridge, reached from the SS12 just before Popiglio, partially makes up for the numerous bends along the way. This dramatic 1922 structure, less than 1m (3 feet) wide, 220m (722 feet) long and 36m (118 feet) high, is suspended over the Lima river bed. Younger visitors will enjoy exploring the paths of the Pinocchio Park, and unexpected encounters with the characters of the story of the puppet.

⑨ Montecatini Terme

Long before Grand Duke Peter Leopold encouraged their modern exploitation in the latter part of the 18th century, the sodium-chloride-sulphate-alkaline waters of Montecatini and their healing powers were known to the ancient Romans. A 'canopy' covered the bath in which Florentine noblemen and gentlemen practised water therapy in 1417. Today, a refined early 20th-century atmosphere surrounds the spas and grand hotels of this airy garden-town. For a real taste of the spa experience, visit the Tettuccio, with its travertine-stone colonnades and the sumptuous tap-rooms rebuilt in 1925; the classical-style Terme Leopoldine, built in 1777; and the art nouveau baths of the Excelsior (the former town casino, converted to a spa in 1915). A scenic route (there is also a funicular railway) climbs to Montecatini Alto.

ⓘ *Viale Verdi 66*

▶ *After taking the A11 motor-
way towards Florence, exit at
Pistoia and take the SS66 to
Poggio a Caiano.*

❿ Poggio a Caiano

Designed by Giuliano da
Sangallo (c1445–1535), the
splendid Medici villa of Poggio
a Caiano was the prototype for
new aristocratic residences. The
formerly inaccessible fortress
was transformed to open on to
the landscape, with a wide
ground-floor portico and a loggia
on Ionic columns surmounted
by a tympanum (the glazed
terracotta frieze is a copy of the
original, inside). The decoration
is rich with humanistic references to the classical period:
characters from ancient Rome
are shown in frescoes in the
central hall, overshadowing the
man who commissioned the
work, Lorenzo il Magnifico, and
his father Cosimo. The villa has
witnessed its share of drama. In
1587, the Grand Duke
Francesco I and his beloved
second wife Bianca Cappello
died here just a few hours apart;
she was unpopular with her
subjects and there was talk of

Water, marble and paintings at
the Terme Leopoldine

poison (although the true cause
of death may have been
malaria). After Italian unification, King Vittorio Emanuele II
(1820–78) stayed here with Rosa
Vercellana (the famous 'Bela
Rosin'), who became his wife.

ⓘ *Piazza Medici 1*

▶ *Follow the signs for the town
of Prato.*

⓫ Prato

The symbolic figure of Prato is
merchant banker Francesco di
Marco Datini (1330–1410), who
created a financial empire with
branches all over Europe.
His mansion is a remarkable
example of a pre-Renaissance
residence, its exterior once
entirely covered in frescoes.
The industrious modern town –
the second most highly populated in the region – seems to
have inherited the manufacturing genius of the 13th century,
when this was the Tuscan capital
of wool cloth, a tradition revived
in the 19th and 20th centuries.
Art treasures adorn the
Romanesque-Gothic Duomo
(13th to 14th century). The
external pulpit by Michelozzo
(1396–1472) has dancing *putti* on
its parapet, sculpted by
Donatello (c1386–1466). Inside
are fresco cycles by Agnolo

Gaddi (1333–96), Paolo Uccello
(c1396–1475) and Fra' Filippo
Lippi (1406–69). The mighty
turreted walls of the Castello
dell'Imperatore, built by
Frederick II between 1237 and
1248, are reminiscent of the
Swabian castles of Puglia and
Sicily. A few steps away is Santa
Maria delle Carceri, a perfect
example of a Greek cross
church, built by Giuliano da
Sangallo between 1485 and
1505.

ⓘ *Piazza Santa Maria delle
Carceri 15*

▶ *Return to Pistoia along the
road running at the foot of
the hills, via Montale.*

SCENIC ROUTES

Much of the route between
Pistoia and Pescia is scenic. If
you have an off-road vehicle,
you can cut out numerous
winding miles by turning left,
just before Lucchio, on to the
rough cart track to Pontito.
From here an asphalt road
descends to Pescia. This is a
magnificent excursion – also
recommended from Pescia –
through picturesque fortified
villages perched on both sides
of the valley.

FROM MAREMMA TO THE SEA

Maremma, in Tyrrhenian Tuscany, stretches from the mouth of the Cècina river to Tarquinia (in Lazio) and beyond, along a sweep of sandy coastline, mainly flat but punctuated with the heights of the Piombino headland, Punta Ala and mounts Uccellina and Argentario. It extends across no fewer than three provinces – Livorno, Pisa and Grosseto – and encompasses a variety of landscapes. In the northern hinterland are the Mediterranean *maquis* and evergreen wood vegetation of the beautiful Livorno hills, parallel to the coast. Central inland Maremma runs to the slopes of the metal-producing hills, where it reaches the greater heights of the Cornate di Girifalco and Poggio di Montieri, which rise above 1,000m (3,280 feet), cloaked with chestnut and other trees.

The region flourished in Etruscan and Roman times, before marshland encroached on the protective dunes of the coastal plain and drove the inhabitants away. In subsequent centuries Maremma was a desolate, malarial wetland, where the average life span before 1840 was less than 20 years. The 20th century brought reclamation (with the Cècina, Cornia, Bruna, Ombrone and Albegna rivers serving as outfall drains), and created the new geometric landscape of roads, canals and hydraulic engineering works that today seems part of the natural landscape. Malaria is a thing of the past, and the Maremma coastline has re-established itself as a holiday venue; but the region's traditional image of silent pools, horses and 'cowboys', reeds and marshy ground beneath *maquis*, water, sky and wind can still be found, preserved in the Uccellina Park.

Volterra, Massa Marittima, Sovana and Pitigliano are just some of the memorable Tuscan locations that provide intriguing insights into the medieval way of life. Off the coast, beyond the Piombino channel, the isle of Elba – the most famous and largest island in the Tuscan archipelago – attracts seaside and other tourism with its extraordinary mosaic of natural scenery.

The wild boar, an animal typical of Maremma (and its cuisine)

Tour 6

Maremma's Livorno coastline is high and rocky as far as Castiglioncello; from there to the Piombino headland it's flat and sandy, and often protected by pinewoods. Having rid itself of its gloomy past as a deserted malarial zone, it has transformed itself into a splendid seaside location. The tour leaves the coast at Cècina and heads for Volterra, before venturing into the metal-producing hills amid the white industrial vapours of the 'Valley of Hell'. Back on the coast, ancient Etruria and the feudal Middle Ages are conjured up by the fascinating remains of two mining centres – Populonia and Rocca San Silvestro – before the tour heads for a poet's birthplace and an ancient coastal sanctuary.

Tour 7

An arm of wind-blown sea, just over 8km (5 miles) wide, separates Piombino from the isle of Elba – an island of beauty and light with a surprisingly mild climate. At 27km (17 miles) long and 18km (11 miles) wide – but less than 4km (2 miles) wide at its narrowest point – this is the largest and most famous tourist destination in Tyrrhenian Tuscany. Starting from Portoferraio, this tour visits the lesser known features – tiny sanctuaries, inland villages, romantic churches, strongholds and fortresses, mountain springs, chestnut groves and disused mines – without neglecting Elba's two best-known attractions: the beaches and Napoleon Bonaparte.

Tour 8

The Etruscans and the Romans managed to do for Maremma what the medieval feudal power of Pisa and Siena could not do. They saved it from disintegrating into marshland by creating *tombolos* (sand dunes) to obstruct the river flow. As the marshes took over during the later period of neglect, the populated centres were abandoned, and their inhabitants withdrew to the hills. The wild Uccellina Park, where this tour begins, is all that survives of that marshy

Sweeping view of Marciana and Capo Sant'Andrea, Elba

world, which was subsequently erased by 19th- and 20th-century reclamation. After exploring the coastline, the route turns inland to retrace the glorious path of a thousand-year history in the magnificent city of Massa Marìttima and the ancient stones of Vetulonia and Roselle.

Tour 9

This tour combines the evocative legacies of a medieval past – at Sovana, Sorano and Pitigliano – with the charm of a landscape covered with *maquis*, furrowed by ravines and gullies and scattered with the Etruscan 'ways' and burial grounds of the 'tufa lands'. On reaching the sea, at Orbetello and the Argentario, the Etruscan and Roman remains blend with the pinewoods and protected wetlands, and provide a contrast with the more obvious attractions of seaside holiday beaches and tourist marinas.

The Maremma
around Livorno

With its sunny squares and breezy seafront, Livorno is the newest Tuscan city – in more than one sense. Originally created in 1577 by Grand Duke Francesco I de'Medici, it was built anew nearly 400 years later, after being destroyed by World War II bombing.

3 DAYS · 324KM · 201 MILES

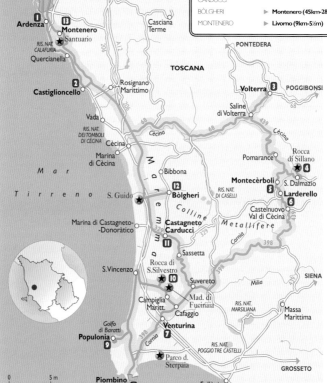

Above: Castiglioncello's beach
Below: alabaster plaque

☐*i* *Piazza Cavour 6; Piazza del
Municipio; Calata Carrara,
Livorno*

▶ *Follow Viale Italia along
the shore, southbound to
Ardenza.*

❶ Ardenza

Drive past the houses and 19th-
and 20th-century kiosks and
bathing establishments, many
built in art nouveau style.
Continue beyond the Accademia
Navale (1878) and hippodrome
(1869) to the semicircular neo-
classical Casini d'Ardenza, built
in 1844 to the model of the 18th-
century Royal Crescent in Bath.
Its several self-contained units
were originally rented holiday
houses. The great seaside holiday boom was just beginning at
this time, in a revival of the 18th-
century tradition of summer
escape captured in Carlo
Goldoni's *Villegiatura Trilogy*
(1761), set on the Montenero hill
(see Tour 13).

▶ *Continue along the coast road
to Castiglioncello.*

❷ Castiglioncello

With its inlets, sandy shores
and rocks shaded by pine and
ilex trees, this is the headland
of the seaside resort of
Castiglioncello, guarded by a
Medici watch-tower. The most
notable sights are the Pasquini
castle (an annual theatre and
dance festival is held in its
grounds) and the National
Archaeological Museum – an
Etruscan temple reconstructed
between 1912 and 1914.

☐*i* *Via Aurelia 632*

▶ *Travel north to the* **SS1**. *Drive
towards Grosseto as far as the
exit for the* **SS68** *and Volterra.*

❸ Volterra

Severe, grey Volterra perches
531m (1,742 feet) on its hill
overlooking the subsid-
ing Cretaceous
chasm of the
Balze. In the 5th
and 4th century
BC, the original
Velathri had
25,000 inhabitants
– twice as many as
the town has now. It was
one of the 12 great Etruscan

towns, exporting wheat, iron
and alabaster all over the
Mediterranean. An exceptional
collection of funerary urns
(including the famous Sposi urn,
1st century BC) and the bronze
Ombra della Sera (3rd century
BC) can be seen in the Mario
Guarnacci Etruscan Museum,
part of which dates from 1732.
The free *Comune* proclaimed in
1193 built the Duomo (cathedral) and octagonal baptistery
facing it, as well as the nearby
square on which stands Palazzo
dei Priori, begun in 1208, and
considered the oldest town hall
in Tuscany. After sacking the
town during the War of Volterra
(1472–5), the Florentines
consolidated their power by
adding the Rocca Nuova to the
14th-century

A spectacular view of the Balze, the landslide close to Volterra

Rocca Vecchia. The whole complex is now used as a prison, and is closed to the public.

Two of Volterra's artistic treasures should not be missed – the Gothic chapel of the Croce di Giorno in San Francesco, entirely frescoed in 1410 by Cenni di Francesco Cenni, and the amazing *Deposition* (now in the Civic Art Gallery), painted for the same chapel by Rosso Fiorentino in 1521.

[i] *Via G Turazza 2*

▶ *Return along the SS68 to Saline di Volterra and turn left on to the SS439. After Pomarance turn left for San Dalmazio and follow the signs to the Rocca di Sillano.*

❹ Rocca di Sillano

After passing the ruins of a 13th-century parish church on the right, the road reaches a barrier and a steep dirt track that leads to the considerable remains of the Rocca di Sillano stronghold; its high tower is visible for miles around. During the 1200s, it belonged to the bishops, then to the *comune* (municipality) of Volterra. Modernised in the 15th century by the Florentines, it is owned by the *comune* and is undergoing restoration. The original three rings of walls are virtually unrecognisable, but the central polygonal construction survives and the top (reached with caution) offers a superb view of the ravines below.

▶ *Return to the SS439 and continue southwards to Montecèrboli.*

❺ Montecèrboli

Clustered around a Romanesque brick parish church, this village sits like a medieval balcony over the steaming landscape of the 'Valley of Hell'. Dense vapour columns rise amid the flaring silhouettes of an electric power station's cooling towers, some up to 75m (246 feet) high, and a great spider's web of silver-coloured pipelines spreads over valley and hill as far as the eye can see.

▶ *Drive on and turn left almost immediately for Larderello.*

❻ Larderello

The Museum of Geothermal Energy, housed in the ENEL (National Electricity Board) management offices while it awaits transfer to the Palazzo de Larderel, is the first stop on a visit to a geothermal power station and its covered lake. The Larderello plants originally extracted boric acid from the lake waters, but since 1905 this work has been increasingly supplemented by the conversion of steam energy into electricity. Boric acid production continues, but now uses colemanite, a boric mineral imported from Turkey and Argentina. It's worth a visit to the unusual church built in 1956–8 by Giovanni Michelucci for the modern residential centre constructed by ENEL.

[i] *Museum of Geothermal Energy, Piazza Leopolda*

▶ *Return to the SS439 and follow it to the SS398, which leads to the right via Suvereto to Venturina.*

BACK TO NATURE

Northeast of Piombino, between the Vignale-Riotorto road and the sea, past an intimidating cluster of smokestacks, lies the well-equipped Sterpaia Park, criss-crossed with paths that venture into the lush vegetation of the dunes behind the beach.

---

7 Venturina

Two large open-air thermal pools are the reason for a stop here. The Terme di Caldana waters maintain a temperature of 32°C (90°F), and the small, crystal-clear, gravel-bed Calidario lake is overlooked by the remains of the old ironworks and the paper mill that exploited the spring waters. Open all year round until late at night, the pools provide a refreshing solution to the strain of long hours at the wheel.

[i] *Via Roma, Castiglione Marittima*

▶ *Continue on the SS398 to the southwest to Piombino.*

FOR HISTORY BUFFS

François-Jacques de Larderel set up his boric acid extracting factory in 1818. In 1827 he had the ingenious idea of building a brick dome over the bubbling 'lake' and using the steam to heat the boilers where the boric solution was concentrated. Grand Duke Leopold II was sufficiently impressed to make him Count of Montecèrboli in 1837; the village that grew up around the plant – an enlightened example of industrial paternalism – was given the name of Larderello in 1846.

The 15th-century Rocca dominates Populonia

8 Piombino

The expansion of the metal and steel industry and the great movement of people and goods to the isle of Elba have practically erased all trace of Piombino's past. From 1399 to 1815 this was the capital of the small independent state run by the Appiani family of Pisa and their descendants. To rediscover it you must climb to Piazza Citadella, converted to a residence by the Appiani family in 1465–70. Near the scenic Piazza Bovio, protruding into the sea, are the 12th-century port and the marble water fountains of the Canali springs, dated 1248.

[i] *Via Ferruccio 4 (seasonal)*

▶ *Drive back along the SS398 and go left for San Vincenzo; turn at the junction signposted on the left for Populonia.*

9 Populonia

At the foot of the Populonia headland, the road skirts the pine-shaded dunes that edge the charming Baratti gulf before arriving, on the left, at the necropolis site (7th–6th century BC), the only large Etruscan centre right on the sea. Here, from the 6th century BC to the

3rd century AD, workers processed the haematite that was brought across from the isle of Elba. The huge mounds of slag that accumulated on various types of tombs (including trench, chamber, tumulus and tambour) were removed by companies exploiting their high mineral residue between the 1920s and 1960s. On the rise behind the site is an Etruscan sandstone quarry, reused as a necropolis in the Hellenistic period (4th–2nd century BC).

The Larderello boric acid fumarole, with vapours pouring out of the cooling towers

Modern Populonia, set 170m (558 feet) up, is a tiny village dominated at the entrance by a 15th-century stronghold constructed by the Appiani family. There are fantastic views from the large grass clearing before it and even better ones from the top of the central tower.

▶ *After reaching San Vincenzo to the north, turn right for Campiglia Marittima and drive to Madonna della Fucinaia; here an unsurfaced road on the left leads to the Temperino Mining Park.*

🔟 Rocca di San Silvestro
A shuttle service leaves from the Temperino Mining Park visitor centre to pass through working quarries to the Rocca di San Silvestro, a spectacular fortified village at the top of an isolated spur. A return on foot allows you to visit mines dating from Etruscan times to the 20th century. The structures of the Rocca are quite clearly visible, thanks to recent excavations. The village was built in the 10th century to exploit the local copper and silver-lead, and was abandoned in the mid-14th century. After the guided tour of the Temperino mine, visit the Etruscan foundry furnaces (5th–4th century BC) on the left at the point where the park road meets the road to Campiglia.

ℹ Via Roma, Campiglia Marittima (seasonal)

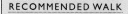

RECOMMENDED WALK

A path descends from the clearing on the left of the road up to Populonia to reach the sea in less than an hour, passing close to the vast Buche delle Fate necropolis (3rd–1st century BC), not equipped for visitors and still plundered by grave robbers (though with extreme care you can enter numerous underground chamber tombs). Along the coast below, wind and water have eroded the rocks into amazing shapes.

▶ *Back on the asphalt road, continue via Campiglia Marittima to Cafaggio; turn left on the SS398 to Suvereto and go left again via Sassetta to Castagneto Carducci.*

⓫ Castagneto Carducci
Coats-of-arms, arches and sculpted decorations are among the numerous reminders in Castagneto of the period between the 13th century and 1749, when the della Gherardesca family ruled the village. Their castle, greatly altered, still stands at the top of the village. Since the last century, however, this rich medieval history has been over-shadowed by memories of cele-brated poet Giosue Carducci (1835–1907), who lived in Castagneto with his family in 1848–9, until his father, Michele, local doctor and member of the independence movement, was dismissed and moved to Florence. An archive museum and the Carducci Centre are dedicated to the poet's memory.

ℹ Via della Marina 8, Marina di Castagneto-Donoràtico (seasonal)

▶ *Follow the SS329 to the SS1; turn right and skirt the dual*

The famous cypress-lined avenue that climbs to Bòlgheri dall'Aurelia

*carriageway to San Guido,
then right again to Bòlgheri.*

12 Bòlgheri

The fame of this village, where
Giosue Carducci spent his
childhood from 1838 to 1848, is
concentrated in the straight
tree-lined avenue that climbs
from the Via Aurelia. Its cypress
trees, lauded by the poet in a
famous work of 1874, still rise
to meet travellers between the
octagonal oratory (1703),
named after the hermit saint
Guido della Gherardesca
(10th–11th century), and the
rural farming village of
Bòlgheri. A turreted gate
provides access to the castle,
which, since the late 19th
century, has incorporated
Palazzo della Gherardesca and
a Romanesque church.

▶ *Return to the SS1 and drive
towards Livorno to the turning
signposted on the left for the
Santuario di Montenero.*

13 Santuario di Montenero

In 1345, a local shepherd found
a picture of the Virgin Mary,
brought it to this spot and
found himself miraculously
cured of a serious illness. The
small oratory, consecrated in
1575, was extended and given a
baroque-style interior in the
18th century. In the sacristy, a
rich collection of ex-votos
(votive offerings), mainly from
sailors, provides an interesting
illustration of the themes of
popular devotion. From the
church square, 193m (633 feet)

*Bòlgheri, in the woody hinterland
of Livorno*

up, the view sweeps over
Livorno and the sea. Set on a
rock off the coast is the Meloria
tower, on the site of a naval
battle won in 1284 by the
Genoese – a victory that
marked the decline of Pisa as a
seafaring power.

▶ *Follow signs for Livorno centre.*

TUSCAN ISLANDS & BEACHES

Elba, Gorgona, Capraia, Pianosa, Montecristo, Giglio and Giannutri – when the necklace adorning Venus' delicate throat broke, its splendid pearls are said to have fallen into the Tyrrhenian Sea and created the seven islands of the Tuscan archipelago. This 'ecological corridor' of islands between the peninsula, Corsica and Sardinia, has been part of a national park since 1989 – currently the largest marine park in Europe. Despite their popularity, they can still offer havens of peace along the coast, especially in June and September.

The gulf of Baratti, just north of Populonia

Elba, at 223sq km (87 square miles), is the largest and most varied island in the archipelago and the subject of Tour 7.

Gorgona is the northernmost island – 34km (21 miles) from Livorno – as well as the smallest (2.23sq km/0.8 square miles) and greenest. It's entirely mountainous and has been home to a prison farming complex since 1869. Gorgona is only accessible on guided nature excursions from Livorno (Cooperativa Parco Naturale Gorgona, tel: 0586 884522).

Capraia lies 53km (33 miles) from Piombino and is volcanic, elliptical in shape and mountainous, culminating in 44m (144-foot) Monte Castello. Most of its coastline is rocky and inaccessible. The rich Mediterranean *maquis* consists of marine rockrose, myrtle, lentiscus and rosemary mixed with oleander and arboreal euphorbias. The wild goats that gave the island its name are now extinct, as is the colony of monk seals that once settled here. From the 15th century onwards the island belonged to Genova (Genoa), but in 1815 it passed to the Kingdom of Sardinia. The only inhabited centre, Capraia Isola, features the Genoese fortress of San Giorgio. There is a lovely walk to the Stagnone, a small lake surrounded with buttercups in spring.

Pianosa is low and flat. A neighbour of the isle of Elba, 14km (9 miles) away, it has been a prison since 1858 and is not accessible to the public.

Montecristo, 40km (25 miles) south of Elba, is a granite mass bizarrely sculpted and smoothed by erosion and culminating in 645m (2,116-foot) Monte Fortezza. Wild and inhospitable, it has never been permanently inhabited apart from a settlement of Benedictine and, later, Camaldolensian monks. Their wealth was spirited away after devastating raids by Barbary pirates in 1553, giving rise to the legend of the buried treasure that inspired Alexander Dumas'

1844 novel *The Count of Monte Cristo*. The Savoy family turned the island into a hunting reserve and it is now a marine and land nature reserve, allowing access to no more than 1,000 visitors per year on organised guided trips (Ufficio Forestale di Follònica, tel: 0566 40019).

Giglio, 14km (9 miles) from the Argentario (ferry service from Porto Santo Stefano, also to Giannutri), is almost entirely mountainous, with a generally high coastline that is rugged to the west and in the east has sandy coves equipped for seaside tourism (Giglio Campese). Fragrant *maquis* alternates with rock, and the cultivated vine terraces produce a strong, prized wine called *Ansonica*. The main commercial centre is Giglio Porto and the *comune* is based at Giglio Castello, 6km (4 miles) from the port in the centre of the island. This charming maze of narrow streets, steep steps and medieval houses is dominated by the Pisan Rocca. It was rebuilt after 1544 when the notorious Barbary pirate Barbarossa (Khair-ed-Din) devastated the island and deported the 700 survivors as slaves.

Giannutri, part of the *comune* of Giglio, 16km (10 miles) away, is the southernmost island in the Tuscan archipelago. Its crescent-shaped coastline is nearly all rocky, with two short pebble beaches. Having served as a Roman commercial port, a sanctuary for monks and a Pisan naval base, it is now a private residential estate. Visitors can land on it but may not stay overnight unless invited.

From Viareggio to the Argentario

Tuscany has approximately 300km (186 miles) of coastline, much of which gets crowded in the summer holiday months, especially July and August. Immediately inland, however, from the Apuan Alps to the historical villages in the Livorno hills, there are many rewarding distractions.

The coastline is generally low and sandy, with large beaches and bathing establishments. The terrain rises briefly to the south of Livorno, then again after Baratti in the Piombino headland, at Punta Ala, after Bocca d'Ombrone in the Uccellina mountains, and in Monte Argentario. Stretches of the original coastal dune

landscape can be seen near the Migliarino *maquis* (see Tour 4), in the Uccellina Park (see Tour 8) and around Orbetello (see Tour 9). The principal seaside (and society) resorts are Forte dei Marmi, Viareggio, San Vincenzo and the Baratti gulf, Castiglioncello, Punta Ala and Castiglione della Pescaia, Porto Santo Stefano and Porto Ercole on the Argentario.

Sun and sea at Punta Ala

The Isle
of Elba

Just an hour's ride on the ferry from Piombino to Portoferraio will bring you to the incredible mosaic of natural scenery that is Elba – gulfs, headlands, precipitous coastline, peaceful bays, Mediterranean *maquis*, abandoned mines, woody mountains and terraced vineyards; and, all around, the deep, blue sea.

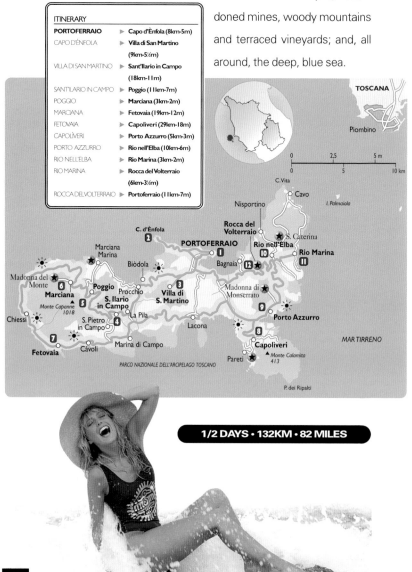

1/2 DAYS · 132KM · 82 MILES

Sansone beach, near Portoferraio

house between 1814 and 1815, and adopted it as his country residence. In fact, he used it only as a stopover during his walks, and never slept here.

▶ *Back on the main road, continue west to Procchio, then left to the Pilà (airport) and right for Sant'Ilario in Campo.*

4 Sant'Ilario in Campo
Leaving the sandy shores of the Biùdola and Procchio gulfs to the right, climb to the village of Sant'Ilario in Campo (202m/663 feet). About 3km (2 miles) further on, towards Poggio, the road passes through fine scenery close to the largest Romanesque church on Elba, the roofless parish church of San Giovanni (12th century). Near by, on a huge granite mound, stands a Pisan defence tower.

▶ *Continue to Poggio.*

5 Poggio
After passing the charming hamlet of Poggio, you will come to the Fonte di Napoleone, set in a cool wood surrounded by granite rocks. This tiny spa is no longer in use, but if you want to test the diuretic properties of the water – sampled by Napoleon himself when he visited the sanctuary of Marciana – you can buy it bottled, or use the highly popular fountain along the road.

1 Portoferraio
Cosimo de'Medici and Napoleon Bonaparte were the two men who shaped this town's destiny. In 1548, the former transformed the medieval mining port of Ferraia into the impregnable Cosmopolis, defended on its seaward boundary by three mighty forts – Linguella, Falcone and Stella – and on land by the grand Fronte d'Attacco bastions. The exiled Napoleon landed in the capital of Elba on 3 May, 1814. The Palazzina dei Mulini was adapted for him, and he lived there until 26 February, 1815, when he set out to try and regain power and face his old enemy at Waterloo.

i Calata Italia 26

▶ *Travel west on the coastal road to Capo d'Ènfola.*

2 Capo d'Ènfola
A strip of land links the island with this sheer, rocky headland (135m/443 feet), covered with shrubbery and edged with the splendid Acquaviva beach. On the approach is a large 18th-century fishery that was in use until a few decades ago.

▶ *Return along the same route and follow the signs for Marciana Marina; turn left for Villa di San Martino just past the Porto Azzurro junction.*

3 Villa di San Martino
Napoleon added a small two-storey neo-classical building to this originally unpretentious

---

FOR CHILDREN

At San Giovanni, near Portoferraio, a pleasant stop can be made at Elbaland, where horses, goats, sheep, donkeys, peacocks, deer, rabbits, ostriches, ducks, geese and swans live in harmony with visitors beside a toddlers' playground. Amadeus is a delightful amusement park, overlooking the Barbarossa gulf at Sassi Turchini, 1km (½ mile) from Porto Azzurro.

▶ *Follow the signs to Marciana.*

❻ Marciana

Set on the slopes of Monte Capanne (at 1,018m/3,340 feet the highest peak on the island, reached by cableway or path), lies Marciana, a pretty village with narrow winding streets, dominated by the picturesque ruins of the castle taken by the Appiani family of Piombino in 1399. From the village, a road and then a path with a Via Crucis (Way of the Cross) of 14 chapels lead in 45 minutes to the medieval Sanctuary of the Madonna del Monte, rebuilt in the 16th and 17th centuries. In 1814 Napoleon was often a guest at the nearby hermitage; on one visit he was accompanied by Maria Walewska, his Polish lover.

▶ *Return to the coast road and follow it around the west of the island to Fetovaia.*

❼ Fetovaia

On the way here the route passes a sheer, rugged coastline

RECOMMENDED EXCURSION

South of Capoliveri a fast road leads to Pareti and the Innamorata Bay, surrounded by dazzling marine landscapes and monuments of industrial archaeology. In the early 20th century, this was a fully equipped quay for the export of minerals; now it's a modern ruin, corroded by wind and salt.

SPECIAL TO...

At the foot of Marciana is Marciana Marina, at just over 5sq km (2 square miles), the smallest *comune* in Tuscany. It forms a crescent along the beach, with its convenient harbour guarded by a round Pisan tower, 25m (82 feet) high.
Between Marciana Marina and Procchio stretches the delightful Paolina beach, where Napoleon's enigmatic sister indulged in the then scandalous practice of nude sunbathing.

and, not far from Chiessi, the lovely 13th-century church of San Bartolomeo, well worth a visit. At the foot of a rocky outcrop you reach the spectacular sandy beach of Fetovaia, framed by pine trees. Also of note, a short distance further to the east, is the Càvoli beach, a particular favourite with young people.

▶ *Continue east towards Porto Azzurro to the turning on the right for Capoliveri.*

❽ Capoliveri

At the Roman *Caput Liberum*, preceded by the remains of the

Along the coast near Marciana

Romanesque church of San Michele (late 12th century), you enter Elba's mining territory. Nowadays, in fact, the local economy relies mainly on tourists, especially from Germany. A scenic road high above the sea offers views of the former iron mines of Monte Calamita (413m/1,355 feet), at the foot of which lie some of the island's wildest and most unspoiled beaches.

▶ *Return the same way, following the signs for Porto Azzurro.*

9 Porto Azzurro

Porto Azzurro lies on a fiord in the Mola Gulf, an area which, during the 17th century, was garrisoned by the Spanish. They built the Focardo fort, to the southeast, and the mighty star-shaped Longone fortress (now used as a prison; the town was called Porto Longone from 1863 to 1947) at the opposite end of the bay. North of Porto Azzurro, today a renowned holiday resort with a leisure-boat marina, a path climbs to the Sanctuary of the Madonna di Monserrato

spurs raised by the Appiani family in the 16th century. To the north of the village is the hermitage of Santa Caterina, surrounded by fragrant rose bushes.

▶ *Descend eastwards to Rio Marina.*

11 Rio Marina

Protected by a 16th-century hexagonal tower, the small bay overlooked by Rio Marina – once a mining centre – is enclosed within red-ochre

ferrous rocks. In the village, where the houses shine with specks of iron, the Elba Mineral Museum displays minerals extracted on the island. Near by, enthusiasts can search for haematite and magnetite crystals among the gigantic tiers of an old open-air mine. The famous beaches of Bagnaia, Nisporto and Nisportino lie to the west of the village.

▶ *Back at the Rio nell'Elba junction, proceed eastwards to the Rocca del Volterraio.*

The Volterraio stronghold

(1606), where a copy of the Black Madonna of the monastery of Monserrat in Catalonia is venerated.

▶ *Continue northeast to Rio nell'Elba.*

10 Rio nell'Elba

Reddish rocks near Rio nell'Elba bear witness to the ancient mining activities of this area. Etruscans came here seeking supplies of iron minerals for the furnaces of Populonia. The church at the centre of the village is defended by fortified

RECOMMENDED WALK

Terranera is an emerald-green lake of sulphurous sodium chloride, sodium iodide and bromine waters. This surreal place is surrounded by red rocks and yellow broom, and separated from the sea by a strip of light-coloured sand. Take the road from Porto Azzurro to Rio nell'Elba and turn right just after the turning for the Madonna di Monserrato, at the sign 'Residenza Reale'. The final descent is on foot; the spectacle of the lake and its setting is without equal.

12 Rocca del Volterraio

After a few kilometres the ruins of the Volterraio stronghold appear, perched on their rock. The complex developed around a Pisan watch-tower (built, according to legend, by the Etruscan Queen Ilva), and its arches, wells, vaults and military patrol walks can be reached along a footpath. Splendid views of the coast accompany the descent to Le Grotte and the remains of a Roman villa dating from the 1st century AD, arranged around a large pool.

▶ *Follow the signs west back to Portoferraio.*

The Maremma
near Grosseto

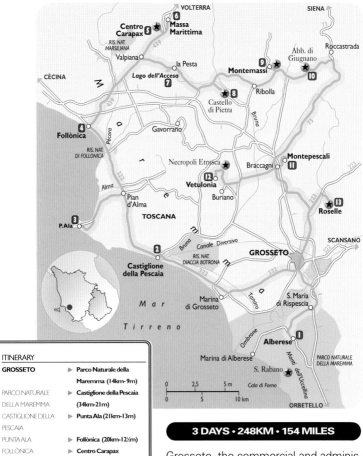

3 DAYS • 248KM • 154 MILES

Grosseto, the commercial and administrative hub of Maremma, is a modern-looking town, though the old centre still survives, enclosed within the strong hexagonal walls erected by the Medici family in 1564–93. A delightful half-hour walk takes you all the way round.

The Maremma Park in Alberese

[i] *Via Monterosa 206, Grosseto*

▶ *Follow the **SS1** southbound to Santa Maria di Rispescia, then signs for Alberese and the Maremma (or Uccellina) Nature Park Visitor Centre.*

❶ Parco Naturale dell'Uccellina

The Uccellina mountains, the Marina di Alberese pinewood, the mouth of the Ombrone river and the Trappola marsh make up Uccellina Park, a microcosm of classic Maremma, where cowboys on horseback oversee the grazing cattle – distinctive for their long lyre-shaped horns – and horses roam half-wild. Paths in the park include a 6km (4-mile) round walk (5 hours) across *maquis* and hills to the ruined abbey of San Rabano (11th to 12th century), and a 5km (3-mile) round walk (3 hours) to the watch-towers (13th and 16th century), taking in all the major ecosystems en route. A 12km (7-mile) round walk (6 hours) runs from the coast to the splendid beach of Cala di Forno.

[i] *Via del Fante*

▶ *Return to Grosseto and take the **SS322** west to Castiglione della Pescaia.*

❷ Castiglione della Pescaia

Climb from the picturesque port-canal, crowded with fishing vessels and leisure craft, to the medieval district, perched on a spur of rock. The formidable ring of Pisan walls and towers (12th to 13th century) was reinforced during the occupation of the Aragonese (1446–60) with the restoration of the triangular stronghold. Today, Castiglione is a renowned seaside resort; to the southeast, it boasts an endless sandy shore framed by the large pines and dunes that skirt the Diaccia Botrona nature reserve.

[i] *Piazza Garibaldi*

▶ *Continue along the **SS322** to the turning on the left for Punta Ala.*

Sunset in the Maremma Park

'*Butteri*', Maremma's cowboys

3 Punta Ala

Until 1932 this resort was known as Capo Troia. It acquired its new name, which means 'Wing Point', when the entire area was bought by the Fascist government and aviator Count Italo Balbo (1896–1940). A luxury tourist zone has developed among the dense *maquis* that covers the headland, and, slightly further north, is Cala Violina, a beautiful bay with sand that crunches musically beneath your feet. The Hidalgo or Barbiere tower (1577) is an outpost of the State of Piombino, on the border with the Grand Duchy of Tuscany; there's also a contemporary tower, known as the Troia (or Balbo castle).

➤ *Back on the **SS322**, continue northwards to Follònica.*

4 Follònica

The highly unusual church of San Leopoldo sits in the centre of town. Its portico, bell tower, altar, candelabra and pulpit all feature extensive use of ornately fashioned cast iron, produced between 1836 and 1838 by the old foundries of Great Duke Leopold II, who encouraged the industry as part of the Maremma reclamation programme. Once a simple hamlet, Follònica is now

---

RECOMMENDED WALK

On the road from Grosseto, a small turning on the right, just before the bridge over Castiglione della Pescaia canal, leads to Casa Rossa. Constructed in 1767–8 by engineer Leonardo Ximenes, it straddles the catchment canal; floodgates, worked from inside, regulated the outflow of stagnant water.
Beyond the adjacent bridge, a signposted path leads between the canal banks and the Diaccia Botrona marsh, all that remains of the ancient Lake Prile.

the second major urban centre of Grosseto province.

i *Via Giacomelli 11*

▶ *Take the SS439 to the foot of Massa Marìttima; turn left and follow the signs for the Centro Carapax.*

5 Centro Carapax

This European centre for the protection of tortoises and

▶ *Return to the junction with the SS439 and follow the signs to the centre of Massa.*

6 Massa Marìttima

Massa Marìttima has two separate centres. The lower Città Vecchia is the hub of civic activities, while the Città Nuova, a development started in 1228, sits higher up. Between the two is the fortress built by Siena to control the people of

which now houses an archaeological museum and contains the superb *Majesty* (1340) by Ambrogio Lorenzetti, celebrating Sienese supremacy. A few steps away, the Mining Museum commemorates Maremma's mining origins, the initial source of its wealth.

i *Via N Parenti 22*

▶ *Back at the junction, continue*

Punta Ala, the Cala Violina beach

turtles studies all imaginable specimens – large and small, terrestrial and marine, Italian and exotic. After taking part in breeding programmes, all are returned to nature. Many belong to unusual species, such as alligator snappers, giant Sahel tortoises and red-footed Amazon turtles. Gentle Monte Amiata donkeys live with the tortoises, taking care not to squash them. There is also a huge aviary for storks, which allows them plenty of space with an area as large as a football pitch and 25m (82 feet) high. In summer, it is best to visit early in the morning or towards evening.

Massa after their subjugation in 1335. To pass from one centre to the other you must go through the Silici Gate; near this, a breathtaking arched bridge, 22m (72 feet) long, connects the Sienese keep to the older Candeliere tower with a fine view from the top. The Città Vecchia boasts a splendid, sloping medieval square, overlooked by the buildings of episcopal and lay power. By a skilful play of perspective, the arches on the façade of the magnificent 12th–13th-century Romanesque-Gothic Duomo (cathedral) of San Cerbone seem to grow narrower as you walk towards the end of the square. Opposite is the Palazzo Pretorio or Podestà (1225–35),

SPECIAL TO...

At Massa Marìttima, the recent restoration of the Fonti dell'Abbondanza (1265, named after the public granary above) uncovered a fresco of a 'fertility tree' with male penises hanging from its branches. Women converse beneath its foliage; two are fighting over one of the unusual 'fruits', while another chases the crows that are about to eat them. This is an exceptionally rare find in Italy: most representations of this theme are more circumspect, depicting men and women hanging from the branches.

along the SS439 towards Follònica; enter Valpiana and follow the signs to the left for Lago dell'Accesa. At La Pesta a short unsurfaced road leads to the lake.

7 Lago dell'Accesa

Crystal-clear blue waters flow underground at a constant temperature of 20°C (68°F) in a hollow surrounded by meadows and wooded hills. The pale sand bed plunges at the centre to a depth of 45m (148 feet). This unspoiled corner of Maremma is a haven for the swimmers who venture into the marsh grass, sedge and water lilies of its shores.

▶ *Drive on and take the provincial road on the left to Ribolla; shortly after the junction, turn right on to an unsurfaced estate road and proceed for 2.6km (1½ miles) to a derelict farm on the right.*

The square in Massa Marittima; on the left are the steps leading up to the Duomo

8 Castello di Pietra

Leave the car and in just a few minutes you can climb to the precipitous ruins of a castle, whose presence was first recorded in 1067. During the 13th century it belonged to the Pannocchieschi family; one of them – Nello – is said to have brought his Sienese wife, Pia dei Tolomei, here and killed her so that he could marry the powerful Margherita Aldobrandeschi. The unfortunate Pia makes an appearance in Dante's *Inferno*, and an ominous sign among the ruins marks the spot known as the Countess's Leap.

▶ *Back on the provincial road, proceed right via Ribolla towards Roccastrada to the turning on the left for Montemassi.*

9 Montemassi

You will already have seen the crenellated silhouette of Montemassi castle. This Pannocchieschi fortress was besieged in a daring campaign by Guidoriccio da Fogliano,

captain of the Sienese army. In 1328 Simone Martini celebrated his victory in a fresco in the Palazzo Public in Siena. Behind the captain, he shows the temporary wood and stone structure erected by the Sienese in the course of the siege. Only the ruins of the stronghold, with its unmistakable octagonal tower, now survive.

Detail of the frescoes at the Fonti dell'Abbondanza, Massa Marittima

marked the beginning of a crisis, when nearby Populonia seized its monopoly of the iron and maritime trades. The ruins of its 5km (3 miles) of polygonal-block walls are all that survives of its past grandeur in the town itself; archaeological sites at the entrance to the town and near the cemetery date from Roman times (2nd–1st century BC). Even the name was lost for a while – it became known as Colonna di Buriano, until a royal decree of 1887 restored the ancient name of Vetulonia.

On the northeastern slopes of the hill are the impressive tombs of a necropolis called Via dei Sepolcri. The Pietrera tumulus (7th century BC) measures 60m (197 feet) in diameter.

▶ *Return to Braccagni and follow the old Aurelia road southbound, turning left for the SS223 Siena-Grosseto; to the north, this leads to the turning signposted on the left for Roselle.*

13 Roselle

The history of Etruscan Roselle mirrors that of Vetulonia. Situated on the opposite shore of Lake Prile, it flourished from the end of the 6th century BC as its rival declined, and based its fortunes on a flourishing farming trade. Conquered by the Romans in 294 BC, it continued to prosper until the 1st century BC and was not abandoned until 1138, when the bishop of Roselle moved to Grosseto.

Straddling two deserted hills, gigantic Etruscan walls surround considerable Roman remains – streets, a medieval tower, the imperial forum, outline of the amphitheatre, and spa (reused as a church in the 5th and 6th centuries), as well as the foundations of houses and public buildings.

▶ *Back on the SS223 travel southwards to Grosseto.*

▶ *Return to the last junction and continue towards Roccastrada for approximately 5km (3 miles). Turn left at the signpost for Tecnobay and drive 200m (220 yards) to the San Guglielmo farm holiday centre, which organises visits.*

10 Abbazia di Giugnano

The ruins of the abbey dedicated to San Salvatore comprise a splendid Romanesque crypt and a colonnade with cross vaults on four columns. You must descend underground to reach it, as the original plan was 3m (6 feet) lower than at present. Near by stand the Gothic remains of a church. A stone hydraulic structure, also in the area, indicates the site of a former foundry. The name of the centre, San Guglielmo, probably derives from Wilhema of Bohemia, who had a strong following in 13th-century Maremma.

▶ *Continue towards Roccastrada as far as the SS73, then turn right and drive towards Grosseto until you come to Braccagni; from here proceed to Montepescali.*

11 Montepescali

Montepescali, set in a dominant position on the plain leading to Grosseto, was a feudal territory

belonging to the Aldobrand-eschi family throughout the 13th century. Ultimately, though, it fell within the orbit of Siena, and the city finally took possession of it around 1300. Of considerable note here are the 14th-century church of San Lorenzo (the square which it overlooks has a sweeping view of Maremma and the Giglio island), and the Romanesque San Niccolò (12th–13th century).

▶ *Descend to Braccagni again and travel westwards following the signs for Buriano and then Vetulonia.*

12 Vetulonia

It may seem unlikely now, but Etruscan *Vetluna* was a seafaring town. In a sculpture dating from the 1st century AD the town is personified as a young man with an oar on his shoulder, and indeed at that time Vetulonia overlooked the large lagoon which extended to the sea and which the Romans called Lake Prile. This was a centre of primary importance in the 8th and 7th centuries BC; it was here that many of the Romans' symbols of power were devised – the curule chair (seat of office for Roman officials), the purple-edged toga, the fasces (symbolic rod denoting a magistrate's power), and the trumpet of war. But the early 6th century BC

The Tufa Lands
& the Argentario

The name Maremma derives from *mare* – the sea. But there is also an inland Maremma – the Maremma of impenetrable *maquis* and shady gorges, of strongholds and rocky sites, of Etruscan burial places and 'quarry ways' cut into the thick layer of tufa, volcanic rock produced when Monte Amiata and the Bolsena mountains spewed lava over the land where the Albegna now flows.

3 DAYS · 267KM · 166 MILES

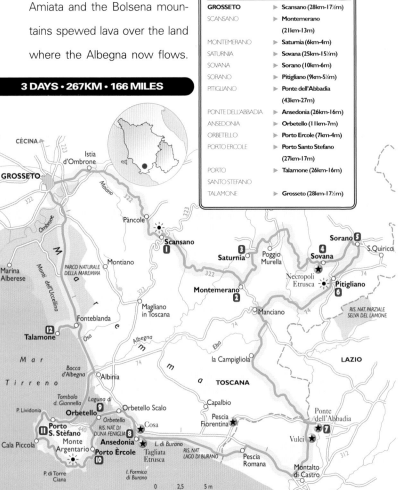

Via Fucini 43/c, Grosseto

▶ *Follow the SS322 to Scansano.*

❶ Scansano
Until 1897, this village was invaded every year from May to September by Grosseto's leading civil, military and religious authorities. This was the 'summering' – an administrative holiday instigated by the Grand Duke of Lorraine Leopold II, known as 'Canapone' for his thick red hair. The purpose of the annual exodus was to avoid the worst of the malaria season – an equivalent of the British flight to the Indian hills during the monsoon. In winter the whole process went into reverse, as shepherds and woodcutters descended from the mountains to the coast. The air really is good up here, 500m (1,640 feet) above sea level in the Maremma countryside. From Scansano you can see Monte Amiata and the sea, from the isle of Elba to Civitavecchia in the distance. The wine is also rather good:

production of the local tipple (*Morellino*) is celebrated with a grape festival in September.

▶ *Continue along the SS322 to Montemerano.*

❷ Montemerano
The narrow streets and tiny squares of this village clustered on a 303m (994 feet) hillock form a charming medieval picture of one of the most well-preserved centres in the Albegna valley. The fine church of San Giorgio (14th century) has an unusual panel, the 15th-century *Madonna della Gattaiola*. It has survived despite years of use as a granary door, complete with a hole at the bottom to let the cat through.

▶ *Go back to the turning for Saturnia.*

❸ Saturnia
As you arrive in the valley at the foot of Saturnia (294m/964 feet), your nostrils are assailed by a strong smell of sulphur. It

Relaxing in the warm waters of Saturnia's natural pools

emanates from the warm, whitish-blue waters of the Gorello falls, which fume and bounce off perfect natural basins of white travertine stone. Enthusiastic bathers flock here summer and winter, day and night (leave your car on the unattended dirt track to the left).

A little further on to the right, Viale delle Terme leads to two magnificent pools, where the water flowing from a rocky spring is even hotter, at 37°C (99°F). Higher up, on a plateau, is a quiet 19th-century farming village, with good visitor amenities. Marks left by the iron rims of ancient cartwheels are still visible in the paving of Via Clodia, which crosses the monumental Etruscan–Roman south gate (ancient Saturnia was destroyed by Silla in 82 BC). From here a 30-minute walk along a lovely path leads to the spa pools (156m/512 feet).

▶ *Proceed eastwards following the signs for Sovana.*

4 Sovana

Beyond a tunnel visitors are confronted with mysterious 'eyes' hollowed in the tufa rock. These are the first signs that you have reached the isolated town of Sovana, birthplace of Hildebrand, who became Pope

Pitigliano's houses are built into the tufa hills

Gregory VII (1073–85). At one end of the village stand the ruins of the Rocca Aldobrandesca (13th–14th century); at the opposite end is the solitary Romanesque Duomo (cathedral, 12th–14th century). Between the two stretches the brick-paved village street. Grouped in the fascinating square are the Palazzo Pretorio (12th–13th century), the adjacent Loggia del Capitano, the Palazzo Archivio, the ruins of an early-Christian church (possibly 4th century) and the Romanesque Santa Maria (12th–13th century). All around Sovana lie large Etruscan necropolises, interlaced with beautiful nature walks. Among the mysterious 'quarry ways' cut precipitously in the tufa is that of San Sebastiano, near the Sirena tomb.

ⓘ *Palazzetto dell'Archivio*

▶ *Follow the signs for Sorano.*

5 Sorano

Watching over the village is the mighty stronghold built by Niccolò IV Orsini in 1552 – one of the most impressive military structures in Maremma. The defensive ring of walls that protect it are reached via a gateway that displays the emblems of the Aldobrandeschi and Orsini families. At its foot, the village, full of unusually decorated old buildings, extends towards Sasso Leopoldino. This remarkable rock was incorporated in the 18th century into a sloping wall surrounded by houses built in tufa. Huddled together or perched on the slope, these are linked by steep streets, covered and underground passages and steps. The whole district, known as Rocca Vecchia, has suffered the worst of the landslides which have threatened the existence of Sorano for nearly 200 years.

Wildfowl in the Monte Argentario nature reserve

$\boxed{i}$ *Piazza Busati*

▶ *Follow the signs to Pitigliano.*

6 Pitigliano

The best place to view this extraordinary spectacle is from the Sanctuary of the Madonna delle Grazie, at the first left-hand bend on the SS74 for Marciano. Even at night, when it's illuminated with floodlights, Pitigliano is an amazing sight.

FOR CHILDREN

Tarot-card characters and mystic visions inhabit the Giardino dei Tarocchi, the park created by Niki de Saint-Phalle in 1979 in an abandoned quarry. The brightly coloured reflecting surfaces of the Wheel of Fortune, the Magician and the High Priestess, the Tower and the Empress combine fun and fairy-tales with an unsettling air of sorcery and spirits. The park is reached along an unsurfaced lane that branches off the Aurelia junction for Pescia Fiorentina.

Its houses sit on the edge of a sheer tufa mass, filled with cavities and dominated by the grandiose arches of the aqueduct (1543–5), designed by Antonio da Sangallo for Gian Francesco Orsini. Set 313m (1,027 feet) up, it was built to a typically Etruscan plan: a spur surrounded on three sides by ravines and fortified on the fourth, with 'quarry ways' leading from the foot of the site. It acquired its medieval-Renaissance appearance thanks to the Orsini family, who ruled between 1293 and the 16th century. They were responsible for the palace-fortress that now houses the Diocesan Museum of Holy Art and the Civic Archaeological Museum. In a side street, a small synagogue (1589) with an unleavened-bread oven is a reminder of the Jewish community that formed here after the expulsion of Jews from Rome by the Papal bull of 1569. The Jewish population diminished as people emigrated to Livorno and Florence, and vanished altogether after the Fascist persecutions. The local

Tha Abbadia bridge across the Fiora river at Vulci

economy now relies heavily on the production of its prized white Pitigliano wine.

$\boxed{i}$ *Piazza Garibaldi*

▶ *Take the SS74 to Marciano where you turn left on to the provincial road to Ponte dell'Abbadia (Vulci).*

7 Ponte dell'Abbadia

Anyone crossing the bridge over the Flora river had to pass under the arched walls and tower of the

The bay and port of Porto Ercole

Badia castle, a 12th-century Cistercian building restructured in the 16th century. This formed the customs post between the Papal State and the Grand Duchy of Tuscany; today it houses the Vulci National Museum. Vulci was – especially in the 7th and 6th centuries BC – one of southern Etruria's main trading and manufacturing centres. The museum houses

what little remained after Lucien Bonaparte started excavating in 1828.

Near by, you can visit the town's remains and necropolis, including the maze-like Cuccummella tumulus and the tomb of François (4th century BC), once famous for containing the only cycle of wall paintings with an 'historical' subject handed down by the Etruscans. The paintings were removed in the 1800s and most of the cycle is on display in the Torlonia collection of Villa Albani in Rome.

▶ *Follow the signs for Montalto di Castro to the SS1 (Aurelia); turn right on to this and exit at Pescia Romana to reach the coast, which leads westwards to Ansedonia.*

8 Ansedonia
Ansedonia does not exist – it was totally destroyed by the Sienese in 1330. Today's elegant resort is made up of villas and visitor amenities dotted across the slopes of a hill, at the top of which stand the ruins of the flourishing Roman town of *Cosa*, founded in 273 BC. Remains of the old quays crumble into the waves, but the silting of the port at the foot of the rise is

prevented by the regulation of the flow and ebb of waters, using the so-called Tagliata Etrusca (Etruscan Channel). Before the Romans dug this tunnel from the rock, drainage was guaranteed by the breathtaking Spacco della Regina Channel, on the other side of the Tagliata and now blocked in its final section. The nearby Torre della Tagliata (15th century), along with the remains of a Roman villa, was occupied by Puccini when composing part of his opera *Tosca*.

▶ *Continue across the Ansedonia hill (signposted to the right is the Cosa archaeological site) and return to the SS1; after 3km (2 miles), turn left for Orbetello.*

9 Orbetello
Orbetello perches on a strip of land extended by a dam built in 1842 and now reaching the Argentario and dividing the lagoon in two. The town's military past is preserved in the remains of Etruscan walls and 15th-century Sienese and 16th- to 18th-century Spanish fortifications. At the town library is the terracotta pediment of the Etruscan temple of Talamone (2nd century BC). It is not

known whether the Argentario ('silver') headland (then an island) was named after the shiny rocks or the office of *argentarii* (bankers) exercised by the Romans who governed the area.

[i] *Piazza della Repubblica*

▶ *After reaching the Argentario, follow the signs to the left for Porto Ercole.*

10 Porto Ercole
This seaside resort and tourist marina sits on a bay overlooked by a circle of 16th-century forts

and bastions. A splendid old village occupies the foot of the headland, where the Rocca (fort) looms. A pointed gate leads to a maze of covered passages, low arches and steps hewn into the rock. The powerful defence system of Porto Ercole (founded by the Romans) comprises the quadrangular Filippo fort (1558, private) and the original Stella fort.

[i] *Via Caravaggio 78*

▶ *Drive around the edge of Monte Argentario, following the signs for Cala Piccola and Porto Santo Stefano, on a splendidly scenic but winding road, with a difficult unsurfaced section approximately 4km (2 miles) long immediately after Porto Ercole. Those wishing to avoid this section can go back along the SS440 to the Tombolo della Giannella.*

11 Porto Santo Stefano
A group of Genoese sailors was shipwrecked here in the 15th century and stayed put to live as fishermen. This is the centre that suffered most damage during the bombing raids of World War II. Its post-war

reconstruction spared the old centre clustered around the 17th-century stronghold, and the village is now kept alive by the busy tourist trade passing through the port, that serves the Giglio and Giannutri islands.

[i] *Archetto del Palio 1*

▶ *Take the SS440 towards Orbetello and turn left for the Tombolo della Giannella as far as the SS1; drive 8km (5 miles) towards the Grosseto exit at Fonteblanda to reach Talamone to the west.*

12 Talamone
This was called *Tlamu* by the Etruscans and *Telamon* by the Romans, when it was the main port of the Albegna valley towns. At that time it extended between the Bengodi and Talamonaccio hills. The site of today's lively fishing village was established in the Middle Ages, and is dominated by the mighty Rocca, erected by the Sienese in the 15th century.

[i] *Via Cala di Forno 7*

▶ *Take the SS1 back to Grosseto.*

Fishing in the Orbetello lagoon

NORTHEAST TUSCANY

This area was historically part of Florence's first dominion; today it lies within the provinces of Florence and Arezzo. Mugello, northeast of the regional capital, is a vast hollow in the mountains, crossed by the Sieve river, which flows through the valley of the same name into the Arno. The hills around Florence gradually dissolve into the alluvial plain of the lower Valdarno, and the river basins of the Elsa and Era also flow into the Arno. Val d'Elsa (the Elsa Valley), wedged between the Chianti hills, which separate it to the east from Val di Pesa and the ridge of heights that extend from San Gimignano to San Miniato, was once one of the main through-routes between northern and southern Tuscany.

Between upper Valdarno and the Sieve are the rounded meadow-covered hills of Pratomagno. To the west lies Casentino, a deep hollow in the upper reaches of the Arno, with a landscape of turreted hill-villages, castles and parish churches, climbing from the vineyards and olive groves of the valley floor to chestnut groves, meadows and extensive, ancient fir woods. Back on the plain, you travel through the Upper Val Tiberina, the Tuscan stretch of the Tiber Valley, past mountain springs and Sansepolcro. After a brief excursion to Città di Castello in Umbria, you cross the farming region of Valdichiana, south-west of Arezzo.

Of the rich and varied attractions found in this part of Tuscany, the foremost are those in Florence; a remarkable Renaissance showpiece, crammed with the very best of that exceptional era's artistic output. In Tuscany a city is wherever there is a square, a church and a mansion; other splendid examples include San Miniato, tiny Certaldo, San Gimignano and Cortona. Out in the countryside there are more treasures: the Medici villas, monasteries and hermitages hidden in the silent, dark green woods. Art is omnipresent, and deserves its own tours – such as that of Piero della Francesca, from Arezzo to Anghiari and Sansepolcro.

Palazzo Pitti seen from the Bòboli gardens in Florence

A wolf in the Casentino forest

Tour 10

Florence is one of the world's most famous cities, a treasure trove of art and architecture. This tour explores it on two circular routes which converge to form a figure of eight on Piazza della Signoria. Make sure you take into account the vast crowds of visitors to museums, churches and chapels (best to book where possible) as well as the incredible wealth of things to see. The Uffizi alone would take several long visits to do it justice.

Tour 11

West of Florence, the urbanised Arno plain was, and still is, a manufacturing, craft and industrial centre. The hunting and the grape-harvests that brought the Medici family here on their holidays are, however, things of the past. Visit the lofty stronghold of the imperial San Miniato before heading south across Val d'Elsa, dotted with its 'dual' towns – the monuments of nobility and power on the hilltops, the merchant houses and markets lower down. Medieval

San Gimignano is an exception, its ancient towers and streets forming an irresistible whole. Monteriggioni, near Siena, and the Charterhouse of Galluzzo, close to Florence, illustrate the themes of secular force and religious spirit that recur, often in fierce opposition, throughout the history of this area.

Tour 12

The centuries-old practice of 'colonisation' conducted by the Florentine capital in the Mugello hills, northeast of the city, created a dense network of parish churches, villas and castles around the vast valley of

the Sieve, a crucial tributary of the Arno. The Medici came here for amusement, but also to attend to their affairs. Today's visitors can indulge their fantasies as they explore ancient 'walled lands' and the scenic delights of the hill of Fiesole, Etruscan precursor of Florence.

Tour 13

This tour winds through one of Tuscany's most extensive and unspoiled 'green lungs', home to numerous hermitages and religious settlements entrusted with care of the majestic fir and beech woods that cover the area. The Franciscan site of Verna and the Benedictine complex at Camàldoli, protected by the turreted castles of the Guidi counts, are followed by the long, rounded mountain ramparts of the Pratomagno hills, watched over by Vallombrosa. Parish churches, abbeys and 14th-century settlements accompany the return to Arezzo.

Tour 14

After passing the small centres of the Arezzo hinterland on the edge of the Romagna-Marches Apennine, this tour crosses into Umbria which, especially at Città di Castello, seems so very Tuscan. It follows a section of the upper reaches of the Tiber, then passes through quiet countryside to emerge in the Chiana Valley and Cortona, on its eastern edge, standing amid olive groves.

The Medici villa at Artimino

Florence

Florence is one of the world's great cities. The sheer concentration of great art – in churches, mansions and museums – almost defies belief, and is matched only in Rome and Venice. The beauty of the city itself, set amid the gentle slopes that descend to the River Arno, is another element in its uniquely Tuscan magic.

3 DAYS

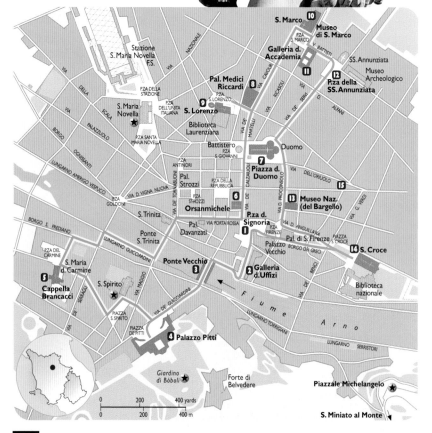

i Via Cavour 1r; Piazza della
Stazione 4a

➤ *Go to Piazza della Signoria on
foot or by public transport. The
closest large car-parks are to
the northwest, beneath Piazza
del Mercato and the Santa
Maria Novella railway station.*

❶ Piazza della Signoria

This became the home of secular
power when, in the early 14th
century, Arnolfo di Cambio built
Palazzo dei Priori. It was later
known as Palazzo Signoria in the
15th century, Palazzo Ducale in
1540, when Cosimo I (1537–74)
took up office here, and Palazzo
Vecchio when he later moved to
Palazzo Pitti (1565). Parliament
sat in Palazzo Vecchio from 1865
to 1871, when Florence was the
capital of Italy. Today, this
massive structure, crowned by a
gallery built for the lookout
patrol (the design was based on
the tower, 94m/308 feet high),

Portrait of a Man by Sandro
Botticelli in the Uffizi Gallery

serves as the city hall, and
contains splendid rooms.

The square before it, scene
of great political events, was
adorned over the years with
symbolic sculptures (most have
been replaced with copies) –
Donatello's *Judith and Holofernes*
(here since 1495) and
Michelangelo's *David* (1504)
mark the victory of democracy
over tyranny, whereas *Hercules
and Cacus* (1534), created for the
first Duke, Alessandro (1532–7),
represents victory over the
Medici's enemies. Dictator
Cosimo I was portrayed in it on
horseback by Giambologna
(1594–8). Far less visible, near
the Neptune fountain (known
as *il B, Biancone* to the
Florentines), an inscription indicates the place where religious
and political reformer Girolamo
Savonarola was hanged and

burnt at the stake in 1498 with
two fellow Dominican friars.

➤ *To the south of the square is
the entrance to the Uffizi
Gallery, at the top of the
loggia on the left.*

❷ Galleria degli Uffizi

Duke Cosimo I planned to take
the state into his own hands,
uniting 13 magistratures (*uffizi*)
in an annexe of Palazzo Vecchio.
Giorgio Vasari (1511–74)
designed two long wings,
connected by a short block overlooking the Arno. When Cosimo
moved to Palazzo Pitti, Vasari
created a corridor running from
there via Ponte Vecchio and the
Uffizi, providing the Duke with
discreet and safe access to
Palazzo Vecchio along a covered
passageway. On completion of
the work (1560–80), the Grand
Dukes started to fill the building with all sorts of 'artifices'
produced by man and nature.
Today the gallery's internation-
ally renowned art collections are
besieged by visitors. Botticelli's
The Birth of Venus is one of the
Uffizi's most popular paintings.
Mention of only the best-known
painters becomes a roll-call of
the masters of Italian art from
the 12th to the 18th centuries.

Piazza della Signoria with Palazzo
Vecchio and the Arnolfo tower

SPECIAL TO...

When it reached the bank of the Oltrarno, Vasari's corridor came up against the Mannelli tower, which had survived 14th-century demolition. A way had to be opened through it but the owners refused to yield to the supposedly omnipotent Cosimo. In the end Vasari used projections on corbels.

▶ *Cross Piazzale degli Uffizi to the Lungarno and continue to the right to Ponte Vecchio.*

❸ Ponte Vecchio
The *madielle* (glass cases) of the shops on Florence's most famous bridge, which crosses the Arno at its narrowest point, are filled with gold. Because of them, the river can be glimpsed only where the bridge widens at the centre. Butchers, fishmongers and greengrocers originally installed themselves on the three solid arches built in 1345, but they were forced out in 1593 by Grand Duke Ferdinando I, who considered gold- and silversmiths more appropriate tenants. His preference may also have had something to do with the fact that they paid higher taxes.

▶ *From the bridge follow Via de' Guicciardini to Piazza de' Pitti.*

❹ Palazzo Pitti
A far smaller version of the Palazzo Pitti was commissioned in or around 1458 by the merchant and banker Luca Pitti, but due to his financial ruin it was never completed. Cosimo I bought it in 1549 to turn it into a palace; it subsequently became the official residence of the Medici Grand Dukes (until 1737), those of Lorraine (1737–1800 and 1814–59) and Vittorio Emanuele II (1865–71). Extended over the centuries, Pitti is the largest palace in Florence and its façade is 205m (672 feet) long. Visit the Royal Apartments, the Costume Gallery and the amazing collections in the Silver Museum.

Ponte Vecchio, with its shops

The greatest attraction, however, is the Palatina Gallery, originally an annexe for the overflowing collections of the Uffizi. It contains a superb range of work by Raphael, Andrea del Sarto and Titian.

▶ *Cross Sdrucciolo de'Pitti and Via de' Michelozzi to Piazza San Spirito (the elegant interior of the church of the same name is by Filippo Brunelleschi); south of the square, Via Sant'Agostino and Via San Monaca lead to Piazza del Carmine.*

❺ Cappella Brancacci
The frescoes painted by young Masaccio in the Brancacci chapel were said to have 'schooled the

RECOMMENDED WALK

Annexed to Palazzo Pitti are the extensive Italian Bòboli gardens – an extraordinary open-air museum of statues, water, grottoes and pavilions, offering a welcome break from the bustling Florentine streets.

Brunelleschi's great dome stands out against the Florence skyline

world' and were studied by all the Renaissance painters. The more traditional Masolino da Panicale helped decorate the chapel (1423–27), which can also be reached from the church of Santa Maria del Carmine. The work was completed by Filippino Lippi in 1480.

▶ *North of the square, turn into Borgo San Friediano, left into Via de'Serragli, right into Lungarno Guicciardini, left on to the San Trinità bridge (the finest in Florence) and Via de' Tornabuoni, right into Via Porta Rossa (picturesque medieval Palazzo Davanzati, now the Museum of the Old Florentine House) and left into Via de' Calzaiuoli to Orsanmichele.*

6 Orsanmichele

The origin of Orsanmichele is unusual, although appropriate to its function as church of the guilds (*arti*). Its name was inherited from the now-vanished Oratory of San Michele in Orto, but the building was initially a loggia designed by Arnolfo di Cambio as a cereal market (1290). The arches were walled in and it was raised another two storeys when converted to a church at the end of the 14th century. Still visible inside are the loading and unloading apertures of the granaries above. All around are statues of the patron saints of the guilds, commissioned in the 15th century.

▶ *Continue along Via de' Calzaiuoli to Piazza Duomo, adjacent to Piazza San Giovanni.*

7 Piazza del Duomo

The great octagonal Baptistery – Dante's 'bel San Giovanni' (he

also claimed to have broken one of its fonts to save 'one who was drowning in it') – dates perhaps from the 11th century. The decoration of this symbol of the city became a competition between its patron, the powerful Merchants' Guild, and the Wool Guild. Vying for prestige, the Wool Guild undertook work on Santa Maria del Fiore, opposite, and may be said to have won, given the exceptional quality of the three bronze doors (the south door is by Andrea Pisano, about 1330; the north and east doors by Lorenzo Ghiberti, 1403–24) and the inlaid marble floor (1207).

The Duomo (cathedral) or basilica of Santa Maria del Fiore was conceived in the late 13th century by Arnolfo di Cambio as a place where the entire community could gather – not only for worship, but also for secular events. Readings of the *Divine Comedy* are still a popular non-religious occasion here. He made it big enough for 30,000 people: 153m (502 feet) long, 90m (295 feet) wide at the transept and

38m (125 feet) at the aisles. The erection of the dome was completed by Brunelleschi in 1436. The much-debated façade was not finished until 1887.

The Museo dell'Opera exhibits works of art never used in, or removed from, the Duomo, the Baptistery and the bell tower, such as the façade sculptures begun by Arnolfo di Cambio and dismissed in 1587 as 'unfashionable'; and the choirs by Donatello (1433–9) and Luca della Robbia (1431–8).

▶ *Go northwards along Via de' Martelli and Via Cavour to Palazzo Medici-Riccardi.*

8 Palazzo Medici-Riccardi

The area around today's Via Cavour became the 'headquarters' of the Medici family in the 15th and 16th centuries. Michelozzo constructed this prototype (1444–62) of the aristocratic Renaissance residence for Cosimo the Elder, and it served as the family residence until 1540. In 1659 it was purchased and then enlarged by the Riccardi family, although the figures of the old proprietors

still appear in the chapel, in the *Procession of the Magi* wall fresco, created by Benozzo Gozzoli in 1459–60.

▶ *To the left of the Palazzo, take Via de' Gori to Piazza San Lorenzo.*

9 Basilica di San Lorenzo

In 1418 the Medici family decided to transform what had been Florence's first cathedral (4th–7th century) into the family church. Brunelleschi designed an admirable interior for them but the façade was left in rough stone. The old sacristy (1421–6) was completely finished – a Brunelleschi cube decorated by Donatello. Michelangelo then intervened to create the new sacristy (1520–56; it serves as the funeral chapel of the family of Lorenzo il Magnifico), which became the prototype for mannerist architecture, made all the more dynamic by the great man's intense sculptures. During the same period, Cardinal Giulio de' Medici commissioned Michelangelo to build the Medici Laurenziana

SPECIAL TO...

The biblical figure of David, symbolising the brain that defeats the brawn of Goliath, is a recurrent theme in Florentine Renaissance art. Although not Italy's strongest state, for decades it dominated the country's political life – to such a degree that Lorenzo il Magnifico, in power from 1469 to 1492, was considered 'the index of the Italian political scale'.

library to house the collection of manuscripts begun by Cosimo the Elder. The Chapel of the Principi, conceived by Cosimo I, is sheer opulence – the Opificio delle Pietre Dure workshop was created in 1588 specifically to fashion the precious materials required, and it remains a leading presence in the field of restoration.

▶ *Continue along Via Cavour to Piazza San Marco.*

The stone façade of San Lorenzo

da Fiesole (better known as Fra' Angelico). Nearly all the painter's works in Florence are now gathered in the rooms of the convent-museum.

▶ *Go south along Via Ricasoli to the Galleria dell'Accademia.*

⓫ Galleria dell'Accademia
The students of the Academy of Fine Arts needed examples of sculpture for reference, and in 1784 Grand Duke Pietro Leopoldo decided that they should have only the greatest Florentine masterpieces. The

---

FOR CHILDREN

To celebrate the nativity of the Virgin Mary, Piazza dell'Annunziata is illuminated on the night of 7 September with the flickering lights of lanterns (*rificolone*) hanging from the tops of sticks. They are carried by worshippers on their way to pay homage to the Madonna of the sanctuary, lighting their way as did the citizens of the past, and by children all over the city.

Above: Piazza della SS Annunziata
Bottom right: the old 'pharmacy' of Santa Maria Novella

⓾ Chiesa e Museo di San Marco
In 1437, Cosimo the Elder called on his trusted architect, Michelozzo di Bartolomeo Michelozzi, to restructure the 14th-century complex of San Marco for the Dominicans. The church apse and sacristy were revamped and the convent layout proved one of the most practical and rational of its time. The undertaking cost more than 40,000 florins, but it's doubtful whether the commissioner was ever recompensed. His inept great-nephew Piero, son of Lorenzo il Magnifico, was chased from the city by the followers of one of San Marco's priors, reformer Savonarola, considered by some the master of the city and a guiding spirit of

the Florentine Republic (1494–1512). Cosimo, who had reserved a double cell for himself in the convent, never saw the sublime frescoes created there by Fra' Giovanni

---

SPECIAL TO...

In Via della Scala, near the railway station, you can buy perfume, spirits, soap, balsam and lotions in the neo-Gothic surroundings of the 'Officina profumo-farma-ceutica di Santa Maria Novella', owned by the Dominican friars until 1866. Just a few steps away, a visit to the Chiesa di Santa Maria Novella (1278) is a must both for its exemplary façade (1458–78), by Leon Battista Alberti, and the frescoes by Paolo Uccello (from 1425–30, in the church museum), Masaccio (1427) and Domenico Ghirlandaio (1485–90).

---

choice was obvious: in time the gallery became a 'Michelangelo museum', also housing the casts of works on display elsewhere. Four of the gigantic *Prisoners* are here – powerful figures sketched for the tomb of Pope Julius II and half imprisoned in the stone itself. They provide a startling contrast to the refined

original *David* moved from Piazza della Signoria.

▶ *Back in Piazza San Marco, turn right into Via Battisti and follow it to Piazza della SS Annunziata.*

12 Piazza della SS Annunziata

The Ospedale degli Innocenti (1419–45), built by Brunelleschi and financed by the Silk Guild, is a masterpiece of precise symmetry: in the portico, the width of the arches is equal to the height of the columns and the depth of the bays. It provided a blueprint for Renaissance architecture – but the building served a daily practical function, too. The abandonment of children was a persistent problem, and the creation of a 'Hospital of Innocents' was the city's way of

addressing the issue. From 1660 to 1875 the children were collected from a rotating stone – 'the wheel' – situated in the Ospedale's portico. Opposite the Ospedale, the Loggiato dei Serviti (1516) imitates Brunelleschi's arches. Between the two is the basilica of the Annunziata (1444–77). To the east of the square, a large vault leads to the Archaeological Museum. Here you can see the oldest Tuscan art – that of the Etruscans – including famous pieces such as the bronze sculptures *Chimera di Arezzo* (5th–4th century BC) and the *Arringatore di Perugia (Orator of Perugia)*, an example of Etruscan realism.

▶ *Walk south along Via de' Servi, around the apse of the Duomo and down Via del Proconsolo to Palazzo del Bargello.*

13 Museo del Bargello

You pass through the 13th-century Volognana tower, whose bell rings only for the passing of a century, to the first public building (13th–14th century) of communal Florence. In 1574 it became the seat of the *shirro*, or the police, and prison. The museum arranged in the rooms of the Bargello comprises works by Donatello (two Davids), Michelangelo, Pollaiolo, Verrocchio and Cellini. It even offers the opportunity to judge between the two bas-reliefs of the *Sacrifice of Isaac*, entered in the 1401 competition between Brunelleschi and Ghiberti to decorate the north door of the Baptistery. Ghiberti won.

▶ *Continuing along Via del Proconsolo you come to Piazza San Firenze (fine late-baroque Palazzo San Firenze,*

The classical view of Florence
from San Miniato al Monte, with
the Fièsole hills in the background

*with the twin façades of the
church and oratory of San
Filippo Neri); turn left into Via
dell'Anguillara and walk to
Piazza Santa Croce.*

14 Chiesa di Santa Croce

The Church of Santa Croce was
begun by Arnolfo di Cambio in
1295 for the Franciscans in a
heavily populated quarter of
wool-workers. The grandiose
Gothic style is at its height on
the sides and on the apse (the
façade is 19th-century neo-
Gothic); the solemn interior
contains the tombs of many
notable Florentine citizens.
Giotto created his last fresco
cycles (1320–5) in the Peruzzi
and Bardi chapels. The adjacent
Pazzi Chapel is Brunelleschi's
masterpiece (1429, included in
the Museum of Works of Santa
Croce). Hanging in the refectory
is a great crucifix by Cimabue,
which suffered in the 1966
flood.

EXCURSION

▶ *To the west of the square, Via
Borgo de' Greci and Via de'
Gondi lead back to Piazza
della Signoria. Take your car or
public transport to Piazzale
Michelangelo, south of the
Arno.*

Piazzale Michelangelo e San Miniato al Monte

Admiring the view from this
large square, built in 1875 and
well connected to the Firenze
Sud motorway exit, is an excellent way to take leave of the city.
Even better, drive up Viale
Galilei (or climb the steps) to
San Miniato al Monte
(1018–1207). Together with the
baptistery – which it echoes in
its distinctive white and green
marble – this church is the
greatest masterpiece of
Florentine Renaissance style.

A Florentine football match, in
Piazza Santa Croce

TOUR
11

From Val d'Arno to Val d'Elsa

Visiting the borderlands of Florence, Pisa and Siena, this tour travels along two important ancient routes: Via Pisana, which follows the Arno, and Via Francigena, the only medieval channel of communication across the peninsula and seen here on its stretch along the Elsa river. Traffic, farming and industry enriched the people who lived along these routes, enabling them to build walls around their splendid towns.

ITINERARY

FIRENZE	▶ **Lastra a Signa (15km-9½m)**
LASTRA A SIGNA	▶ **Artimino (9km-5½m)**
ARTIMINO	▶ **Montelupo Fiorentino (7km-4m)**
MONTELUPO FIORENTINO	▶ **San Miniato (21km-13m)**
SAN MINIATO	▶ **Castelfiorentino (18km-11m)**
CASTELFIORENTINO	▶ **S. Vivaldo (14km-9m)**
S. VIVALDO	▶ **Certaldo (15km-9½m)**
CERTALDO	▶ **San Gimignano (14km-9m)**
SAN GIMIGNANO	▶ **Colle di Val d'Elsa (14km-9m)**
COLLE DI VAL D'ELSA	▶ **Monteriggioni (11km-6½m)**
MONTERIGGIONI	▶ **Certosa del Galluzzo (50km-31m)**
CERTOSA DEL GALLUZZO	▶ **Firenze (5km-3m)**

2/3 DAYS • 193KM • 120 MILES

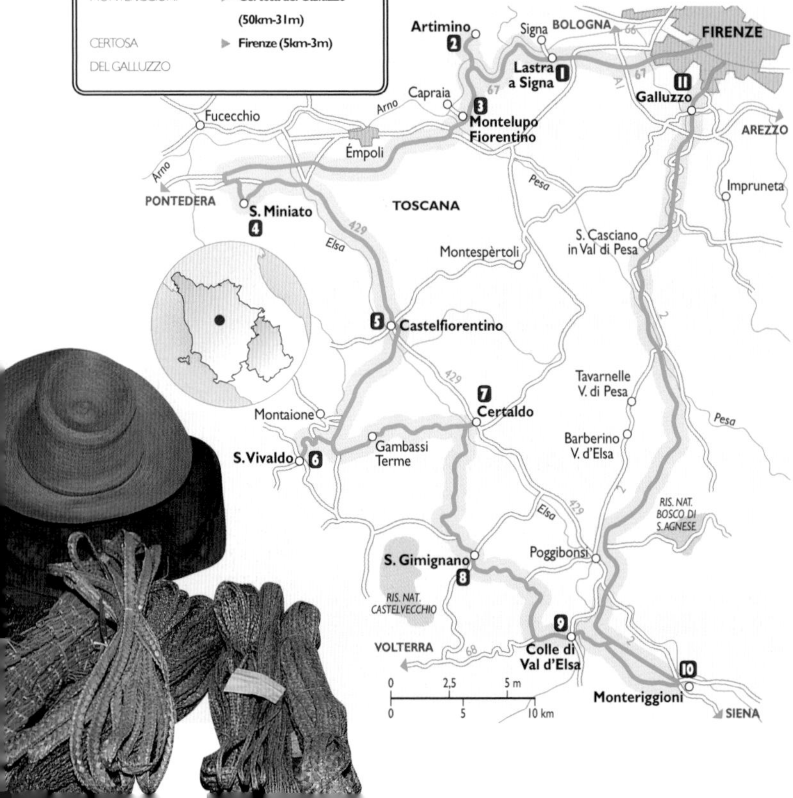

Church of San Leonardo, Artimino

[i] *Via Cavour 1r; Piazza della Stazione 4a, Firenze*

▶ *Take the SS67 westbound to Lastra a Signa.*

❶ Lastra a Signa

The countryside hereabouts has been heavily urbanised from the Middle Ages on. Florentine expansion took the form of new 'walled lands', of which Lastra a Signa is a classic example. In 1424 Brunelleschi worked on the ring of walls originally built on the instruction of the Florentine authorities in 1377. Below the village is the starting point of the narrow Golfolina gorge, Arno's route to the Tyrrhenian sea.

[i] *Via Diaz 116*

▶ *Continue along the SS67, then cross the Arno and follow the signs to Artimino.*

❷ Artimino

Good wine and an abundance of game attracted the Medici family here every autumn. In 1594, Grand Duke Ferdinand I asked Bernardo Buontalenti to erect a 'hunting and grape-

---

SPECIAL TO...

Florence is famous for its elegant straw hats, first introduced at Signa in 1718, when a man from Bologna planted 'March wheat' to be harvested before the ear ripened. This was then used to weave hats of far superior quality to those made using ripe wheat straw. A cottage weaving industry flourished during the 19th century and the province of Florence had 100,000 workers, living on starvation wages. In the early 20th century, traveller Edward Hutton noted: 'One of the finest ladies' sun hats…costs 15 lire, and the woman who makes it only gets 2 or 3'.

---

harvesting' villa on a hill site. Bizarre chimneys in various shapes and sizes adorn the roofs, and the view sweeps over the Arno Valley to Florence and Pistoia. Not far away is the lovely Romanesque church of San Leonardo, founded in 1107.

▶ *Back on the SS67, continue westwards to Montelupo Fiorentino.*

❸ Montelupo Fiorentino

A market-place developed at the point where the Pesa river flows into the Arno, and in the late Middle Ages Montelupo became a flourishing ceramic centre. Before yielding to temptation in the craft shops, visit the restored Palazzo Podestà and see pottery produced over the centuries by local kilns, and now on display in the Archaeological and Pottery Museum.

[i] *Via Baccio 74*

▶ *Take the Florence-Empoli-Pisa dual carriageway eastbound, exit at San*

FOR HISTORY BUFFS

The Florentines were vexed by the presence of Capraia, an outpost of their Pisan rivals nestling on a rugged crag across the Arno. They decided that 'a wolf (*lupo*) is needed to destroy this goat (*capra*)'. So in 1203 they created their wolf – the castle of Montelupo, whose ruins can be glimpsed at the top of a hill southeast of the village.

down towards the coast. San Miniato Basso (26m/185 feet), the lower, modern town, is now a busy leather-processing centre. The four original districts on the ridge were restructured and fortified in 1226 by Frederick II. Of the stronghold he built at the highest point (192m/630 feet) only the tower survives, rebuilt after bombing in 1944. This is probably the scene of the tragic downfall of jurist, poet and king's representative Pier delle Vigne (*c*1190–1249), who fell into disgrace, was blinded and – according to Dante – committed suicide to 'escape contempt'. Two spectacular squares are linked by steps around the 13th-century cathedral. In November, the town is packed for the national white truffle fair.

i **Piazza del Popolo**

▶ *After descending to the foot of San Miniato, travel east to the SS429, which to the right leads to Castelfiorentino.*

5 Castelfiorentino

Like other towns in Val d'Elsa, Castelfiorentino consists of a modern and industrialised centre on the plain and an older settlement on the hill. Roman in origin, it was a Carolingian fief before coming under Florentine influence and taking its present name in 1149. Two visits are especially worthwhile. The

Church of Santa Verdiana, a showpiece of early-18th-century architecture and painting, has an underground cell where Verdiana (1178–1242), patron saint of the town, lived the last 34 years of her life – in the company of two snakes, according to legend. In the town's Cultural Centre you can admire two fresco cycles by Benozzo Gozzoli (1420–97) and his assistants, depicting the life of the Virgin Mary.

i **c/o Railway Station**

▶ *Proceed south, following first the signs for Montaione and then those for San Vivaldo.*

6 San Vivaldo

In 1320, a Franciscan monk, Vivaldo Stricchi, who had retired here to lead a hermit's life, was found dead in the hollow trunk of a chestnut tree. He was later canonised and a small church was built for him and consecrated in 1416. The Franciscans, guardians of the Holy Places in Palestine, arrived in the 16th century, and created a 'holy mount', reproducing the sanctuaries of Jerusalem and marking stages in the life of Jesus. Thirty-four chapels were built over a 30-year period (17 survive), scattered in the woods and containing large tableaux

Miniato and follow the signs to the town.

4 San Miniato

The nucleus of the old town is distributed on three rises overlooking the Arno plain, with wide views over the valley and

One of the chapels of San Vivaldo, at Montaione

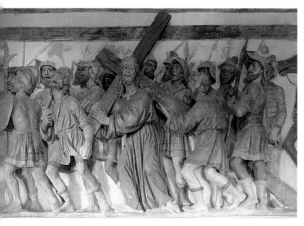

fashioned in multicoloured terracotta by local artists of the Robbia school.

▶ *Go back and take the road signposted on the right for Gambassi Terme and Certaldo.*

7 Certaldo

In the 13th century Certaldo's low-lying *borgo* (village) began to develop around Via Francigena; this commercial and residential area is now known as Certaldo Basso. Up on the hill, the institutions of power centred around the castello, and this area, Certaldo Alto, is the most interesting quarter for visitors today. The warm tones of its medieval brick architecture have survived the tribulations of centuries, not least the destruction wrought by World War II. Rich in scenic views, the upper town culminates in Palazzo Pretorio, revamped in the 15th century. Inside, the walls of the cells used for a men's prison (there is also a women's version) still bear messages written by past prisoners. The adjacent 13th-century former church has a remarkable fresco cycle completed in 1466–7 by

The view around San Gimignano from the top of the Torre Grossa, beside the Palazzo del Popolo

Benozzo Gozzoli and other painters for the *Tabernacolo dei Giustiziati*. A bust dating from 1503 marks the tomb of Giovanni Boccaccio, author of the *Decameron*. Originally from Certaldo, his family moved to Florence in the late 13th century; Boccaccio is thought to have been born in 1313 on the banks of the Arno, and is known to have returned in or around 1361 to live in the ancestral

home until his death on 21 December, 1375. The house still stands: restored after the war, it contains an interesting research library.

ⓘ *Via Cavour 32*

▶ *Cross the Elsa again and follow the signs for San Gimignano to the left.*

8 San Gimignano

The first sight of San Gimignano takes your breath away. Its perfectly preserved medieval towers and streets

> SPECIAL TO...
>
> Awaiting visitors to San Gimignano's Palazzo del Popolo (1288) are precious paintings and at least two rarities. The first is a rug knotted in Cairo in the 15th to 16th century to resemble three rugs piled on a table (the only other known specimen is in the Victoria and Albert Museum in London).
> The second is a series of unusual scenes of married life, chosen by Memmo di Filippuccio for his frescoes in the Podestà chamber at the beginning of the 14th century.
> After a visit to the Civic Museum, climb to the top of the 54m (177-foot), 14th-century Torre Grossa to enjoy the sweeping view of the town and surrounding countryside.

seem to take you back to another age. Orginally there were no fewer than 72 towers (15 survive). They were built thanks to the immense wealth of this free *comune's* merchant and financial classes, gleaned from their principal trades of saffron and usury (as 13th-century canonical law defined financial speculation).

San Gimignano fell into decline in the 14th century, when its population was decimated by wars, civil strife, famine and plagues. In 1351 the town relinquished its independence and surrendered itself to Florence. In the meantime, an abundance of houses, towers and tower-houses, springs and reservoirs, churches, warehouses, hospices, convents and elegant mansions had grown up along the urban stretch of Via Francigena. Protected by strict monument restrictions since 1929, San Gimignano is an extraordinary living museum. Perhaps it does have a few too many souvenir shops and tourists but come in the low season, on weekdays or at quiet times for an unforgettable visit.

[i] *Piazza Duomo 1*

Above: rafting in Val d'Elsa
Right: Monteriggioni's ring of walls

▶ *After driving 5km (3 miles) towards Poggibonsi, turn right for the SS68 which, to the left, leads to Colle di Val d'Elsa.*

🟨 Colle di Val d'Elsa

Three areas make up Colle di Val d'Elsa, developed between the 10th and the 13th century. The lower section, known as Piano, specialised in the manufacture of paper in the Middle Ages, using energy from the waters of the Elsa river. Today Colle Bassa is a major producer of glass and crystal. The other two sections, Castello and Borgo, together form Colle Alta, and feature splendid architecture of medieval origin with Renaissance additions. Via del Castello is the site of the centres of secular power, old tower-houses (one is said to have been the birthplace in 1245 of the architect and sculptor Arnolfo di Cambio) and fine 15th- to 16th-century mansions.

[i] *Via Campana 43*

▶ *Proceed towards Siena to the SS429, which to the right soon*

takes you to the turning on the left for Monteriggioni.

🔟 Monteriggioni

Dante was profoundly impressed by Monteriggioni's superb 'round circle' of towers, which he likened to the abyss guarded by 14 giants described in his *Inferno*. The citadel was erected by the Sienese, who founded this outpost against Florence in 1203. It took 70 years to complete the ring, which is 570m (1,870 feet) long and incorporates 14 towers. The village's medieval atmosphere and intact fortifications, arranged along an axis running from the gate facing Florence to that facing Siena, make it the most significant example of a 'walled land' on Sienese territory.

ⓘ *Largo Fontebranda 3*

▶ *Take the Siena–Florence motorway northbound and exit at Firenze Certosa, then follow the signs to the Certosa del Galluzzo.*

🔟 Certosa del Galluzzo

Founded in 1342 by the Florentine Niccolò Acciaioli, the Certosa (Charterhouse) is surrounded by high walls and looks like an inaccessible fortress. Once inside, though, this impression is soon dispelled. Large cloisters and slender porticoes – mainly 15th-century – open on to the light and landscape. Initially the rich benefactor had intended to reserve a normal cell for himself (actually, they are two-storey mini-apartments). Then, ignoring the monks' objections, he started to build himself a mansion beside the monastery,

but died before its completion. Today, a picture gallery contains the frescoes removed from the grand cloister, where Jacopo Pontormo created them in 1522–4.

During the Napoleonic occupation, the charterhouse was stripped of most of its treasures. In 1958, the Carthusians were replaced by Cistercian Benedictines who now organise guided visits to the complex.

▶ *Continue northwards to return to Florence.*

SPECIAL TO...

In San Gimignano look out for the delicious ice-cream flavoured with saffron pistils, a traditional local crop.

WINE & OIL

Wine-making has a long and respected history in Tuscany, kept alive by local skills and the initiatives of some of its oldest aristocratic families. A great way of learning more about its traditions is to follow the wine routes – tourist trails that concentrate on nature, culture and good food, visiting museums, restaurants and wine cellars. So far the Tuscan regional authorities have approved 11 such routes – Carmignano, Chianti Colli Fiorentini, Chianti Rufina e Pomino, Colli di Maremma, Colline Lucchesi e Montecarlo, Colline Pisane, Costa degli Etruschi, Monteregio di Massa Marìttima, Montespertoli, Vernaccia di San Gimignano and Vino Nobile di Montepulciano. Details are found in local town halls.

Chianti and much more

By far the most popular grape in the region – used in almost 80 per cent of Tuscan wines – is Sangiovese. This is followed by Trebbiano Toscano (11 per cent), Brunello (2 per cent – a local variety of Sangiovese) and Ciliegiolo (1.2 per cent). The undisputed champion wines are Chianti and the renowned Brunello di Montalcino (Chianti and Chianti Classico constitute

Chianti country grape harvest

a 'regional' wine that extends beyond the mountains from which it takes its name to more than 100 *comunes* in six different provinces). The other DOCG (origin controlled and guaranteed) wines are Carmignano (Prato), Vernaccia (San Gimignano) – the region's only white wine – and Vino Nobile di Montepulciano. There are also 29 DOC (origin controlled) wines. Below is a list of DOC and DOCG wines in their order of appearance in the tours.

Northwest Tuscany
Colli di Luni (La Spezia, Massa-Carrara), Candia dei Colli Apuani (Massa-Carrara), Colline Lucchesi, Montecarlo (Lucca), Bianco Pisano di San Torpè (Pisa, Livorno), Bianco della Valdinièvole (Pistoia), DOCG Carmignano, Barco Reale di Carmignano and Carmignano (Carmignano and Poggio a Caiano, Prato).

Maremma Montescudaio (Pisa), Bòlgheri (Castagneto Carducci, Livorno), Val di Cornia (Livorno, Pisa), Elba (Isle of Elba), Monteregio di Massa Marìttima, Morellino di Scansano, Bianco di Pitigliano (Grosseto), Ansonica Costa Argentario (Grosseto and Isle of Giglio) and Parrina (Orbetello, Grosseto).

Northeast Tuscany DOCG Vernaccia di San Gimignano (San Gimignano, Siena),

Pomino (Rùfina, Florence), Colli dell'Etruria Centrale (Arezzo, Florence, Pisa, Pistoia, Siena), Bianco Vergine della Valdichiana (Siena, Arezzo).

Inland Tuscany Val d'Arbia (Siena including its capital town), DOCG Chianti Classico (Florence and Siena), Vin Santo del Chianti (Siena, Florence, Pistoia, Arezzo, Pisa, Prato), Vin Santo del Chianti Classico (Siena, Florence), DOCG Chianti (Florence, Siena, Arezzo, Pistoia, Pisa, Prato), DOCG Brunello di Montalcino, Moscadello di Montalcino, Rosso di Montalcino, San'Antimo (Montalcino, Siena), DOCG Vino Nobile di Montepulciano, Rosso di Montepulciano, Vin Santo di Montepulciano (Montepulciano, Siena).

Umbrian wines

The DOC wine-producing areas of Umbria are concentrated in and near the Umbra Valley, the upper Tiber Valley to the north, the central Orvieto area and Ternano to the south. Umbrian vines are influenced by their proximity to Tuscany; three-quarters of the region's production comes from the Trebbiano and Sangiovese vines, although Umbrians tend to prefer white to red; two indigenous grapes, Sagrantino and Grechetto, produce prized wines. There are also two DOCG wines – Montefalco Sagrantino and Torgiano Rosso Riserva. DOC wines (nine in all) are dominated by Orvieto, which alone constitutes two-thirds of the total. Other DOC-producing zones are the Altotiberini hills, the Trasimeno hills, the Perugia hills, Assisi, Torgiano, Montefalco, the Martani hills and the Amerini hills (in the province of Terni).

Oil, from Lucca to Trasimeno

Tuscan olive oil is the best-known extra virgin oil in Europe. With an intense green colour, tending towards golden yellow, it has a fruity smell with a touch of almond, and quite a

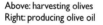

Above: harvesting olives
Right: producing olive oil

tangy flavour. Its quality varies according to the type of olive, microclimate and soil (or *cru*). Elegant, delicate, golden oils with a hint of green are produced in the Lucca area, and more robust versions in Maremma. The oils of Chianti and the Sienese hills are tangy and bitter, with a herbal aftertaste. In the Florentine hills the olives produce oils with a pleasant almondy smell; Pratomagno's is tangy, and Rùfina's (north of Florence) has body. A light, fruity taste distinguishes the oil produced in the Pisan mountains, an intensely sweet product not unlike oils from the province of Livorno.

Umbrian olive oil is one of the most refined in Italy, with an amber colour, very slight acidity and high oleic content. Around Trasimeno and Perugia, on the calcareous slopes of the mountains that extend between Assisi and Spoleto, the olive trees form a dense and continuous band between 250 and 550m (820 and 1,804 feet) above sea level. Particularly fine is the oil of Spoleto, a town that boasts the most efficient oil industry in the region, although those of Foligno and Terni are also excellent.

Mugello
& Fièsole

2 DAYS · 148KM · 92 MILES

Etruscan tombs and sweeping views, Medici villas and old parish churches, romantic cypresses and symmetrical Italian gardens, the birthplaces of Giotto and Fra' Angelico, artistic ceramics and even knives – this tour, winding through the beautiful hills to the north of Florence, reveals a host of surprises to visitors.

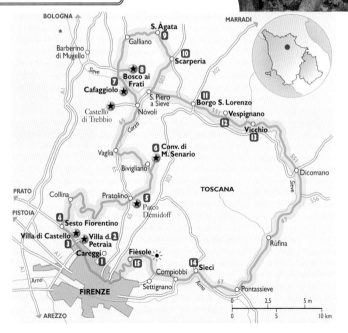

A view from the garden of the Medici Villa della Petraia, originally owned by the Brunelleschi family

> [i] Via Cavour 1r; Piazza della Stazione 4a, Florence

▶ After reaching Piazza Dalmazia at Rifredi take Viale Morgagni and Viale Pieraccini to the Careggi hospital (responsible for the Medici villa).

❶ Villa di Careggi

The Medici family bought a building on this hill in the early 15th century and had it restructured by Michelozzo. It then became the seat of the Accademia Platonica Fiorentina and was, from the middle of the century, patronised by the best-known scholars, philosophers and artists of the Medici circles, including Marsilio Ficino, Pico della Mirandola and Michelangelo.

▶ Back in Piazza Dalmazia, proceed along Via Giuliani, Via delle Panche and then, following the signs, Via della Querciola, Via di Castello and Via della Petraia to Villa della Petraia.

❷ Villa della Petraia

This villa, originally a castle, was built in the 14th century and came into the hands of the Medici family after 1530. Bernardo Buontalenti (1536–1608) redesigned it in the last decades of that century. There is a beautiful three-tiered garden and a courtyard which was covered with iron and glass by the Savoy family after 1865 to create a ballroom. Frescoes inside created in the 17th century celebrate the splendours of the Medici house.

▶ Return along Via della Petraia and take Via del Castello to Villa di Castello.

❸ Villa di Castello

Obtained by the Medici family in 1477, the villa was converted for Cosimo when he became Duke (1537), with subsequent additions by Bernardo Buontalenti (1536–1608). It is now closed to visitors – but you can see the magnificent gardens, laid out to symbolise the territory of the Duchy. Since 1974, the building has been the base of the Accademia della Crusca, an institution created in 1583 to publish the famous *Vocabolario* that established the conventions of the Italian language.

▶ Return to Via delle Panche and follow this before taking Via Gramsci to Sesto Fiorentino.

❹ Sesto Fiorentino

Today, this is a major industrial town, having seen substantial urbanisation in recent decades.

Villa di Cafaggiolo, where Lorenzo the Magnificent came to relax

Its name indicates its position at the sixth Roman mile (approximately 9km/6 miles) from the centre of Florence. Two notable legacies of the town's ancient past still survive – 7th-century BC Etruscan tombs with false domes. One, called the *Montagnola*, is in the gardens of Villa Manfredi (Via Fratelli Rosselli) and the other, known as *Mula*, is situated in the grounds of the villa of the same name (Via della Mula).

▶ In Via Gramsci turn right into Via Matteoti and take Via dei Colli Alti to Pratolino and the Demidoff Park.

5 Parco Demidoff
The Villa Medici-Demidoff park lies close to Pratolino. Bernardo Buontalenti was commissioned to create the sumptuous residence in 1569 for the Venetian Bianca Cappello, unscrupulous lover and later wife of the Grand Duke Francesco I de' Medici. It fell into disrepair under the Lorraine family and was demolished in 1824. The park, formerly full of 'wonders' (fountains, grottoes, statues

enlivened with flowing water and even an automatic organ), was redesigned to suit romantic tastes. The famous Appennino fountain, created between 1579 and 1589 by Giambologna, depicts a colossal crouching old man 11m (36 feet) high, which incorporates a number of spaces inside. From here you can see the garden and activate unexpected water 'tricks'.

▶ Return to Pratolino and follow the signs northeast to the Convent of Monte Senario.

6 Convento di Monte Senario
Situated 815m (2,674 feet) above sea level, this convent was founded in 1234 by seven Florentine noblemen who had formed the Servite Order. Of the original structure, only the chapel – where the Virgin Mary is said to have appeared to the Servites in 1240 – remains. The church, with its rich baroque interior, the bell tower and the convent were repeatedly altered during the 17th and 18th centuries. The terrace surrounding the complex overlooks the Mugello Valley.

▶ After reaching Vaglia and the SS65 (Futa), take this road

northbound past the Nòvoli turning (left for the castle of Trebbio) to Cafaggiolo.

7 Villa di Cafaggiolo
Architect Michelozzo Michelozzi (1396–1472), who built the castle of Trebbio (visits by request) on a hillock between 1427 and 1436 for Cosimo the Elder, was commissioned by Lorenzo de' Medici in 1454 to create Villa di Cafaggiolo. Crowned with crenellations and corbels and featuring a large tower with a monumental gate, it was a favourite bolt-hole for Lorenzo the Magnificent.

SPECIAL TO...

The Medici villas were places of amusement and delight – as described in the *Nencia da Barberino*, a poem composed by Lorenzo de' Medici at Cafaggiolo, around 1473–6. In it, the magnificent lord of Florence, disguised as a peasant, does his utmost to seduce a local peasant girl. He imagines her accompanying him to the pastures, where 'I would put my beasts among yours / and we would seem one, although we were two'.

▶ *Continue north towards Barberino di Mugello, turning right for Galliano and right again for Bosco ai Frati.*

8 Bosco ai Frati

The same Medici client and the same architect reappear in the convent of Bosco ai Frati. Occupied first by Basilian and then by Franciscan monks in the 13th century, it was almost entirely rebuilt in the 15th century. This small complex created for Cosimo the Elder is admired more for its enchanting position, amid hills and Adriatic oak woods, and a dramatic wooden crucifix attributed to Donatello, than for the work of Michelozzo (visible in the choir and ribbed cross vaults).

Scarperia's 14th-century Palazzo dei Vicari with crenellated tower

▶ *Go back and continue north-wards to Galliano, where you turn right for Sant'Àgata.*

9 Sant'Àgata

Ashlar stone alternates with serpentine green in this typical example of Tuscan Romanesque style. The parish church of Sant'Àgata – nave and two aisles divided by monu-mental columns – is the most important and one of the oldest holy buildings in Mugello, dating from 984. An enterprising 17th-century parish priest made the baptistery using the panels of a 12th-century pulpit. He was also responsible for the striking painting of the martyrdom of Sant'Àgata, on a gold back-ground, which hangs above the reliquary of the saint, at the centre of an incredible collage of saints painted on fragments

FOR CHILDREN

While at Sant'Àgata, make sure you see the unusual craft and folk exhibition. A scaled recon-struction of the village contains small moving figures that re-create moments of everyday life in years past.

of old panels. The date and provenance of the pieces have proved baffling.

▶ *Take the southbound road to Scarperìa.*

10 Scarperìa

Scarperìa is a 'new land' founded in 1306 by the Florentines against the Ubaldini, vassals of Mugello, and has preserved much of its medieval past. It still retains its grid plan, a section of medieval walls, and the imposing Palazzo dei Vicari, bearing the coats-of-arms in stone and majolica of successive governors of the village. It has also kept alive the trade that made its knife-makers famous all over Tuscany. Their history is recorded in the Knife Museum in Palazzo Vicari; an old knife shop survives a short distance away. To the southeast of the village is the Mugello racing circuit, opened in 1974, which hosts Formula 1 races.

i *Palazzo dei Vicari*

▶ *Take the SS503 southbound and, before reaching San Piero a Sieve, turn left for Borgo San Lorenzo.*

11 Borgo San Lorenzo

Lying in a large hollow formed by the Sieve river, the most important and industrialised town in Mugello is visited for the Romanesque parish church of San Lorenzo (1263), which has a hexagonal bell tower. Inside, a Madonna's head painted on a panel by Giotto in the 1300s is the only work by the painter preserved here in his homeland.

The view of Florence from San Francesco in Fièsole

☐ *Via Togliatti 45*

▶ *Take the SS551 eastwards and go left at the turning for Vespignano-Casa di Giotto.*

12 Vespignano

Painter, architect and sculptor Giotto di Bondone was born here, probably in 1267. The story of his life is told in various documents, records and

---

SPECIAL TO...

The Rèmole fulling mills are virtually all that survives of the numerous works that used to full woollen cloth. Heavy hydraulic hammers would beat the fabrics day and night to soften and strengthen them with the aid of solutions containing soda, soap and urine. The mills were initially installed on rafts anchored in the centre of Florence, but after the disastrous Arno flood of 1333 they transferred their evil-smelling industry up- and downstream of the city.

---

reproductions of his works at the house where he is said to have been born, now restored.

▶ *Back on the SS551 continue to Vicchio.*

13 Vicchio

Set on the border between Mugello and Val di Sieve, Vicchio, like Scarperìa, was founded by the Florentine Republic in the early decades of the 14th century as a strategic base and to control the roads to Romagna. The old centre, enclosed within pentagonal walls in 1324, was the birthplace of Fra' Angelico (*c*1400–55). The museum named after him shows holy works from the Mugello area – but none by his own hand.

☐ *Corso del Popolo*

▶ *Continue towards Florence via Dicomano and Pontassieve to Sieci.*

14 Sieci

Standing in the centre of the village is the Romanesque parish church of San Giovanni Battista a Rèmole, dating from

---

the first half of the 12th century. On the opposite side of the Arno, two massive, crenellated towers mark the Rèmole fulling mills, recorded since 1425 but certainly much older.

▶ *Continue towards Florence to Compiobbi, where you turn right and follow the signs for Fièsole via Montebeni.*

SPECIAL TO...

Michelangelo's wet-nurse was the wife of a stone-cutter from Settignano; he later claimed that he had absorbed his love of the art with her milk. The people of Fièsole were said by Dante to have a character 'of mountain and stone', and the colour of the rock (*bigia* or *serena*) cut from the Monte Cèceri quarries still dominates Fièsole, Maiano and Settignano. Here, the stone-cutting trade created great sculptors such as Desiderio da Settignano (1428–64), Mino da Fièsole (1430–84), Giuliano (1432–90) and Benedetto da Maiano (1442–97).

---

15 Fièsole

A beautiful archaeological site reveals the origins of Fièsole. At the end of the 4th century BC Fièsole was already an important Etruscan town with megalithic walls – thought in the Middle Ages to be the work of giants – temple and necropolis. Having become a Roman colony in 90 BC, it acquired a forum, temples, spas and, in Augustan times, a theatre for 3,000 spectators. It fell into decline under the Lombards, but was brought back to prominence when Florence came to ascendancy in 1125. During the 18th and 19th centuries, the town was embellished with villas and gardens, and became a favourite destination of foreigners visiting Florence. The wealth of art and history, the historic Borgunto

The Roman theatre on the Fièsole archaeological site

quarter and the magical view from a clearing on the road up to the Gothic church of San Francesco add to its attraction.

Along the road to Florence stands the monastery of San Domenico, to which Fra' Angelico belonged. The church, begun in 1406, contains a much-altered triptych by the young artist (1425). From San Domenico a short walk descends to the old Badia Fiesolana, residence of the bishops of Fièsole from the early Middle Ages until 1028. In 1456 Cosimo the Elder – who was so fond of the Badia that he spent the last years of his life here – decided to enlarge it, but on his death in 1464 the new façade, incorporating the elegant marble geometry of the 12th century, was still incomplete.

i *Via Portigiani 3/5*

▶ *Follow the signs to Florence.*

Casentino
& Pratomagno

The uncertain course of the Arno has few parallels among the great rivers. From the Monte Falterona springs, it flows south in the Casentino Valley, but within sight of Arezzo 'it takes a fright and turns back' (as the Florentines used to say), encircling the long Pratomagno ridge to the north. Not until Pontassieve does it finally choose its route – west to the sea.

2 DAYS · 220KM · 137 MILES

Image of Dante before the
mansion of the Guidi counts

[i] *Piazza della Repubblica 28,
Arezzo*

▶ *Take the SS71 to Ràssina,
then turn right on to the
provincial road and drive via
Chitignano, following the signs
for Chiusi della Verna and the
Eremo della Verna.*

❶ Eremo della Verna

The wooded calcareous peak of
Monte Verna, with sheer drops
on three sides, is visible all over
Casentino and from the upper
Val Tiberina. In 1213, Count
Orlando Cattani made a gift of
it to Francis of Assisi, who
embedded the little church of
Santa Maria degli Angeli
(1216–18) on its slope. Today
the church itself is set in the
side of a larger church, Chiesa
Maggiore, which dates from the
14th to 15th century. Splendid
glazed terracottas by Andrea
della Robbia (1435–1528) adorn
the interior of both buildings.
Corridors, cells and grottoes
lead to the Chapel of the
Stigmata, built where the saint
is said, in 1224, to have
received the divine stigmata

from an angel with six blazing
wings. The sanctuary, home of
the Franciscan Minorites and
visited by many pilgrims, is
surrounded by a beautiful
forest of fir, beech, maple and
ash trees. The forest has been
tended by the monks since the
14th century, and some trees
are more than 400 years old.

▶ *After descending to the
SS208 once more, proceed
westwards to Bibbiena and
then take the SS70 to Poppi.*

❷ Poppi

The soaring tower at the centre
of the crenellated mansion of
the Guidi counts, built in the
second half of the 13th century

BACK TO NATURE

Wolves, bears, fallow deer, roe
deer, water lynx, day and noc-
turnal birds of prey and even a
colony of white Asinara
donkeys (a species at risk of
extinction) await visitors to
Poppi's small zoo of European
fauna, on the edge of the
Foreste Casentinesi-Monte
Falterona-Campigna
National Park.

FOR HISTORY BUFFS

'Those of Arezzo attacked the
field so vigorously…that the
ranks of Florentines recoiled
sharply. The battle was bitter
and harsh…The daggers rained
down…the air was covered
with clouds, the dust was
great. Those on
foot…crouched under the
bellies of the horses with
knives in hand and ran them
through…those of Arezzo
were broken not for being
faint-hearted or for lack of
courage, but for the excess of
foes, and were driven away and
killed; the Florentine soldiers,
accustomed to defeat, slayed
them; the scoundrels had
no mercy.'
Thus the chronicler Dino
Compagni described the
battle of Campaldino on
11 June, 1289.

by Jacopo di Cambio, is the
distinguishing feature of Poppi,
isolated on a green hill in the
Arno Valley. Jacopo's son
Arnolfo is said to have copied
his father's masterpiece when
designing Palazzo Vecchio
in Florence.

A forester in the Foreste
Casentinesi National Park

North of the town, at the junction for Stia (SS310) and the Consuma Pass (SS70), a 20th-century column marks the Campaldino plain where, in 1289, 1,300 horsemen and 10,000 foot-soldiers of Guelph Florence routed the 800 horsemen and 8,000 foot-soldiers of Arezzo (see panel on page 81). Even Dante was there, as a 'lightly-armed knight' in the vanguard. Arezzo suffered 1,700 casualties, with another 2,000 plus taken prisoner. This heavy defeat marked the beginning of the decline of Ghibelline fortunes in Tuscany.

ℹ️ *Via Cavour 11*

▶ *Follow the signs north for Camàldoli.*

🄱 Camàldoli
Count Maldolo d'Arezzo is said to have donated the land on which San Romualdo constructed the original hermitage in 1012. A few years later, 3km (2 miles) further south, the pilgrims' hospitium (now the guests' quarters) was built, followed by the monastery of Fontebuona. The monastic community flourished here, especially between the 12th and 15th centuries, extending its influence all over Casentino.

Camàldoli was an important cultural centre. From the binding presses of its printing works came the *Costituzioni Camaldolesi*, a tract that included the planting and care of the surrounding fir woods among the duties of religious practice.

▶ *Continue northwards to the Eremo of Camàldoli.*

🄳 Eremo di Camàldoli
The hermitage, standing solitary 1,104m (3,622 feet) above sea level, is reached through a monumental forest of soaring fir trees. You can visit the church, renewed in the 17th and 18th centuries (including that of the founder's cell). Other cells are clustered to form a sort of village based on the model of eastern monasticism, with about 20 one-storey houses arranged in five rows, divided by right-angled paths. Each has a small portico, vestibule, bedroom, latrine, study, oratory, wood store and vegetable garden. Francis of Assisi himself stayed in one of them.

▶ *Take the road to the west (bear right at the next two main junctions) that leads via Lonnano to Pratovecchio; here cross the SS310 and follow the signs for Castello di Romena.*

🄴 Castello di Romena
Built around the year 1000 on a scenic site already inhabited in Etruscan and Roman times, the castle came under Florentine occupation, and from the 12th to the mid-14th century it was one of the major fortified bases of the Guidi counts. Inside, visitors are greeted by the remains of the mighty ring of walls, the castle keep and three of the original 14 towers (donjon, postern and prison).

Above: Vallombrosa Abbey in its present 17th-century guise
Below: San Romualdo, Camàldoli

▶ *Return to the junction signposted for the Pieve di Romena.*

6 Pieve di Romena

Isolated in the most beautiful countryside, the parish church of San Pietro di Romena (12th century) is one of the most interesting Romanesque buildings in Casentino – despite having been mutilated over the centuries by landslides and earthquakes. Particularly attractive is the exterior of the apse, adorned with two rows of arches featuring a pair of two-mullioned windows and a three-mullioned one. All works of art have been removed from the interior for safety (if closed, knock at the country house near by).

▶ *Continue to the **SS70**, which to the right goes over the Consuma Pass (1,060m/ 3,478 feet) amid mountain scenery. After passing the village of Consuma turn left for Vallombrosa.*

7 Vallombrosa

The road that climbs the northern tip of Pratomagno passes through boundless woods of

SPECIAL TO...

Born in Ravenna to an aristocratic family around 952, the restless Romualdo was always torn between the importance of community life and his fascination with the hermit's solitude.

Every monk in the community can ask to be transferred to the hermitage; the theory runs that only those who have developed their own spirituality through contact with the world have the strength to cope with the solitude that leads to perfection. However, the hermit can also ask to return to the Benedictine 'communal house', a hive of monastic industry.

silver fir trees (planted over the centuries by monks), mixed with beech, chestnut and Corsican pine trees. Florentine San Giovanni Gualberto, disappointed by the lack of rigour at Camàldoli, founded the abbey for a Vallombrosian

S. ROMUALDO

congregation in 1055. Driven by the desire for poverty and the eradication of hierarchy, the Vallombrosian Benedictines distinguished themselves for their uncompromising opposition to the corrupt Florentine bishopric. The grandiose complex today presents a severe, almost military appearance, a result of its restoration in the 17th century. Inside the monastery, open to visitors on request, a monumental pyramid-shaped fireplace (1786) dominates the kitchen.

i *Piazza Roma 7, Saltino (seasonal)*

▶ *Travel via Saltino and Pietrapanna, following the signs for Reggello and Cascia.*

8 Cascia

The treasure of tiny Cascia is the parish church of San Pietro, a well-preserved Romanesque structure in ashlar sandstone (12th–13th century). At the end of the left-hand aisle, a triptych dated 1422 is said to be the first work by Masaccio, who painted it at just 21 years of age, already showing his innovatory sense of volume and mass.

i *Saltino (seasonal)*

▶ *Turn around and take the first road on the right that leads via Pian di Scò to Castelfranco di Sopra; after*

passing through the village, follow the signs for San Giovanni Valdarno.

9 San Giovanni Valdarno

A square gridplan, enclosed within rectangular walls broken by four gates, is a clue to this town's origins as a 'new land', founded by the Florentines on the left bank of the Arno in 1299. Like the nearby Terranuova Bracciolini and Castelfranco di Sopra, it was designed by Arnolfo di Cambio (1245–1310); he was also responsible for Palazzo Pretorio, altered from the 15th century on. In 1401, San Giovanni Valdarno was the birthplace of Tommaso di Ser Giovanni Cassai, better known as Masaccio and destined to revolutionise Florentine

---

RECOMMENDED WALK

For a fine view of Vallombrosa (958m/3,143 feet) climb to the left of the monastery up a lovely path past small shrines and shelters – the scene in the past of miracles and harsh hermit asceticism – to the so-called Paradisino terrace (1,032m/3,386 feet). The English poet John Milton, who mentioned Vallombrosa in his *Paradise Lost*, stayed in this hermitage in 1638.

SPECIAL TO...

On the outskirts of Castelfranco di Sopra stands the former abbey (Badia) of Soffena, built in the 14th century by the Vallombrosian monks, abandoned in the 18th century and today restored and designated a national monument. Frescoes by 15th-century Tuscan artists decorate the walls of the Greek cruciform interior.

painting during his brief, intense life (he died at the age of 27). Recently reappraised works by his brother Giovanni are kept in the 14th-century church of San Lorenzo. The Museum of the Basilica of Santa Maria delle Grazie houses an *Annunciation* painted by a young Fra' Angelico.

i *Piazza Cavour 3*

▶ *Proceed southeast along the SS69 for Arezzo, turning left at the junction signposted for Terranuova Bracciolini and Loro Ciuffenna.*

10 Loro Ciuffenna

As you leave Loro Ciuffenna, a medieval village situated on a chasm cut by the Ciuffenna river, an asphalt road to the left leads to the Romanesque parish church of San Pietro di Gròpina, built around 1000 on an existing religious site. Of note inside is the pulpit, sculpted with a lion, a deacon, and an eagle that serves as a lectern. It's now time to return to Arezzo but, just before you cross the Arno at Ponte a Buriano, the grassy bank of a bend in the river on the right is an enchanting spot for a little relaxation.

▶ *Follow the signs for Arezzo to the southeast.*

Above: view of Loro Ciuffenna
Right: the central panel in the triptych of San Giovenale, at Cascia, attributed to Masaccio

Upper Val Tiberina
& Valdichiana

Before embarking on this tour visiting locations associated with Piero della Francesca, enjoy an introduction to his art by viewing the Legend of the True Cross, his fresco cycle in the Gothic church of San Francesco in Arezzo, created between 1453 and 1466.

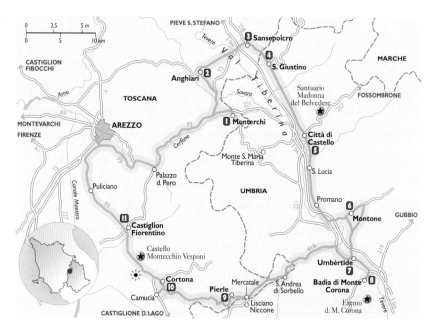

2/3 DAYS • 166KM • 103 MILES

The old village of Anghiari, within
its walls

[i] *Piazza della Repubblica 28,
Arezzo*

▶ *Take the SS73 towards
Sansepolcro-Città di Castello,
turn right on to the SS221 for
Città di Castello and continue
to the turning signposted on
the right for Monterchi.*

❶ Monterchi

From the pretty walled village
on a hillock, descend to the
former school to see the fresco
Madonna del Parto, one of Piero
della Francesca's masterpieces.
An excellent exhibition illustrates the phases of its recent
restoration. It was completed
around 1455 for a chapel in what
is now the cemetery; at some
point the fresco will be returned
to its original location.

[i] *Piazza Umberto I*

▶ *Return along the SS221
to the junction with the
SS73 and follow the latter
to the turning on the left
for Anghiari.*

❷ Anghiari

The Tarlati family, 14th-century
lords of Arezzo, built the long
straight stretch of road to
Sansepolcro, and Anghiari developed in its wake, becoming a
Florentine domain after a
famous battle fought in 1440. It
has steep, narrow streets, charming little squares and the
wonderful atmosphere of the
Renaissance Palazzo Taglieschi
(home of the State Museum),
combined with several old tower-
houses. An unusual collection of

SPECIAL TO…

At least as ferocious as that
between Livorno and Pisa, the
age-old rivalry between
Sansepolcro and Anghiari was
immortalised around 1684 in
the mock-heroic poem *Il catorcio di Anghiari*, by Federigo
Nomi. In 1425 the people of
Borgo Sansepolcro stole the
catorcio (bolt) from a gate in the
walls of Anghiari; the expedition
from Anghiari to retrieve it
yielded no more than
underwear stolen from some
unfortunate laundry-women.

---

stretchers is on display in the
16th-century rooms of the
Confraternita di Misericordia,
not far from the old Camaldolese
church of Badìa.

On the edge of the town
stands the church of San Stefano
(7th–8th century). This brick
Byzantine structure has a square
plan with three semicircular
chapels that project like apses.

[i] *Corso Matteotti 103*

▶ *Follow the signs northeast for
Sansepolcro.*

❸ Sansepolcro

Borgo Sansepolcro (as it was
once called) is said to have
developed after two 10th-
century monks returning from
the Holy Land founded an
oratory here to house the relics
of St Sepolcro. This lovely little
town, packed with houses and
mansions in pure Renaissance
style, is renowned for its crafts
(embroidery, wrought iron,
gold-work), for the Palio della
Balestra (crossbow shooting
competition) in 15th-century
dress and, above all, as the
birthplace of Piero della

Francesca (1415/20–92). His works – all sublime – can be admired in the Civic Museum (from the outside, you can see the detached fresco of the *Resurrection* through a window). The Renaissance church of San Lorenzo contains a Deposition painted by Rosso Fiorentino (1528–30).

ⓘ *Piazza Garibaldi 2*

▶ *Follow the old Tiberina state road southeast to San Giustino.*

❹ San Giustino
Make sure you visit the Bufalini castle, now owned by the state. Built in 1480–92 as a fortress with corner towers, drawbridge and moat, it was converted in the 16th century by the Bufalini family, who turned it into a stately residence. Paintings, furniture, majolicas, marble busts and furnishings (accumulated between the 16th and 19th centuries) reflect the tastes of the former owners.

▶ *Continue southeast along the old Tiberina road to Città di Castello.*

❺ Città di Castello
This rarity among the towns of medieval Umbria is essentially Renaissance in style – flat, with wide, straight streets. All this is revealed when you climb to the top of the Civic (Vescovo) Tower, or – for a wider view – take the SS257 Apecchiese road to the sanctuary of the Madonna del Belvedere (17th century). In the 1st to 2nd century AD Pliny the Younger owned a villa and vast estates here; the modern urban layout was developed during the rule of the Vitelli family, from the middle of the 15th to the 16th century. Their power was symbolised in four grandiose mansions, each dominating a district, and the face of the town was changed by their redesigning, demolition and restructuring work. The Vitelli family called on outstanding artists such as Luca Signorelli from Cortona, Raffaello Sanzio (Raphael) from Urbino (who painted four of his masterpieces here), Giorgio Vasari from Arezzo and Rosso Fiorentino to embellish their residences and churches. Some of these works, now mainly scattered, remain in the town's Picture Gallery, arranged in Palazzo Vitelli alla Cannoniera, whose elegant façade overlooking the garden

The round bell tower of Città di Castello's Duomo

was designed by Vasari. In the museum of the Duomo (beneath which lies a 'lower' church with sunken vaults on stocky pillars) you can admire a *Transfiguration* painted by Rosso Fiorentino. Lovers of contemporary art can enjoy numerous works by Alberto Burri (1915–95) donated by the artist to his fellow citizens from 1978 onwards. These are displayed in the 15th-century Palazzo Albizzini and, outside the town, in the disused Seccatoi Tabacchi sheds.

ℹ️ *Piazza Matteotti, Logge Bufalini*

▶ *Continue along the old Tiberina road to the*

turning signposted on the left for Montone.

6 Montone

At the end of the 13th century the Fortebracci family of Perugia took possession of the fortress of Montone, founded in the early Middle Ages on the road between Città di Castello and Gubbio. Their rule is recalled in a costume ceremony that re-enacts the 'donation of the Holy Thorn', a relic which the son of the famous Braccio da Montone (see box) gave Montone in 1473. It is displayed on Easter Monday beneath the gilded baroque coffered ceiling of the collegiate of Santa Maria. At the top of the village stand the ruins of the Rocca di Braccio, destroyed in 1478. On another rise, the Gothic San Francesco (14th century with important votive frescoes) is today used as the town museum. Holiday flats have been created in the adjacent cloister.

ℹ️ *Via San Francesco 4*

The Tuscan countryside surrounding Arezzo

▶ *After a short stretch to the northeast, turn right on to the road for Umbèrtide.*

7 Umbèrtide

Devastated by bombing in 1944, Umbèrtide was rebuilt as a

FOR HISTORY BUFFS

Many Umbrian adventurers roamed Italy during the restless period of transition from city-state communal government to the feudal Signoria. The ambitious Braccio da Montone (born Andrea Foretebracci in 1368) was one notorious example. Having served as a mercenary under Alberico da Barbiano, he worked his way into high society, becoming lord of Bologna and later of Perugia (1416) and Città di Castello (1422). Veering between alliance and enmity with the Papacy, he is said to have cast his sights on the throne of Italy. In 1424, however, he was wounded beneath the walls of L'Aquila and lay there for three days, refusing food and medicine before dying without a word.

A street in the hilly town of Cortona

signposted on the right for the Badia di Monte Corona.

thoroughly modern town, but it has ancient origins. It was the site of the 14th-century Rocca (feudal stronghold) of Fratta, in whose dungeon the young condottiere Braccio da Montone was incarcerated in 1393 for causing the family financial difficulties. The nearby octagonal collegiate, surmounted by a large dome, dates from the 16th century. A few steps away, across the Tiber, is the secluded Piazza San Francesco with its picturesque row of three old churches. Umbèrtide gained its current name in 1863, in honour of the then Crown Prince and future King Umberto.

▶ *Follow the old Tiberina road southeast to the turning*

8 Badia di Monte Corona
Founded by San Romualdo in 1008 as the headquarters of the Camaldolesi Coronesi order, this grew to be the centre of a vast estate that has survived the centuries, and is still the base of one of the region's largest farming companies. Beneath the Romanesque church is a half-lit crypt with three apses and five aisles. Inside the church is a fine 8th-century sculpted ciborium. From the abbey, a sandstone block path known as the *mattonata* (there is also an 8km/5-mile unsurfaced road) climbs through beech and chestnut trees to the Monte Corona hermitage. The present occupants belong to the Carthusian Order, which forbids visits by members of the public.

▶ *Return to Umbèrtide on the old Tiberina road, turn left on to the SS416 to Mercatale, then turn right for Cortona and stop at Pierle.*

9 Pierle
As you climb the slopes of Monte Maestrino, the white castle of Pierle with its few surrounding houses stands out against the greenery. According to tradition this was, in the 5th century, the birthplace of Pope St Leo I the Great. In the 12th century it belonged to the Del Monte marquises, from whom it was taken by the Milanese Bernabò Visconti around the middle of the 14th century. Rebuilt in 1371 and then abandoned, it became a den of bandits until 1574, when Duke Ferdinando I de' Medici ordered its destruction. The imposing ruins are not open to visitors but the location is one of unquestionable charm.

▶ *Proceed to Cortona.*

10 Cortona
Cortona stands on a series of man-made hills known as 'the melons'. The Camucia tumulus, never fully explored, measures 200m (656 feet) in diameter and 14m (46 feet) high, and the Sodo hills are both around 60m (197 feet) across. Opening out of the hills are Etruscan tombs dating

---

SPECIAL TO...

Tanella di Pitagora (Pythagoras' Den) is the name given to a small Etruscan tomb of the Hellenistic period (2nd century BC), built with a barrel vault on a round stone tambour on the lower slopes of the Cortona hill. What was the Greek philosopher (570–490 BC) doing in Valdichiana? Nothing: he was never there. The scholars of the 16th and 17th centuries wrongly interpreted a source that spoke of the foundation of the Pythagorean school, mistaking Crotone for Cortona.

RECOMMENDED WALK

At Cortona, a shady avenue known as the 'flat stroll' extends for more than 1km (0.6 mile) after the scenic Piazza Garibaldi. Only the fit should attempt the ascent up steep Via Berrettini and Via Santa Croce to the imposing Medici fortress (open to visitors; contact the tourist office for details) of Girifalco (651m/2,136 feet) built in 1556. There is an exceptional view from the clearing in front of it. Near Via Berrettini, in a magical courtyard lined with cypresses, the 15th-century church of San Nicolò houses an altar flanked by paintings by Signorelli.

from the 6th to the 4th century BC. Do not miss the step-altar, unique in Etruria. It could be said that modern Etruscology was born here in 1727, when the Accademia Etrusca was founded. Surprising finds in its museum include the famous Etruscan bronze oil chandelier of the 5th to 4th century BC.

The Etruscan town, *Curtum*, was a powerful centre in

A detail of a capital in the old centre of Cortona

Valdichiana, and the late medieval and Renaissance Cortona was equally prosperous. The cobblers' guild commissioned Francesco di Giorgio Martini to build the majestic church of the Madonna del Calcinaio in 1485, to honour a picture painted outside the walls near a vat used to tan hides. Completed in 1513, the church and its harmonious lines evoke the clarity of Brunelleschi's architecture. A wealth of monuments and haunting views can be found throughout the town. The Diocesan Museum in front of the cathedral contains a sculpted sarcophagus of the 2nd century AD, a masterpiece by Fra' Angelico and a magnificent collection of works by Luca Signorelli and his school.

i *Via Nazionale 42*

▶ *After reaching the SS71 proceed towards Arezzo to the turning on the right for Castiglion Fiorentino.*

⑪ Castiglion Fiorentino
The well-preserved medieval structure of this village reaches a Renaissance peak in the square that overlooks the countryside through the stone arches of the 16th-century Vasari loggias. A

few steps away, a narrow street descends steeply to a solitary little square surrounded by three churches. Luca Signorelli painted a fresco, *Deposition*, in the oldest – the Pieve Vecchia, dating from 1451.

i *Piazza del Municipio 12*

▶ *Return to the SS71 and follow it to Arezzo.*

RECOMMENDED EXCURSION

Isolated in a hillside meadow to the right of the SS71, between Cortona and Castiglion Fiorentino, is the Castello di Montecchio Vesponi (owned by the Arezzo family in the 11th century). The castle was passed to Florence after the battle of Campaldino (1289), and later entrusted to Englishman John Hawkwood (1325–94), forerunner of the Italian mercenaries who led the Florentines to victory at Càscina in 1364. In honour of Giovanni Acuto, as the Tuscans called him, Paolo Uccello created an equestrian portrait fresco at Santa Maria del Fiore in Florence, in 1436.

INLAND TUSCANY

Central inland Tuscany more or less corresponds to the province of Siena, one of the Tuscan areas most given over to tourism and yet still for the most part uncrowded and full of surprises. You start with the hills of the Chianti region, between Siena and Florence. This is a magical landscape of olive groves, vineyards blanketing exposed slopes, fields and wooded *maquis* and rows of cypresses climbing towards hilltop farmhouses, turreted castles and villages.

The Crete represents another typical Tuscan landscape – undulating clay hills extending as far as the eye can see between Siena and Asciano, irrigated by the Arbia river and forming a patchwork of erosion furrows, barren clay and a multitude of colours. The same can be said of the whole Sienese hill landscape – from Val d'Orcia, cut in two by the ancient (and modern) Via Cassia, on the edge of the metal-producing hills, to the slopes of Monte Amiata, the extinct volcano that dominates the southern Tuscan landscape with its belt of woods and villages.

Between these hills, the area is bisected by the River Ombrone, from the lofty Chianti mountains in the east to the Uccellina mountains in the west.

Apart from the visit to Siena, a medieval and Gothic delight established in the few brief decades straddling the 13th and 14th centuries, the key to this region's charm is its humanised landscape – Chianti, with its villages and wines, and the seaside resorts of the Siena hills, each marked by unique episodes of history and art, with the high points of Pienza, Montepulciano, Sant'Antimo and San Galgano.

Celebration in Siena

Roads and cypress trees trace an 'S' in the Tuscan countryside

Tour 15

No fixed itinerary is needed to tour Siena. The whole city has such appeal, and its areas are so uniformly medieval, that the whim of the moment is as useful a guide as any other. What you will need, though, to appreciate its charms to the full, is information. Behind every stone, every piece of iron or wood and every patch of colour is a history of centuries of a city's development and of enthusiastic participation in its traditions, as well as a background of devotion to Sienese culture.

Tour 16

The prime reason for Chianti's worldwide fame, and the principal feature of its farming landscape, are the slopes covered with row upon row of grapevines. Alternating with the wine-growing area is the extensive wooded *maquis* of oaks, chestnuts and ilex. This tour

visits the most interesting Chianti centres, historically divided between Siena and Florence but all telling the story of a battle to grow crops in a predominantly mountainous and stony terrain. Modern viticulture has absorbed most of the sharecroppers' farms, after centuries of settlement by the urban bourgeoisie. Chianti-lovers can choose from a range of different kinds of hospitality, including elegant farm holiday centres and many opportunities to taste and buy local food and drinks.

Tour 17

The Crete is an area of barren hills, making up a strange, rolling landscape southeast of Siena. The Montalcino plateau, closed on three sides by the Ombrone and Orcia rivers, features one of the finest, and perhaps the most fascinating, Romanesque monuments in all Tuscany – Sant'Antimo. Other highlights include a spa town with a pool set in its square, a miniature Renaissance

town and the Palazzo Comunale built as a copy of the Palazzo della Signoria in Florence. Between visits you can relax in the picturesque surroundings with a glass or two of the great wine produced on the local hills.

Tour 18

This tour takes you around the territories once ruled by Siena, before it was taken by the Spaniards in 1555. In parts, this surprisingly varied scenery has a northern European feel – especially the countryside around remote San Galgano. After taking in views of inland Maremma, the route climbs the great wooded pyramid of Monte Amiata. Dark volcanic stone is used in the buildings of the towns that encircle it, seen at a distance from the bare peak of Monte Labbro and the towering Rocca di Radicòfani. There's a gentler feel to the scenery around San Casciano and the Etruscan Chiusi, the only major urban centre along a mainly rural route.

Siena

Siena is a medieval city *par excellence*, crammed with rich treasures, and for many people it is infinitely more appealing than Florence, the Tuscan capital. All over the city, statues of Romulus and Remus being suckled by a she-wolf serve as a reminder that, according to legend, it was founded by Senius, the son of Remus.

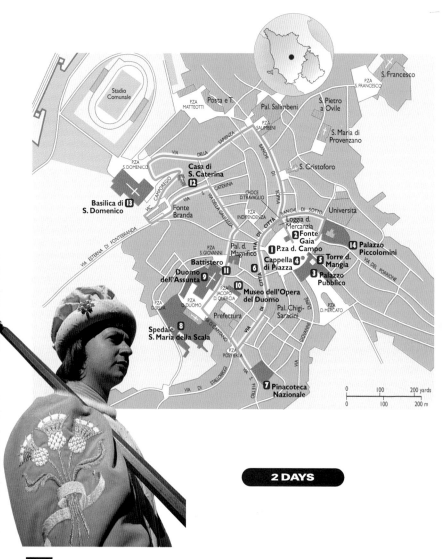

2 DAYS

i̇ *Piazza del Campo 56*

▶ *Leave your car in one of the outlying car-parks and take the shuttle service to the old centre and Piazza del Campo.*

❶ Piazza del Campo

Sloping to the south, this square has been likened to the valve of a shell, divided into nine sections by lighter strips. It could also be compared to a theatre, with the imposing Gothic Palazzo Pubblico (the Town Hall) as the stage. In the 12th century, livestock, chickens and wheat were traded here; during the first half of the 14th century the inner section was paved with bricks and the outer ring flagged. The latter measures 333m (1,092 feet) and provides the track for the Palio (see panel), a horse-race between the city's *contrade*, or districts. During this time, the ring is covered with a thick layer of soil to provide better grip for the horses' hooves.

❷ Fonte Gaia

The popular jubilation that greeted the first gushes of water conveyed to the city by the *bottini* (approximately 30km/19 miles of underground passages

---

SPECIAL TO...

The Palio in Siena comes from the Latin *pallium*, or cloth; or, in this case, a banner. The race is run around Piazza del Campo, a breathtaking piazza at the heart of the city, twice a year (2 July and 16 August) – horses are ridden bareback by tiny jockeys with a crop that is used frequently and ruthlessly. Ten of the historic 17 Sienese *contrade* (districts) still in existence compete in turns, cheered on by the entire city. Preparations are made all year round.

---

and cisterns) in 1346 prompted the name of this 'fountain of joy'. In 1868, the rectangular marble basin sculpted by Jacopo della Quercia (1374–1438) between 1409 and 1419 (the lovely original panels are in the Spedale di Santa Maria della Scala) was moved to the centre of the square from its original position, slightly further back.

❸ Palazzo Pubblico

In the last decade of the 13th century, the merchant oligarchy,

---

represented by the Council of Nine (1287–1355), started this Gothic masterpiece. Its design marks the transition from the fortress, built purely for defence, to the city mansion, a domestic residence with space for guests. When the building was completed in 1310 the Nine called in major artists to paint frescoes for its rooms (now housing the Civic Museum).

Above: Palazzo Pubblico
Below: Piazza del Campo during the biennial Palio

4 Cappella di Piazza

The chapel loggia, constructed in front of the Torre del Mangia (see below), is the result of a vow made during the catastrophic Black Death, which carried off three-quarters of the city's inhabitants between 1328 and 1348. It proved to be an extravagant way of fulfilling a promise, making a deep hole in the Sienese economy.

5 Torre del Mangia

The 88m (289-foot) high brick tower, the second tallest medieval campanile in Italy after Cremona, was built between 1338 and 1348. In 1666 the great bell known as 'Sunto' (an abbreviation of its dedication to Our Lady of the Assumption) was cast. Its majestic peals still mark special events, such as the Palio. The view from the top is breathtaking, as are the steps that lead up to it.

▶ *From the square, Passaggio San Pietro leads to the Croce del Travaglio where the main thoroughfares of the terzieri (Siena's three wards) cross – Via di Città (Terzo di Città), Banchi di Sotto (Terzo di San Martino) and Banchi di Sopra (Terzo di Camollia).*

6 Via di Città

Dominating the Croce del Travaglio (which in the event of war was barricaded with beams to prevent incursions by enemy cavalry) is the Loggia della Mercanzia (1417–44), built for the merchants' tribunal. During the 17th century it became the meeting place of the city's nobility. Of note among the aristocratic mansions that line Via di Città is Palazzo Patrizi (14th century), now housing the Accademia degli Intronati, founded in 1525 by a group of scholars who declared themselves deafened (*intronati*) by the noise of the world. Also dating from the 14th century is the curvilinear Palazzo Chigi-Saracini; this houses the prestigious Accademia Musicale Chigiana (1932), which organises concerts for Siena's Music Week in late July.

▶ *From Piazza della Posteria, turn left into Via San Pietro.*

7 Pinacoteca Nazionale

Arranged in two stately 14th- to 15th-century mansions, the Picture Gallery offers an exhaustive review of the Sienese school of painting between the late 12th century and the first half of the 17th century, exemplified by artists such as Guido da Siena, Duccio di Buoninsegna, Simone Martini and brothers Pietro and Ambrogio Lorenzetti (both victims of the Black Death), as well as Sassetta, Sano di Pietro, Sodoma and Domenico Beccafumi.

▶ *Return along Via San Pietro, Piazza della Postierla and Via del Capitano to Piazza del Duomo.*

8 Spedale di Santa Maria della Scala

This hospital, according to tradition, was founded by a cobbler in 898 to tend to pilgrims, the poor and foundlings. Thanks to alms, bequests and public contributions, by the 14th and 15th centuries it had become a formidable economic and political influence; its emblem, a staircase surmounted by a cross, is seen on numerous fortified farms in the Sienese area. Indeed, such was its power that the *comune* decided to take control of it in the late 14th century. Inside the building, don't miss the Pellegrinaio Hall,

Spedale di Santa Maria della Scala

with frescoes illustrating life in a 15th-century hospital.

9 Duomo dell'Assunta (cathedral)

The construction of this splendid Romanesque-Gothic cathedral took 200 years (13th–14th century). The Pisano family were called upon to embellish it; the father, Nicola, created the famous octagonal pulpit (1266–8) and his son, Giovanni, devoted himself to the bottom of the façade (1285–96). Inside is the Piccolomini library, built by Cardinal Francesco for the books inherited from his uncle, the humanist Pope Pius II. Its frescoes were created by Pinturicchio in 1502–9. The most extraordinary masterpiece in the cathedral is beneath your feet – the floor, all marble inlay and graffiti, divided into 56 panels designed between 1369 and 1547 by skilful Sienese artists. Domenico Beccafumi, the most prolific, completed 35 between 1517 and 1547.

▶ To the right of the cathedral, pass into Piazza Jacopo della Quercia.

10 Museo dell'Opera del Duomo

The cathedral's Museum of Works is really an artistic extension of the cathedral. Among its treasures are the *Madonna dagli occhi grossi* (*Madonna of the Large Eyes*), before which, on the eve of the battle of Monteaperti in 1260, the Sienese dedicated the city to the Virgin Mary; the enormous *Majesty* by Duccio which replaced it in 1311, on the main altar of the cathedral; the statues made by Giovanni Pisano for the façade; and works by Donatello, Jacopo

An aerial view of the Duomo

della Quercia and Pietro Lorenzetti. The building stands in the bays of the right aisle of the 'new cathedral' of 1339, which involved erecting the largest church in Christianity (and turning the hated Florence green with envy). A central axis 55m (180 feet) long was added to the side of the already completed 89m (292-foot) cathedral, turning it into the transept of a church 110m (361 feet) long. The great façade was built, but errors, lack of funds and the Black Death all intervened. Reluctantly, in 1355, the Sienese relinquished their dream. Enormous walls and arches remain, better appreciated from the top of the great façade, reached via the museum.

Duccio di Boninsegna's *Majesty* in the Museo dell'Opera del Duomo

SPECIAL TO...

The elegant Piazza Salimbeni, enclosed by three medieval and Renaissance mansions 'reassembled' in period style at the end of the 19th century, has, since 1866, been home to the still extremely powerful Monte dei Paschi. Founded in 1624 as a lending bank, its operations were guaranteed by revenue from the pastures of the Sienese Maremma.

▶ *Pass beneath the lovely side doorway (1345) of the 'new cathedral' and descend the marble staircase leading to Piazza San Giovanni.*

⓫ Battistero

Perhaps as consolation after the aborted 'new cathedral', the entrance to the baptistery at the rear of the cathedral was transformed into a second façade between 1355 and 1382, incomplete, yet almost as imposing as the main façade, and totally hiding the apse. Inside is the great baptismal font (1417–30) by Jacopo della Quercia, with additions by Lorenzo Ghiberti and Donatello. Standing on the square is Palazzo del

The Santa Barbara fortress

Magnifico, dedicated to Pandolfo Petrucci, lord of Siena between 1487 and 1512.

▶ *From Via dei Pellegrini (the main street between the cathedral and Piazza del Campo, reached along the Costerella dei Barbieri), turn into Via di Diacceto, Via della Galluzza and Via Santa Caterina, all on the left.*

⓬ Casa di Santa Caterina

Caterina Benincasa (1347–80) was the daughter of a dyer, whose eloquence enabled her to convince Gregory XI to return to Rome after the popes' long exile in Avignon (1308–77). The kitchen, bedroom, cell and indeed the saint's whole house were turned into a sanctuary by the *comune* of Siena in 1464. Slightly further on are the arches of the fine Fonte Branda spring, rebuilt in 1245.

▶ *After the Fonte Branda, take the steps of Vicolo di Camporegio to the right then Via di Camporegio, to climb to Piazza San Domenico.*

⓭ Basilica di San Domenico

This massive church, founded by the Dominicans (1226–1465), looms up like a fortress from the Camporegio hill; mendicant

orders often chose outlying locations suited to mass preaching. It deserves a visit for Sodoma's masterpieces of St Catherine in *Ecstasy* and *Swooning* (1526).

▶ *Walk eastwards along Via della Sapienza to Piazza Salimbeni, then turn right into Via Banchi di Sopra and left into Via Banchi di Sotto to come to Palazzo Piccolomini.*

⓮ Palazzo Piccolomini

The name of Piccolomini was synonymous during the Renaissance with money-changing and high finance. Their mansion (1469) was inspired by the styles prevalent in Florence, where this very wealthy family lived. Today, visitors come to see the *bicchernè* of the State Archives. These are wooden covers used to bind the books of the Biccherna administration (the Treasury of Siena). Every six months the outgoing magistrate would have the registers of his half-year period bound, and the covers painted by leading Sienese artists. They now provide an archive of exceptional documentary and artistic value; more than 100 survive from the period between 1258 and 1682.

▶ *Via Rinaldini leads back to Piazza del Campo.*

The Chianti
Hills

Woods, wheat fields, olive trees, vines on hillside slopes, black cypresses beneath farmhouses and villas, walled villages, castles, parish churches and abbeys – all add to the charm of the Chianti hills.

1/2 DAYS • 175KM • 109 MILES

ITINERARY

SIENA	▶	Castelnuovo Berardenga (21km-13m)
CASTELNUOVO BERARDENGA	▶	Castello di Brolio (12km-8m)
CASTELLO DI BROLIO	▶	Gaiole in Chianti (11km-7m)
GAIOLE IN CHIANTI	▶	Badia a Coltibuono (5km-3m)
BADIA A COLTIBUONO	▶	Radda in Chianti (10km-6m)
RADDA IN CHIANTI	▶	Greve in Chianti (21km-13m)
GREVE IN CHIANTI	▶	Impruneta (16km-10m)
IMPRUNETA	▶	Castellina in Chianti (58km-36m)
CASTELLINA IN CHIANTI	▶	Siena (21km-13m)

Brolio Castle dominates the Chianti landscape

i *Piazza del Campo 56, Siena*

▶ *Take the* **SS73** *for Arezzo-Perugia and turn off left after 14.5km (9 miles) for Castelnuovo Berardenga.*

❶ Castelnuovo Berardenga
In the 10th century, the area between the Arbia and Ombrone rivers, on the border with Sienese territory, was subject to the authority of Berardo, a nobleman of Frankish descent. Now little more than a tower remains of the castle, built in the late 14th century. Repeatedly captured by the Florentines and recaptured by the Sienese, it finally fell into disuse after Siena's collapse in 1555. Local industries include wine production and wrought-ironwork.

i *Via del Chianti 61*

▶ *Proceed north on the* **SS484** *towards Radda to the turning on the left for the Castello di Brolio.*

❷ Castello di Brolio
Brolio stands on a solitary hillock, within the mighty 15th-century ramparts erected by Florence and at the centre of the territory that belonged for centuries to the family of Baron Bettino Ricasoli, prime minister of the Kingdom of Italy (1861–2 and 1866–7). In 1860 he built a crenellated mansion in the romantic style, where he died 20 years later. The baron – an expert in wines – devoted himself to wine production in the estate cellars from 1838.

▶ *Return to the* **SS484** *towards Radda then turn right on to the* **SS408** *for Gaiole.*

❸ Gaiole in Chianti
Lying on the valley floor, framed by vineyards, this market town developed in the mid-13th century. A hundred years later it joined the Chianti league and its emblem was the black cockerel, still found on DOC bottle labels. Above the town of Gaiole, you can pay a visit to Spaltenna and the 12th-century Romanesque parish church of

Santa Maria, as well as to the timeless village of Vèrtine, which developed in the 12th and 13th centuries and belonged to the Ricasoli family.

i *Via A Casabianca*

▶ *Continue along the* **SS408** *northbound to the turning off for the Badia a Coltibuono.*

❹ Badia a Coltibuono
The Romanesque church of San Lorenzo is all that remains of the abbey that, from 1095 to 1810, belonged to the Vallombrosian Benedictines.

FOR HISTORY BUFFS

Amid the cypresses of a hillock near Monteaperti, east of Siena, a small pyramid commemorates the 1260 battle in which the Sienese Ghibellines (supporters of the Holy Roman Emperor), led by the Florentine exile Manente degli Uberti, inflicted a bloody defeat on the Guelphs, Florentine allies of the papal cause.

The monastery complex, surrounded by green age-old fir trees, now houses a wine-producing estate along with a restaurant.

▶ *Follow the signs for Radda.*

5 Radda in Chianti

High on the hill that separates the Pesa Valley from that of the Arbia, Radda (530m/1,239 feet above sea level) was an important castle controlled by Siena until 1176. Under Florence it was fortified and made the capital of the Chianti league (1384). Fine 15th-century and 16th-century buildings stand out in the medieval centre, which has an elliptical plan. Radda combines traditional production of wine and oil with its recently developed role as a resort and farm holiday centre. A lovely detour north from the road to Greve leads to the small fortified village of Volpaia and its castle.

[i] *Piazza Ferrucci 1*

▶ *Drive a little way back and turn left, following the signs for Greve.*

6 Greve in Chianti

Now named after the navigator Giovanni da Verrazzano (1480–1528, family castle slightly further north), Greve's large square was once the venue for a major market. Goods were displayed and business was conducted beneath the two wings of terraced porticoes that converge like a funnel towards the church of Santa Croce. Today, it makes a delightful place to rest. In the Middle Ages the town was controlled by the ancient castle of Montefioralle, just west of Greve. The lovely stone village with streets cobbled in a circular pattern and picturesque closed passages is a great place to wander around.

[i] *Via G da Verrazzano 59*

▶ *Continue along the SS222, turn left after 3.8km (2 miles) and drive north following the signs for Impruneta.*

7 Impruneta

In the event of human or bovine plagues, drought, wars and persistent rainfall, the devout Florentines would rush to the miraculous picture of the Madonna dell'Impruneta and accompany it in procession to Florence. Built on a site that had been a place of worship since Etruscan times (6th century BC), the sanctuary was consecrated as a parish church in 1060, then rebuilt and enlarged several times, until its final restructuring in the mid-15th century. The

The market in the lovely Piazza di Greve in Chianti

SPECIAL TO...

Produced since Etruscan times, Chianti wine is made according to the proportions set down by Bettino Ricasoli (see Castello di Brolio, opposite): 75–90 per cent Sangiovese grapes (black), to which are added 5–10 per cent Canaiolo (black), and 5–10 per cent Malvasia del Chianti and Tuscan Trebbiano (white) grapes.

entrance portico and adjacent loggias, funded by pilgrims' offerings, date from the 16th century. The streets of this large village radiate from the square, where the ancient agricultural fair of San Luca, a major event, is held in mid-October. The parade of floats for the grape festival held here at the end of September is, by contrast, only about 70 years old.

[i] *Piazza Buondelmonti 30*

▶ *Follow the signs for the A1 northwest to Firenze-Certosa and here take the motorway for Siena leaving it at Poggibonsi Nord; the SS429 for Radda leads to Castellina.*

8 Castellina in Chianti

From Val d'Elsa, you pass the ilex and cypress trees of lovely

Sant'Agnese wood (nature reserve) to return to the domains of the Chianti league, of which Castellina was an important centre. Magnificently positioned in beautiful country-side scattered with buildings from the era of the grand dukes (many now converted into holiday homes), the town still has its medieval square plan and 15th- to 16th-century houses, dominated by the crenellated tower and castle-keep (14th–15th century). Picturesque views can be enjoyed from the medieval Via delle Volte. On the road to Greve, four Etruscan tombs dating from the 7th to 6th century BC have been excavated from Montecalvario's tumulus.

[i] *Piazza del Comune 1*

▶ *Return to Siena on the SS222.*

**Above: Impruneta's Sanctuary
Below: celebrating the wine festival in Impruneta**

SPECIAL TO...

Weary of armed conflict, rivals Florence and Siena came up with an alternative means of dividing Chianti between them. At the first cock's crow, two horsemen were to set off at full speed from their respective cities; the point where they encountered each other was to mark the new border. The wily Florentine entrusted with the task skimped on the feed of his cockerel, which started to sing with hunger when it was still dark. The Florentine rider set off earlier, as a result, and this is why – so they say – Florentine Chianti is larger than that of Siena.

The Crete
to Val d'Orcia

2 DAYS • 187KM • 116 MILES As well as the harsh and gently undulating Sienese Crete, meaning 'craters' – one of Tuscany's great landscapes – this tour winds past fortified towns, castles, abbeys, country churches, farms, storehouses, magnificent Renaissance cities of art and delightful spas, offering a journey through the Sienese Middle Ages.

i Piazza del Campo 56, Siena

▶ Take the **SS326** for Perugia
and turn right on to the
SS438 to Asciano.

❶ Asciano

An extraordinary landscape
known as the Crete – an expanse
of rounded hills devoid of trees –
awaits visitors who venture
south of Siena. Often used just
for pasture, they're made
bizarrely uneven by erosion
furrows and outcrops of greyish
clay (known as *biancane*). The
sunshine and the shadows colour
them a thousand unusual
shades, depending on the season
and the time of day. The shapes

A summer scene in the Crete
near Asciano

and colours of the Crete appear
in the pictures of the Sienese
school, and interesting works by
its 15th-century artists (such as
Matteo di Giovanni and the
Master of the Osservanza) can
be admired in the Civic
Museum of Casa Corboli, in
Asciano. At the other end of this
fortified Sienese town stands the
fine collegiate of Sant'Agata
(11th-century).

i Corso Matteotti 18

▶ Return along the **SS438** and
turn left on to the **SS451**,
then follow the signs for the
Abbazia di Monte Oliveto
Maggiore.

❷ Abbazia di Monte Oliveto Maggiore

Founded in 1319 by the Blessed
Bernard, this Olivetan
Benedictine monastery stands
in a wooded park on a scenic
rise, protected on three sides by
the steep Crete and barred on
the fourth by a crenellated
tower. Most visitors come to
Monte Oliveto to see the frescoes in the abbey's main cloister.
These form one of the most
important Renaissance cycles,
painted between 1495 and 1505

by Luca Signorelli and by
Sodoma (whose real name was
Giovan Antonio Bazzi; the nick-
name is a reference to the artist's
eccentric behaviour). The 36
scenes depict episodes from the
life of St Benedict. In the adjacent church, a magnificently
inlaid wooden choir portrays
16th-century scenes of Siena.
It's also worth visiting the abbey
library, which has a basilica plan
and three aisles and is rich in
14th- and 15th-century illuminated choir-books.

▶ Follow the **SS451** to
Buonconvento, then take the
SS2 (Via Cassia) south before
turning right for Montalcino.

❸ Montalcino

The bastions of the pentagonal
Rocca (stronghold) that crowns
the Montalcino hill (the Roman

SCENIC ROUTES

The loveliest part of this tour
is the road between Siena and
Asciano, used on both the out-
ward and return journeys, and
therefore caught in changing
light at different times of the
day. The rolling hills that disap-
pear on the horizon are green
with wheat and sweet-smelling
meadows in spring but bare
and arid in summer.
Spectacular views of the Crete
can be enjoyed both before
and after the Abbey of Monte
Oliveto.

SPECIAL TO...

The fish farmed in the large
brick pool in the Abbey of
Monte Oliveto's park allowed
the monks to respect the rules
prohibiting the consumption of
meat at certain periods. This
traditional dietary expedient
was adopted to alleviate the
rigours of the Christian
lifestyle.

mons Ilicinus or Hill of Ilex Trees) offer splendid views of the village and vineyards, spread across the uneven plateau between the Ombrone and Asso valleys. Inside it reveals evidence of the past and present importance of the village. A wine cellar on the ground floor of the keep invites visitors to taste famous local wines such as Brunello and Rosso di Montalcino. In a hall above, a threadbare standard is a reminder that this fortress, built in 1361, was the last bastion of Sienese independence. When the city fell into the hands of Florence in 1555, the steadfast defenders of the republic barricaded themselves inside and for four years resisted the superior Medici forces. Of note in the square are the Palazzo dei Priori and the nearby Gothic loggia. All along the main street shops

housed in late-medieval buildings tempt wine-lovers with their merchandise.

[i] *Costa Municipio 8*

▶ *Continue south, following the signs to Sant'Àntimo.*

❹ Sant'Àntimo

Descend through the vineyards of the legendary Brunello wine to the splendid abbey church of Sant'Àntimo, standing solitary in a small valley near a stream. According to legend, it was founded by Charlemagne in 781; in the Middle Ages the abbey controlled another 38 churches besides Montalcino, scattered as far as Grosseto, Florence and Pistoia. The present church dates from the 12th century and has travertine stone walls, given a remarkable brilliance and golden reflections

by the onyx used as decoration. A fine sculpted doorway (bearing the name of the monk and architect Azzone dei Porcari) leads to the irregular interior, with a nave and two aisles divided by round arches, on to which open the elegant, double-lit apertures of the women's gallery. Of note among the capitals, all covered with symbols and fantastic creatures, is that portraying *Daniel in the Lion's Den*. There is an attractive semicircular apse with radiating

Above: the abbey of Sant'Àntimo
Left: the Montalcino stronghold

FOR HISTORY BUFFS

Around the middle of the 19th century, a local vinedresser, Ferruccio Biondi Santi, decided not to blend Sangiovese grapes but to leave them instead to mellow in oak or chestnut barrels. Thanks to its strictly circumscribed production area – officially limited to 800 hectares (1,977 acres) – and refined ageing process (at least three years, on average seven), Brunello became, in 1980, the first wine in Italy to be labelled DOCG (Origin Controlled and Guaranteed).

Spa delights in the waters of
Bagno Vignoni

chapels – a design of French
inspiration rarely found in
Italian churches.

▶ *Continue southeast and turn
left on to the* **SS323**, *which
climbs north to Castiglione
d'Orcia and Rocca d'Orcia.*

5 Rocca d'Orcia
Nestling at the foot of the vertig-
inous remains of the Rocca di
Tentennano, whose windy
summit offers a breathtaking
view of Monte Amiata, the Orcia
Valley and the Rocca di
Radicòfani, this village retains its
medieval character in its little
stone houses. St Catherine of
Siena stayed in one of these
houses in 1377, while trying to
restore peace to two branches of
the Salimbeni family, powerful
lords of Val d'Orcia between
1274 and 1419. The small, irregular square features a wonderful

old polygonal water basin.
Those who climb towards the
overhanging Rocca can visit the
small church of San Simeone,
with its paintings and frescoes of
the 14th-century Sienese school.

ⓘ *Via Marconi 13, Castiglione
d'Orcia*

▶ *Follow the* **SS323** *north, then
turn left on to the* **SS2** *and,*

FOR CHILDREN

Today, use of the pool in the
square at Bagno Vignoni is
prohibited, but a hotel with a
fine swimming pool on the
outskirts of the village
commands beautiful views of
the Orcia Valley below. Open
summer and winter, it offers
relaxation to the weary
traveller even on the coldest
days, and has a splendid water
games area for tiny tots.

---

*shortly afterwards, left again
for Bagno Vignoni.*

6 Bagno Vignoni
Bagno Vignoni, a spa that developed in the Middle Ages, is a
true surprise to visitors. The
town square is surrounded by
old houses and occupied by an
enormous pool of steaming
sulphurous water. It has seen
illustrious guests – even the 13-
year-old Caterina da Benincasa,
the future St Catherine, came
here from Siena. The loggia
with a small shrine that closes off
one side of the square is named
after her. She was brought here
by her mother, who hoped to
distract her from her solemn religious vocation, but she apparently went so close to the hot
springs – the water flows out of
the pool at 51°C (124°F) – that
she turned even the pleasure of
the spa into religious penitence.
In 1490 the gout-ridden
Lorenzo de'Medici came here.
Not all visitors, however, were
satisfied in times past (in 1581
Michel de Montaigne considered the spa 'a hole') but in
recent times the unusual charm
of Bagno Vignoni has led several
directors to set their films here –
Andrej Tarkovskij filmed
Nostàlghia (1983) here, and Carlo
Verdone used it for part of his *Al
lupo, al lupo* (1992).

▶ *Rejoin the* **SS2** *and continue
left to San Quìrico d'Orcia.*

7 San Quìrico d'Orcia
Situated along the ancient
pilgrims' way, Via Francigena,
San Quìrico was an important
stopping place between
Florence and Rome. Its walls,
broken at intervals by towers,
surround the shady park and
Italian garden of the Horti
Leonini family, created around
1540. The main attraction in
this village is a 14th-century
collegiate with three extraordinary carved doorways. The
main portal, dating from 1080,
features clustered columns,
tied with a loop at the centre,
resting on lionesses, with
mythical monsters grappling in

the bas-relief on the architrave. The first of the two, on the right side, presents powerful lions beneath caryatids, sculpted in the 13th century. Inside, there is a fine 16th-century wooden choir.

☐ *Via Dante Alighieri 33*

▶ *Take the SS146 to Pienza.*

8 Pienza

Pienza was known as Corsignano until Pope Pius II ordered Bernardo Rossellino, a pupil of Leon Battista Alberti, to turn his native country village into a vision of rationalist beauty. In 1459 work began on the 'Utopian town' that was even named after its patron, Pienza. The planned architectural transformation – sadly interrupted by the deaths of both Pius II and Rossellino in 1464 – was accomplished in the square, paved in brick and strips of stone, on which stand a cathedral in travertine stone (the interior glitters with the gold of splendid Sienese altarpieces

Strolling through the castle at Pienza, with sweeping views of Val d'Orcia

ordered by the Pope) and Palazzo Piccolomini (similar in design to Alberti's Palazzo Rucellai in Florence). The loggia overlooking the mansion's hanging garden offers a splendid view of the Orcia Valley; all around are the residences that the erudite Pope forced the cardinals to build, to add lustre to his magnificent extension of the Roman court.

☐ *Piazza Pio II*

The collegiate of San Quirico

▶ *Continue along the SS146 to Montepulciano.*

9 Montepulciano

Montepulciano lies along the crest of a hill between the Orcia Valley and Valdichiana, When, in the 12th century, Valdichiana turned into marshland, traffic shifted towards Montepulciano, resulting in expansion of trade and manufacturing. The town started to accumulate great riches in the 14th century and over the next 200 years, under Florentine rule, spent lavishly on secular, religious and military constructions. An enviable art heritage was amassed and the creators of the town include names such as Michelozzo, Antonio da Sangallo, Baldassarre Peruzzi and Jacopo da Vignola. Stylish aristocratic homes line the two main streets, which culminate in the monumental Piazza Grande. Here, alongside Palazzo Comunale (a small-scale copy of Florence's Palazzo Vecchio), stand the Duomo (cathedral), Palazzo Tarugi, Palazzo Contucci and that of the Capitano del Popolo; facing this is the Pozzo dei Grifi e dei

Above: market in Montepulciano
Right: an invitation to the town's
famous Vino Nobile

Leoni fountain. A short distance
away is the 18th-century Regio
Poliziano theatre, named after
Agnolo Ambrogini, commonly
known as Poliziano. This
humanist poet and close friend
of Lorenzo the Magnificent was
born in Montepulciano in 1454.
Lower down, on Via di
Gracciano, is the tower
surmounted by a metal-covered
figure of Pulcinella, which
strikes the hours. Monte-
pulciano's most famous church,
San Biagio, stands isolated
outside the town on the side of a
hill. This austere Renaissance
masterpiece in travertine stone
has, over the years, turned a
mellow golden colour. Erected
by Antonio da Sangallo the
Elder between 1518 and 1545, it
has a Greek cross plan and a
high central dome; the exterior
is decorated in recurring classic
orders, seen also in the two bell
towers (the right one unfin-
ished) set in the intersections
between the arms of the cross.

[i] *Via Gracciano nel Corso 26*

▶ *Follow the signs to Siena to
the north via Torrita di Siena,
Sinalunga and the SS326, to
the second turning on the left
for Serre di Rapolano.*

⑩ Serre di Rapolano

This was the site of a Byzantine
fortress in the 6th century; at
the time of Frederick
Barbarossa it acquired an imperial palace, which, under 13th-
century Sienese rule, was
turned into a *grancia* – a fortified storehouse with barns, vat-
rooms, olive-store and hayloft.
The building is said to have
been purchased from the
Cacciaconti family by the
Sienese merchant Giovanni
de'Rossi as a home for the
beautiful Ciambragina, a young
girl he had married in Cambrai.
Between the first two Sundays
in May, the silent maze of
streets and alleys that branch
out around the *grancia* come
alive with a medieval market
filled with craftspeople, musicians, falconers, magicians,
beggars, jugglers, genteel ladies
and valiant cavaliers.

▶ *Take the SS438 and continue
via Asciano to Siena.*

Visitate le
Antiche-Cantine
Contucci

BACK TO NATURE

About 6km (4 miles) north of
Serre di Rapolano, near the San
Giovanni Battista spa pool, is
an impressive *mofette* – a
fissure in the earth, exhaling
volcanic gas. Contained in an
enclosed hollow, 80m (262
feet) wide and 6–7m (20 feet)
deep, stagnating toxic vapours
of hydrogen sulphide and
carbon dioxide prevent all
vegetation growth. In the pleasant grove before the baths, sur-
face springs rich in calcium
(now piped) have produced a
bizarre 'mountain' of white
travertine stone, set amid
broom bushes and oak woods
– a wild but delightful spot.

Monte Amiata

This tour takes in the majestic volcanic dome of Monte Amiata, an extinct volcano. The impermeable layer of sedimentary rocks that was covered with magma about 300,000 years ago has produced wonderful, gushing, hot springs in the area. Covered in snow for several months of the year, it is also a popular skiing centre.

2/3 DAYS • 323KM • 201 MILES

ITINERARY	
SIENA	▶ **Abbazia di S.Galgano** (33km-20½m)
ABBAZIA DI S.GALGANO	▶ **Bagni di Petriolo** (29km-18m)
BAGNI DI PETRIOLO	▶ **Monte Amiata** (69km-43m)
MONTE AMIATA	▶ **Santa Fiora** (15km-9m)
SANTA FIORA	▶ **Piancastagnaio** (12km-7½m)
PIANCASTAGNAIO	▶ **Abbadia San Salvatore** (4km-2½m)
ABBADIA SAN SALVATORE	▶ **Radicòfani** (20km-12½m)
RADICÒFANI	▶ **San Casciano dei Bagni** (16km-10m)
SAN CASCIANO DEI BAGNI	▶ **Cetona** (16km-10m)
CETONA	▶ **Chiusi** (16km-10m)
CHIUSI	▶ **Siena** (93km-58m)

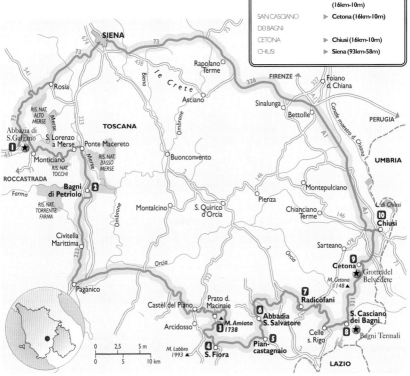

The Abbey of San Galgano stands open to the skies

ℹ️ *Piazza del Campo 56, Siena*

▶ *Follow the SS73 to the south-west to Bivio del Madonnino, where you take the SS441 to the turning on the left for the Abbazia di San Galgano.*

❶ Abbazia di San Galgano
This abbey stands alone in the depths of the countryside, with the sky for a roof and a meadow for the floor. The Gothic vaults of this grandiose Cistercian monument (69m/226 feet long and 29m/195 feet wide) were erected between 1224 and 1288, but collapsed towards the end of the 18th century. Of particular beauty a few steps away, on the hilltop of Monte Siepi, is the dome of an unusual circular church. It covers the stone into which nobleman Galgano Guidotti is said to have thrust

---

SPECIAL TO…

The sword in the rock on Monte Siepi is believed to be modern. None the less, there are enigmatic analogies between San Galgano and King Arthur and his sword Excalibur. Some believe Galgano is none other than the valiant Gawain, Arthur's nephew.

---

his sword to make a cross in around 1180.

ℹ️ *Via Umberto 2, Chiusdino*

▶ *Back at Bivio del Madonnino, turn right and continue to Monticiano, then go left via San Lorenzo a Merse to Ponte Macereto, right for a short way on the SS223 and then left, following the signs for Bagni di Petriolo.*

❷ Bagni di Petriolo
Hidden in the remote Farma gorge, the spa is still surrounded by sections of walls erected between 1404 and 1419. The cross vaults of a portico cover three baths, once filled with the hot sulphurous water that now flows through small natural pools on the riverbanks.

▶ *Continue and turn south-bound on to the SS223 Siena-Grosseto road, then, at the Pagànico exit, go east, following the signs for Castel del Piano; from here go via Prato delle Macinaie, skirting the northeastern slopes of Monte Amiata to the end of the road. The peak (1,738m/ 5,702 feet) is reached on foot in just a few minutes.*

❸ Monte Amiata
The peak of Monte Amiata is made up of a pile of bare reddish rocks, topped with a

large 1910 iron cross. There's a truly extraordinary view – through a mass of aerials.

▶ *Descend the south slope, following the signs for Arcidosso/Santa Fiora, to the turning on the left (to the right you go to Arcidosso, continuing southwards to Monte Labbro) for Santa Fiora.*

❹ Santa Fiora

This village, built with the dark grey volcanic stone that distinguishes all the centres on Monte Amiata, extends from the foot of the Aldobrandeschi's castle. Between the 11th and 15th centuries this family chose Santa Fiora as its county seat. After passing to the Sforza family in 1439, it was the only mountain village to escape Sienese rule. Grand Duke Pietro Leopoldo I did not abolish the fiefdom until 1789. From the castle, after passing the Romanesque parish church of SS Fiora e Lucilla, with its splendid polychrome altar frontals by Andrea della Robbia (1435–1525/8), you descend to the crystal-clear Peschiera (fish pond) built in the 18th century on the Fiora springs. Its cool

Monte Amiata, a peak in Tuscany south of the Arno river

surrounding park offers an inviting and pleasant interlude.

ⓘ *Piazza Garibaldi 17*

▶ *Follow the signs eastwards for Piancastagnaio.*

❺ Piancastagnaio

Piancastagnaio also culminates in an Aldobrandeschi stronghold (13th–14th century), which, from the edge of a scenic plateau, dominates the old centre, with its compact arrangement of streets sandwiched between austere buildings built in volcanic trachyte. As you leave the village, on the right is the church of the Franciscan convent of San Bartolomeo, founded

in 1278. Facing it is a huge chestnut tree hollowed out by lightning.

▶ *Take the road north for Abbadia San Salvatore.*

❻ Abbadia San Salvatore

The new residential districts of Abbadia San Salvatore reveal its present role as the largest summer holiday and winter sports resort on Amiata. Its recent past, however, is illustrated in the museum opened in the cinnabar mines. These were worked between 1897 and 1977, during which time they produced the world's second largest output of mercury. The past is represented not only by the vast medieval centre full of Gothic and Renaissance buildings, blackened by time, but also by the Benedictine abbey of San Salvatore, whose territories extended from the Tyrrhenian Sea to Valdichiana between the

---

BACK TO NATURE

At Arcidosso, near Podere dei Nobili, the paths of the Monte Amiata Fauna Park allow the observation of birds (121 species), deer, fallow deer, chamois and moufflon, and the rare Amiata mouse-grey Crociato donkey. There is a covered terrace for these animals after sightings of the unapproachable Apennine wolf. A history and nature route approximately 3 hours long leads to the bare scenic peak of Monte Labbro (1,193m/3,914 feet; the plateau below can also be reached by car).

late 8th century and the 12th century. The façade of the Romanesque church was begun in 1036 and the interior altered in 1590. Its remarkable column-filled crypt dates from the Lombard foundation of the complex (traditionally attributed to King Ratchis, in 743).

i Via Adua 25

▶ *Continue northwards to the turning on the right which passes over a tunnel on the* **SS2** *to Cassia to reach a road on the right climbing to Radicòfani.*

FOR HISTORY BUFFS

At the top of Monte Labbro, a round tower, walled spaces and an altar at the back of a cave are reminders that this was the home of the Giurisdavidica Church, a sect halfway between the socialist ideal and religious mysticism, founded in 1872 by a carter from Arcidosso called David Lazzaretti (1834–78). The visionary 'Christ of Monte Amiata' preached brotherhood, education, shared property and a woman's right to vote. Mountain-dwellers joined in droves, but the hostility of the authorities, sustained by the local landowners, earned Lazzaretti a bullet in the forehead as he was leading a peaceful procession. A few followers keep his memory alive.

7 Radicòfani

Sienese exile Ghino di Tacco was notorious for levying heavy taxes. From 1297 to 1300 he was master of Radicòfani and anyone passing through the surrounding territory was likely to be set upon and robbed by his marauders. Immediately before the village is La Posta, a late-16th century Medici hunting lodge, subsequently turned into a resting place for travellers on the Via Cassia; Charles Dickens was among those who stayed here. In the typically medieval centre, the Romanesque church of San Pietro (13th century) has fine terracottas by Andrea della Robbia. Radicòfani's greatest attraction, however, is the massive, looming Rocca (stronghold), founded by Pope Adrian IV in 1154, turned into a fortress in 1417 and rebuilt and strengthened by Cosimo I de' Medici after 1565 (today's version is a recent reconstruction).

i Via R Magi 31

▶ *Leave Radicòfani and drive east towards Sarteano/Chiusi to the turning on the right, which leads, via Celle sul Rigo, to San Casciano dei Bagni.*

8 San Casciano dei Bagni

A fine little town of medieval origin on the southern slopes of Monte Cetona, San Casciano stands on a plentiful spa basin, and is considered the third most productive spa in Europe after Karlovy Vary (Karlsbad) and Aix-les-Bains, with over 40 hot springs. South of the town, clustered around a 19th-century villa in the form of a castle, is the luxurious Bagno di Portico spa. The establishment's hot pool overlooks the undulating hills around the town.

i Via San Cassiano 11

▶ *Follow the Monte Cetona road north for Sarteano to the turning on the right signposted for Grotte del Belverde and Cetona.*

The tower atop of Monte Labbro

SCENIC ROUTES

The whole central section of this tour, from San Galgano to Paganico and from Castel del Piano to Cetona, winds through unchanged landscapes and splendid views. Particularly scenic are the mountain roads on mounts Amiata and Cetona.

9 Cetona

Above the hermitage of Santa Maria a Belverde (1367), arranged around three oratories entirely decorated with frescoes, are some gloomy refuges and caves used as a shelter during the Bronze Age (2nd millennium BC). Those wishing to visit the beautiful Belverde caves – St Francis stayed in one – must contact the Civic Museum in Cetona. This is found on the

RECOMMENDED WALK

The Anello della Montagna is a 28km (17-mile) route that goes all the way around Monte Amiata at heights of 1,050m (3,445 feet) to 1,300m (4,265 feet), through monumental woods of beech and chestnut trees. It takes about 12 hours to complete the route, but you can pick it up and leave it from roads, hotels and refuge huts served by public transport.

Above: Radicòfani's stronghold
Below: the Palio at San Casciano

vast 16th-century square that acts as a spectacular introduction to the village, arranged in concentric circles to imitate the dual ring of walls erected by Siena in 1458.

☐ *Piazza Garibaldi 63*

▶ *Leave Cetona to the east on the secondary road that passes over the A I to reach the SS146 for Chiusi.*

🔟 Chiusi

Chiusi has a long history. It was an important centre until around AD 1000, when Valdichiana succumbed to the marshes and malaria, and went into irreversible decline. To learn about this past you must go underground: the hydraulic network of intricate tunnels, reached from the cathedral museum, dates from the time of Etruscan *Chamars*, which in the 6th century BC saw the splendours of Lars Porsena's reign. The route, 120m (394 feet) long, leads out into a huge 1st century BC Roman reservoir, from which

you climb to the top of a 13th-century tower that acts as a bell tower, and gives fine views all around. The museum organises guided visits to the impressive

RECOMMENDED EXCURSIONS

The Etruscans dug a mass of tombs and underground passages in the tufa of the steep Poggio Gaiella, north of Chiusi, between the 7th and 3rd centuries BC. This area was identified by 19th-century scholars as the labyrinthine mausoleum of Lars Porsena, the sovereign who managed to take control of Rome between 509 and 504 BC, as described in Latin sources. This theory has long been discarded, but some swear they have heard, in the vicinity, the cheeping of the 5,000 golden chicks said to have accompanied the great King of *Chamars* to his last resting place. In the absence of the chicks, consolation can be found in the exquisite *brustico* fish, prepared on the traditional reed fire by restaurants on the shores of the nearby lake.

catacombs of San Mustiola (3rd–4th century), outside the town. Contact the National Archaeological Museum for visits to the Etruscan tombs.

☐ *Piazza Duomo 1*

▶ *Take the A I towards Arezzo and leave it at Val di Chiana to take the SS326 Bettolle-Siena road westwards.*

TUSCANY'S HOT WATER SPAS

'For more than 600 years the Romans had no doctors other than their baths' wrote Pliny the Elder (AD 23–79). Actually it wasn't the Romans who discovered hot water spas in Tuscany. The Etruscans already knew a thing or two on the subject; they had special magistrates, called *aquilegi*, who were responsible for protecting the spas – whose sites often coincide with modern centres.

It can't be denied, though, that the ancient Romans were great lovers of water – hot water in particular. The wealthy made sure they had a constantly heated supply by installing household systems; and the therapeutic properties of water were widely accepted, with careful distinctions drawn between various types of mineralisation, each related to the treatment of a specific condition. Indeed, the Romans developed a whole lifestyle in which shared hot baths played an important role. Spas were believed to restore and purify the body and the spirit; they were places in which to relax and socialise. In imperial times, luxurious spa buildings became synonymous with well-being, and refined and cultured tastes.

In the Middle Ages, mineral water therapy went through a period of decline. The barbarian invasions destroyed aqueducts and springs, the bathhouses were stripped and abandoned. The Christian religion waged war on them as pagan sites and places of promiscuous licentiousness. At a local level, none the less, use of the Roman *balnae* (pools) continued; some were even restored in the early Middle Ages. What changed was the purpose and manner of mineral water therapy. It became purely a treatment – no longer recreation – and was carried out solemnly as a medical necessity, without luxury, marble or statues: just baths, mud and lots of sweat. The practice of hygienic and curative baths came back into fashion during the *comune* period. Hydrology appeared as a subject of study at the newborn universities of medicine; in 1292 an *ordinamentum balneorum* issued by the Podestà of Siena regulated the use of spas, introducing partitions between the different sexes. In 1337, Siena renewed the Petriolo spa, sending guardians to maintain it and collect payment from users. Large communal pools, covered with roofs, canopies or branches, were the norm, although some spas had socially differentiated pools. Those of San Giovanni at Bagni di Lucca had one pool for each rung on the social ladder – knights, ladies, male citizens, female citizens, Jewish men, Jewish women and servants.

From past to future

The Renaissance saw a flurry of treatises on the curative virtues of Tuscan waters, by scholars such as Ugolino da Montecatini (1348–1429). The Medici family's involvement in spas was temporary (late 16th century to

The open-air Saturnia spa

amusement, and pleasure, as
well as treatment.

Treatment and pleasure

There's no need to be suffering
from an ailment to visit a spa.
Just stop along the way and try
immersing yourself in a lovely,
steaming, open-air pool, perhaps
after a day's driving and walking. Here's a very brief selection
of baths (waters 30–40°C/
86–104°F and 40°C+/104°F+
respectively), divided by
province. Check opening times.

Massa Carrara: the Equi
Terme pool, in the mountains
north of Carrara (see Tour 1,
only 24°C/75°F but pleasant).

Lucca: the fine pools of Villa
Ada at Bagni di Lucca (see Tour
3) and the small Lake Pra' di
Lama, at Pieve Fosciana in
Garfagnana (see Tour 3, cloudy
but inviting).

Casciana Terme: southeast of
Pisa is the Casciana Terme pool
(36°C/97°F in a garden in the
town centre);
also of note is
the luminous
indoor pool of
Larderello (see
Tour 6).

Livorno: at
Venturina (Tour
6), the Terme di
Caldana pool and the welcoming
Calidario; on the isle of Elba is
the small Lake Terranera at
Porto Azzurro (see Tour 7).

Siena: the pools of San
Giovanni Battista and the Antica
Querciolaia, at Rapolano (see
Tour 17); Bagni di Petriolo (see
Tour 18; not many 'pools' but a
splendid environment); the very
scenic hotel pool of Bagno
Vignoni (see Tour 17) and that
of Bagni San Filippo, between
Abbadia San Salvatore and
Radicòfani (see Tour 18); the
elegant pool of San Casciano dei
Bagni (see Tour 18).

Grosseto: Saturnia (see Tour 9;
the best known spa).

Two ways of taking the waters

early 17th century), and
restricted to those of San
Giuliano, San Casciano and San
Filippo. Although the 17th
century brought a sharp drop in
attendance at spas, there was a
recovery in the second half of
the 18th century. Inspired by
European models, the Grand
Dukes of Lorraine created
splendid spa towns at San
Giuliano and Montecatini. In
the early 19th century,
Napoleon's sister Elisa
Baciocchi spent her time at
Bagni di Lucca. In the 19th
century, these three spa centres
became renowned all over
Europe for their society life and
frivolous encounters between
scholars, politicians, royal

families
and the
grand bourgeoisie. The middle
classes visited small spa towns
scattered over the territory.
Unpretentious rural establishments, often with multiple
communal pools, satisfied the
needs of the less well off.
The golden age of spas
extended into the 20th century
– Montecatini was renewed in
the 1920s and the Chianciano
spa also took off. After World
War II, spas experienced a new
popularity (fuelled partly by
health service reimbursements),
but by the mid-1970s they were
in decline again, and have recov-
ered only partially in recent
years. The future lies, perhaps,
in a return to the past, with spas
being seen as places of

UMBRIA

Enclosed by Tuscany, Marche and Lazio, Umbria is the only Italian mainland region with no outlets to the sea. It extends over 8,456sq km (5,255 square miles) and has just over 800,000 inhabitants (the fourth smallest region in terms of population). A predominantly hilly territory, few peaks rise above 1,500m (4,921 feet); the highest mountains are in the southeast, near the Sibillini and Terminillo ranges. Then there are the fluvial basins: the 'Umbrian Valley', in particular, between Perugia and Spoleto; the valley of the Tiber; and the plains of Gubbio, Norcia and Terni. But the landscape of hills, fields, high towns and villages and mountain settings has a magic beyond dry statistics – and a reputation for great wine, especially in the Orvieto area, and olives, grown in the Trasimeno region.

Umbria has only been a unified region since the mid-16th century, when it became part of the Church State. In ancient times the axis of the River Tiber divided it into a western Etruscan area (Perugia, Orvieto) and an eastern one, initially the land of the Umbrians and later of the Romans (from 295 BC). This division was reimposed in the 6th century, when it was shared between the Byzantines (who controlled a narrow corridor between Rome and Rimini, including Amelia, Narni, Perugia, Gubbio and, further west, Orte, Orvieto, Chiusi and Cortona) and the Lombards, who installed themselves from 576 in the Duchy of Spoleto (with Terni, Foligno, Spello and Assisi). Subsequently the temporal power of the popes waned, and in 1860 Umbria became a region with a single province – with Perugia as its capital. The province of Terni was created in 1927.

Small, lush, neat and civilised, Umbria has appealing locations with a fascinating medieval atmosphere. Assisi is bound to the life of St Francis but also to the work of major western artists, including Giotto, Cimabue, Simone Martini and Pietro Lorenzetti. Then there are Gubbio, Spoleto, Orvieto, Spello, Montefalco, Bevagna and Todi, each with its own particular charm. Museums are found all over the region, some housing tiny collections but all providing a testimony to the Umbrian people's love for their native land. The scenery here is gentle, verdant and largely unspoilt in the hill areas and, along with Lake Trasimeno, comprises one of Italy's most fragile and important wetlands.

Umbrian pottery – a tradition that lives on all over the region, from Orvieto to Gubbio

Tour 19

Founded by the mythical Etruscan Euliste (whose brother, Ocno, founded Bologna and Mantua), the ancient town of Perugia remains enclosed within the 3km (2-mile) perimeter of colossal walls that date from the 4th to the 3rd century BC. The route followed by this tour is similarly confined within those walls, taking advantage of the fact that most of Perugia is a pedestrian zone.

Tour 20

Retracing the steps of the young Francis of Assisi, this itinerary explores the monuments and surroundings of Gubbio, an ancient gem of a town, built in grey calcareous stone. It then ventures across the border with Marche to the breathtaking gorges of Monte Càtria and the abbey of Fonte Avellana. Smoother roads lead back into Umbria and a special destination: Nocera Umbra, which will not fail to move you.

Tour 21

Those who are curious to discover how many shades of green exist in nature can do so on the Lake Trasimeno tour (some have counted more than a hundred). Changing with the angle of observation, the scenery that inspired the Umbrian painter Perugino (*c*1450–1523) is dominated by the delicate light reflected from the waters on to the hills. With a little luck and some patience you may even see the spectacular dives of the ospreys.

Tour 22

The fertile plain of the Umbrian Valley, from Assisi to Spoleto, has changed considerably over the last 50 years. Industrialisation has almost erased all signs of history, and fields of tobacco, beetroot, maize and sunflowers abound. But the hillside has, none the less, managed to preserve its gentle beauty, and vines are now cultivated alongside the area's traditional olive trees.

Tour 23

The main objective of this journey into the heart of Umbria stands on red tufa walls that plunge down between the green vineyards and golden crops of the Paglia Valley. This is the unequalled spectacle of Orvieto, particularly lovely when viewed from the SS71 from Bolsena. The scenery and even the speech seem closer to the Etruria of Pitigliano and Sovana than to the region Orvieto has belonged to since 1860. The Tiber forms a winding boundary that once separated Etruria and the Umbrian territory. Todi, perched on its triangular hill, is

Hill scenery with olive trees, one of the symbols of Umbria

a delightful sight, and on the return journey you can go shopping for ceramics and great wines.

Tour 24

This tour explores the area between the Tiber and its tributary, the Nera, and between Terni and Narni, where urbanisation and industrial development contrast with islands of unspoilt hill country. In the countryside you can still see small fiefs and villages dominated by the lord's mansion or castle, as in the cases of Alviano, Lugnano and Baschi.

Tour 25

Winding past rugged mountain backdrops, Valnerina – an ancient sheep-track once used to move flocks between the Tyrrhenian and the Adriatic seas – presents very different scenes from the gentle slopes and rounded peaks so typical of the Umbrian landscape. This tour climbs the valley and ventures on to the unspoilt 'little Tibet' of the Castellucio plateau, on the Sibillini mountain range. Norcia and Cascia are old towns with long histories, and the sanctuary of Madonna della Stella is the last surprise planned on this tour.

Perugia

Perugia is a modern, cosmopolitan town with an ancient heart. Sharing the space within its walls is 1970s and 1980s architecture designed by Aldo Rossi for the Fontivegge district; flourishing food and textile industries; fine shops; and two universities (one reserved for foreigners). The town comes alive with regular music festivals – and a chocolate festival in October.

1 DAY

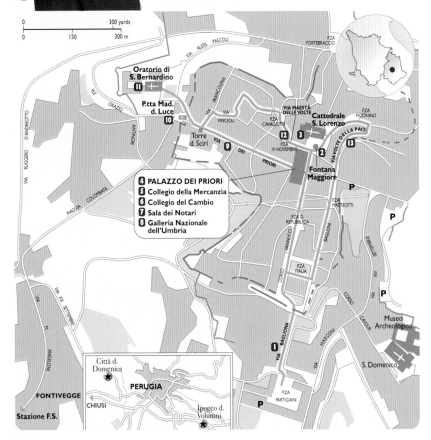

4 **PALAZZO DEI PRIORI**
5 Collegio della Mercanzia
6 Collegio del Cambio
7 Sala dei Notari
8 Galleria Nazionale dell'Umbria

The Fontana Maggiore, a 13th-century masterpiece by Nicola and Giovanni Pisano

i *Via Mazzini 21; Via Mazzini 6; Palazzo dei Priori, Piazza IV Novembre 3*

▶ *Leave your car in the underground car-park in Piazza dei Partigiani and follow the so-called Via Bagliona which rises the 50m (164 feet) up to the centre on escalators.*

❶ Via Bagliona

Entering the remains of the Rocca Paolina and the medieval Baglioni quarter, this underground route recalls two crucial moments in Perugia's history. Churches, convents, 300 houses and 26 towers were demolished and partially buried to make room for the Rocca (fort), built in 1540 by Paolo III Farnese to confirm papal control of the town. Still visible are alleyways, wells, stores and squares, overlooked by furnaces and workshops. The truncated skeletons of tower-houses vanish in the shadows of the vaults. Little more than the embrasures remain today of the once formidable fortress, into the walls of which the architect Antonio da Sangallo the Younger managed to set the arch and loggia of the Marzia gate (3rd century BC). All the rest was demolished in 1860

Detail of the Marzia gate; point of access to Via Bagliona

during Italian Unification by the people of Perugia, who were protesting against massacres perpetrated the previous year by the papal Swiss guards.

▶ *Having come out on to Piazza Italia proceed along Corso Vannucci to Piazza IV Novembre.*

❷ Fontana Maggiore

This monumental fountain, the visual focus of the square, was created between 1275 and 1278 to mark the completion of the 20-year construction of the 4km (2-mile) aqueduct. Its design and decoration are by Nicola Pisano (*c*1225–84) and his son Giovanni (*c*1250–1320). Sculptures are set on two marble basins, surmounted by a bronze one. Below is an

agricultural calendar, the signs of the zodiac and representations of the arts, above 24 statuettes celebrating the town's Etruscan foundation, and combining biblical characters and contemporary figures; at the top are three nymphs. The whole work embodies the ambitious political and cultural programme of the *comune*, in its portrayal of history and universal knowledge. Beside the fountain, a drain cover bearing the inscription 'medieval well' conceals an Etruscan-Roman well more than 47m (154 feet) deep. However, the Etruscan town's main water source is found to the right of the cathedral, in Piazza Danti (once known as 'Piazza della Paglia' because straw (*paglia*) and bread were sold here; now the

Deruta-Ripabianca ceramics market is held here twice a week). An ancient well, with a diameter of 5.6m (18 feet) and lined with travertine blocks, plunges 36m (118 feet) below Palazzo Bourbon-Sorbello.

❸ Cattedrale di San Lorenzo

Despite more than two and a half centuries' work – from 1300 to 1569, the year of its consecration – the cathedral was never completed. Its left side is partially covered with pink and white marble, and forms one side of Piazza IV Novembre, behind the fountain. In the 17th century it was raised with bricks and the façade itself has remained incomplete. In the luminous interior you can admire an *Enthroned Madonna* (1484), a masterpiece by Luca Signorelli, and a *Deposition* (1567–9) painted by Federico Barocci. To the left the cathedral extends into a loggia built in 1423 by Braccio da Montone, then lord of Perugia, 'so that the nobility of Perugia may stroll there at its pleasure and conduct transactions'. Under the first arch are the remains of the 12-sided bell tower demolished in the 14th century in a search for the *palladium*, the mythical Homeric shield that made the city of Troy invincible.

❹ Palazzo dei Priori

The construction of this imposing building, the seat for the town's judiciary, lasted from 1293 to 1443. As was the case for many stately mansions in the region, adjacent tower-houses were bought from craftsmen and

merchants and then converted to the new requirements. Housed within are the Collegio della Mercanzia, Collegio del Cambio, Sala dei Notari and Galleria Nazionale dell'Umbria.

❺ Collegio della Mercanzia

In 1390, the merchants' guild took one of the properties on the ground floor of the Palazzo dei Priori. During the first half of the 15th century, the Collegio della Mercanzia audience chamber (entrance on Corso Vannucci) was covered with splendid inlaid pine and walnut panels. Visible in a lunette is the griffin of Perugia above a bale, the guild's emblem.

❻ Collegio del Cambio

Between 1452 and 1457, money-changers installed themselves in the rooms to the right of the Collegio della Mercanzia. Their audience chamber became a Renaissance showcase, thanks to the frescoes painted by Perugino (1497–1507), which, in keeping with his humanistic approach, combined classical figures (pagan gods, sibyls, illustrious men) with Christian themes (virtues, prophets, the transfiguration and a crib). The painter probably availed himself of the assistance of, among others, the young Raphael (1483–1520). Apparently, both portrayed themselves on the walls of the chamber – the master from Città della Pieve in an explicit self-portrait and his pupil from

Statue of Pope Julius III on the cathedral of San Lorenzo

Strolling in Piazza IV Novembre, the social heart of the town

Urbino as Daniel. This chamber leads to the lovely chapel of San Giovanni Battista, entirely covered in frescoes by Giannicola di Paolo in 1515–18.

7 Sala dei Notari

In 1582 the notaries also moved into Palazzo dei Priori, occupying the Sala del Popolo, a large, vaulted room which they had sumptuously frescoed. It is reached through a doorway in front of the Fontana Maggiore. Hanging from the corbels, supporting the griffin of Perugia and the Guelph lion, are the chains and a long bar that the people of Perugia removed from the gates of Siena after defeating its militia in 1358. To the right of the portico, the narrow Via della Gabbia is a reminder of the times when wrongdoers were suspended in an iron cage and exposed to public ridicule.

8 Galleria Nazionale dell'Umbria

The Umbria National Gallery is the latest tenant of note in the mansion, where it was installed on the third floor in 1878. It exhibits works in well-ordered, chronological sequence, divided by schools. Duccio di Buoninsegna, Gentile da Fabriano, Beato Angelico, Benozzo Gozzoli, Piero della Francesca, Perugino, Pinturicchio and Pietro da Cortona are among the painters, and Arnolfo da Cambio and the Pisano family among the sculptors. These few names show that this is one of Italy's richest museums, particularly important for its work from the Umbrian, Tuscan and Marche areas.

▶ *Return to Corso Vannucci and turn right into Via dei Priori.*

9 Via dei Priori

Descending along this major medieval thoroughfare, you come to the Torre degli Sciri (46m/151 feet), Perugia's tallest intact tower/fortress. Exploring the winding narrow side streets that lead off Via dei Priori, often with steps and covered with vaults, is like stepping back in time.

10 Piazzetta della Madonna della Luce

This irregular square is noteworthy for its mix of architectural styles – Gothic houses and the remains of a postern stand opposite the Renaissance façade of the church of the Madonna della Luce (1513–19).

A few steps away, on its original Etruscan columns, rises the Porta Trasimena (gate), the old exit on the route to Trasimeno and Tuscany.

11 Oratorio di San Bernardino

The medieval stone austerity of Via dei Priori brings you out into the Piazza San Francesco, which is a splendid setting for the masterpiece of Perugian Renaissance architecture across the lawn – the oratory of San Bernardino, with refined bas-reliefs on its polychrome façade, sculpted by Agostino di Duccio in 1457–61.

SPECIAL TO…

The Sandri pastry shop in Corso Vannucci is a Perugian institution, greeting customers in regal surroundings – old furnishings, a frescoed vault and crystal cases containing perfect pastries, the results of combining the original central European proprietors' recipes with regional tradition.

Above: looking out over Perugia
Below: detail from the Volumni
hypogeum

▶ *Return to the Sciri tower and
take Via Francolina to the left,
Via Vincioli to the right, Via
della Pernice to the left and
Piazza Morlacchi to the right,
leading to Piazza Cavallotti,
where you turn into Via
Maestà delle Volte.*

⓬ Via Maestà delle Volte
The Via Maestà winds along
one of Perugia's medieval
streets, past 13th- and 14th-
century houses and beneath
dark vaults. A red-and-white
banded Gothic arch is all that
remains of the oratory built in
1335 to protect the *Majesty*
fresco there.

▶ *Once in Piazza IV Novembre
proceed through Piazza
Danti, Piazza Piccinino and
Via Buontempo, and turn
right into Via Volte della Pace.*

⓭ Via Volte della Pace
Following the curve of the
Etruscan walls is the
picturesque covered Via Volte
della Pace. In the Middle Ages,
treaties with nearby towns were
contracted here. It opens into
the elongated Piazza del
Sopramuro, now Piazza
Matteotti, created in 1247
to house the market, fish-

SPECIAL TO...

In the first ten days of July
Perugia holds Umbria Jazz
Estate, preceded by a mini-
festival in the Trasimeno
villages. A more specialised and
experimental event is Umbria
Jazz Winter, held between
Christmas and New Year at
Orvieto. Since 1986, Rockin'
Umbria, a multimedia rock
festival, has reviewed music,
video, graphics, photography
and cartoons in Perugia and
Umb'rtide (June–July).

---

mongers and abattoir. Until
the 15th century the inhabitants
of Perugia flocked to this
square to watch their favourite
sport – violent stone fights
between teams from the various
districts.

▶ *From Piazza Matteotti
continue along Via Baglioni to
Piazza Italia, where the
mechanised 'Via Bagliona'
leads back to the car-park.
The following excursions are
made after a short drive
following the signs (the
hypogeum is southeast of
the centre; the Città della
Domenica to the northwest).*

EXCURSION I

Ipogeo dei Volumni
An impressive row of house-
shaped cinerary urns found in
the surrounding necropoli dominates the steps descending into
the underground tomb of the
Velimna Etruscans. The 2nd
century BC hypogeum repro-
duces the plan of a noble house.
Three *cubicula* (bedrooms) open
off each side of a large rectangular atrium with a pitched roof; at
the end is the *tablinium*, the
sitting room, with seven urns.
The central urn shows the head
of the Arunte family, watched
over by funerary demons that
guard the door to the next
world; around this lie other
members of the family, with
Arunte's daughter Velia sitting
on an elaborate seat.

EXCURSION 2

Città della Domenica
Step into Pinocchio's village,
Snow White's house, Swan
Lake, the Witches' Wood,
Sleeping Beauty's Castle and
the Far West. The amusement
park, created in 1955 northwest
of Perugia on
the slopes of
Monte
Malbe, was
planned as a
mini Umbrian
Disneyland.
Other attrac-
tions include
an aquarium,
animals roaming
free and a
miniature rail-
way that
crosses the
park.

Northeast
Umbria

This tour winds up and down the Umbria-Marche Apennine ridge, through hills, woods, valleys and harsh mountain gorges, encountering tantalising fragments of a distant past. Visits to isolated hermitages add a touch of mystery.

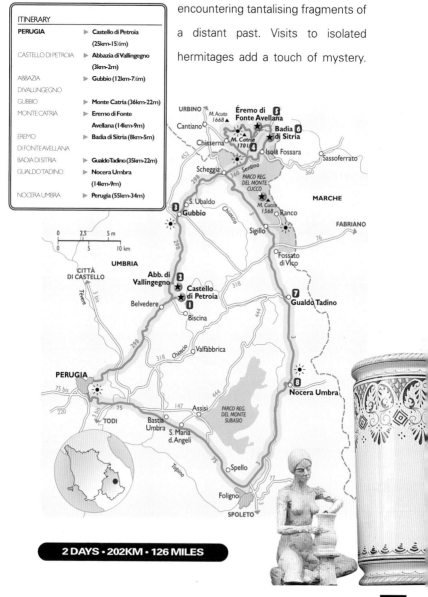

2 DAYS · 202KM · 126 MILES

ℹ️ *Via Mazzini 21; Via Mazzini 6; Palazzo dei Priori, Piazza IV Novembre 3, Perugia*

▶ *Take the SS298 towards Gubbio, passing Belvedere and then turning right for Biscina-Fratticciola Selvatica to the short, unsurfaced road, signposted on the right for the Castello di Petroia.*

❶ Castello di Petroia

Together with the castles of Biscina to the southeast and Vallingegno to the north, the tiny fortified village of Petroia formed the defence system organised by Gubbio in the Middle Ages on the right bank of the Chiascio river. In 1414 Duke Guidoantonio da Montefeltro, whose family controlled Gubbio from 1384, sold the castle to Matteo Accomandugi of Urbino. Eight years later, a granddaughter of the buyer, the young Elisabetta, lady-in-waiting to Duchess Rengarda in Urbino, chose remote Petroia to give birth to her lover Guidoantonio's illegitimate son Federico, the future duke and magnificent patron of Renaissance Urbino.

▶ *Back on the SS298, continue towards Gubbio to the sign on the right for the Abbazia di Vallingegno.*

❷ Abbazia di Vallingegno

St Francis' early biographers tell how the young man from Assisi, travelling to Gubbio after leaving his paternal home, stopped cold and hungry at a monastery along the way. This was probably Vallingegno Abbey, rebuilt by the Benedictines in the 13th century. In the crypt, a late imperial arch contains the remains of San Verecondo, stoned to death in the 5th century by local pagans, worshippers of Genius, the god who presided over the destiny of new-born babies (hence the name Vallingegno, or 'genius valley'). Slightly lower down is the medieval castle. The 'miraculous' spring on the side of the main road was apparently made to gush forth by Ubaldo Baldassini, the bishop-saint who controlled Gubbio between 1130 and 1160.

▶ *Return to the SS298 and proceed right to Gubbio.*

❸ Gubbio

Even from afar the grey calcareous stone buildings of Gubbio stand out, huddled at the foot of Monte Ingino. This was where the Umbrians constructed the *Tota* (town) *Ikuvina*, mentioned on seven bronze tablets (2nd–1st century BC), now in the Civic

RECOMMENDED WALK

Leaving Gubbio in the direction of Scheggia, you soon reach the Bottaccione basin, created in the Middle Ages to fuel the mills below. The presence of rare iridium in the rocks of the gorge has prompted theories of a huge asteroid falling and having catastrophic effects on the vegetation and climate. The upper town can be reached from the Bottaccione dam by walking 2km (1 mile) along the stones of the overhanging aqueduct (1327). Less precarious is the ascent to the Basilica di Sant'Ubaldo on Monte Ingino, which can also be reached by cableway or car.

Gubbio's Palazzo dei Consoli

Museum. The Romans moved their town to the plain, where you will find the well-preserved remains of their 1st century AD theatre, and the urban nucleus did not return to the slopes of the mountain until the Middle Ages. On Piazza Quaranta Martiri stand Gothic San Francesco (1255; site of the Spadalonga family, who welcomed St Francis on his arrival in Gubbio) and the 17th-century Loggia dei Tiratori (wool-workers responsible for ironing the cloth). From here climb to Piazza Grande, a windy, scenic balcony supported by arches. The *comune* started building this, their new centre of civic power, in 1321. Angelo da Orvieto and Gattapone built the tall, graceful Palazzo dei Consoli (1332–49), now a museum. Even higher up is the 15th-century Gothic Duomo (cathedral), near Palazzo Ducale, which the town donated to Federico da Montefeltro, Duke of Urbino, in 1480. The court of honour bears the mark of Francesco di Giorgio Martini, and is the only real Renaissance space in Gubbio.

This is an ancient town, proud of traditions such as the ancient and extremely popular Corsa dei Ceri (see below) and the Palio della Balestra (last Sunday in May), during which local crossbowmen in costume

The crowded Corsa dei Ceri in Gubbio

challenge those from Sansepolcro. At the 14th-century Palazzo del Bargello you may see people walking three times around the fountain while some-one else splashes them with water from the basin – this is the 'madman's fountain' and the ceremony gives participants the right to adopt the honorary title of 'madman'.

ℹ️ *Piazza Oderisi 6*

▶ *Follow the **SS298** to Scheggia and then the **SS360** towards Sassoferrato, turning left (towards Cantiano) for Chiaserna, where a road sign-posted for Monte Catria climbs to the grassy saddle between Monte Acuto and*

SPECIAL TO...

The Corsa dei Ceri is a race held in Gubbio every 15 May, featuring three *ceri* – wooden structures, each weighing 200kg (441 pounds) and standing 4m (13 feet) high. The statue of a different saint is attached to the top – Sant'Ubaldo, San Giorgio and Sant'Antonio. Each *cero* takes its eight carriers and their two team captains between 9 and 11 minutes to climb the course from the city gate to the Basilica di Sant'Ubaldo. During World War I, when there were no men, the *ceri* were carried by women.

SPECIAL TO...

Many of the 13th- to 14th-century ashlar stone houses that line the streets of Gubbio feature strange pointed doors, raised above street level, on the main entrance side (see those on Via dei Consoli and Via Baldassini). According to tradition, this is the 'door of the dead', reserved for funerals. A more prosaic explanation is that they were raised for safety reasons and provided independent access to the upper floors.

The Fonte Avellana hermitage, a Camoldolensian abbey at the foot of Monte Catria

SCENIC ROUTES

The most spectacular part of this tour (in particular the ascent and descent of Monte Catria, on unsurfaced roads) requires caution. Rough, narrow roads run along the edge of unprotected precipices; it's best to stop if you want to enjoy the views. Always sound your horn on the narrow stretch between Isola Fossara and Scheggia that skirts the Sentino river gorge.

Monte Catria. Here the asphalt ends and you bear right at the next two forks to come, near the Vernosa shepherds' hut, to a path that leads in half an hour to the top of Monte Catria (1,701m/5,581 feet).

❹ Monte Catria

Views of Umbria and the Marche as far as the Adriatic sea open out from the plateau on the summit of Monte Catria,

which is dominated by an enormous metal cross. Stretching out to the south is the regional park that culminates in the conical Monte Cucco (1,566m/5,138 feet), an ideal destination for keen hikers, hang-gliders and pot-holers.

▶ *Descend to the last fork and continue to the right along the unsurfaced road (bear left at a fork after 5km/3 miles) to Fonte Avellana (those who prefer surfaced roads can avoid the ascent of Monte Catria and remain on the SS360 as far as Isola Fossara before turning left for Badia di Sitria and Eremo di Fonte Avellana).*

❺ Eremo di Fonte Avellana

Founded in 980 in the woods at the foot of Monte Catria and prosperous in the Middle Ages,

RECOMMENDED EXCURSION

Monte Cucco is a hang-gliders' and pot-holers' paradise. The famous Cucco underground system extends for 30km (19 miles) to a depth of 922m (3,025 feet). It is reached from Sigillo (on the SS3 south of Scheggia) along a scenic road that leads in 9km (5 miles) to the beech woods and meadows of Val di Ranco (1,040m/3,412 feet). The entrance to the cave (no access) opens sheer above a gorge at a height of 1,390m (4,560 feet).

the Camaldolensian abbey of Fonte Avellana now comprises a Romanesque-Gothic church with presbytery, built over a dark crypt dating from the 11th century. As well as the cloister, chapterhouse and library, you can visit the *scriptorium*, where a barrel vault with 13 windows ensured plenty of even light for

the scribes. The famous illuminated manuscripts of Fonte Avellana are now kept in the Vatican library.

▶ *Leave the hermitage in the direction of Pergola, then turn right towards Scheggia to come to the Badia di Sitria.*

⑥ Badia di Sitria

The abbey of Santa Maria di Sitria, a satellite of Fonte Avellana, was founded in the early 11th century by San Romualdo, a nobleman turned monk. Its interesting Romanesque church has a nave with barrel vaults and raised presbytery. The crypt below is supported at the centre by a Roman column with a Corinthian capital.

▶ *Continue to Isola Fossara, where you turn right on to the SS360 for Scheggia and then take the SS3 (Via Flaminia) towards Rome to the turning for Gualdo Tadino.*

⑦ Gualdo Tadino

Roman *Tadinum* lay on the plain, near the Via Flaminia; the town was moved to the hillside during the 12th century. San Benedetto cathedral, dating from 1256, has a lovely façade with three doorways and a rose window. A few steps away is Gothic San Francesco (deconsecrated), with frescoes by Matteo da Gualdo (*c*1430–1507). Notable triptychs by him and other Umbrian painters are exhibited in the picture gallery in the Rocca Flea, a massive fortress built by Federico II in the 13th century.

ⅰ *Via Calai 39*

▶ *Continue along the SS3 southbound to Nocera Umbra.*

⑧ Nocera Umbra

Since a disastrous earthquake in 1997, prefabricated homes have filled the Topino Valley. The hilltown of Nocera Umbra looms above them, now a ghost town to which access is forbidden after dusk. Huge metal girders shore up the clusters of houses perched on the rise, and silence reigns in the covered Via di San Filippo, built into the medieval walls. The museum of the former church of San Francesco is closed. Higher up, opposite the Duomo (cathedral), also closed, the stronghold's only surviving tower has collapsed. This is where, in 1421, the lord of the castle, Pasquale di Vagnolo, murdered his adulterous wife along with his feudal lord, Trinci di Foligno. A view of the valley and mountains opens up between cathedral and tower.

ⅰ *IAT del Folignate*

▶ *Continue south on the SS3 to the slip road leading to the SS75 dual carriageway for Perugia.*

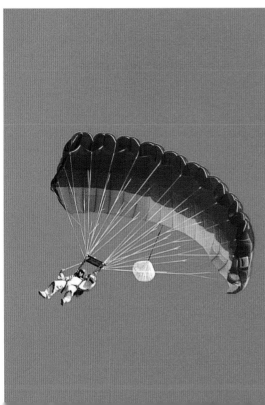

The thrill of parascending. Monte Catria and Monte Cucco are well known to lovers of free flying

Shores & Hills
of Trasimeno

With its low shores, in places thick with reeds, lying amid gentle hills of olive trees, vines and castles, Trasimeno – Italy's fourth largest lake, though only 6m (20 feet) deep – has been poetically described as 'a veil of water on a meadow'.

1/2 DAYS• 128KM • 80 MILES

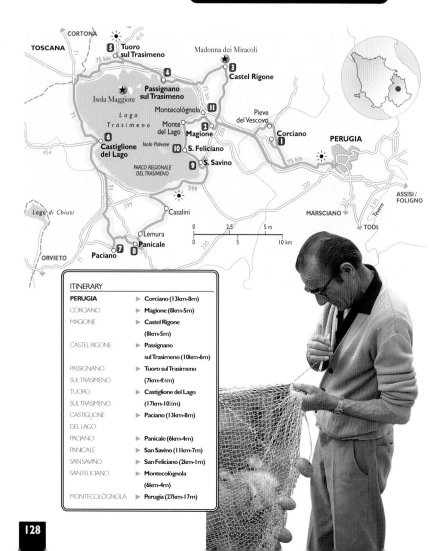

ITINERARY

PERUGIA	▶	Corciano (13km-8m)
CORCIANO	▶	Magione (8km-5m)
MAGIONE	▶	Castel Rigone (8km-5m)
CASTEL RIGONE	▶	Passignano sul Trasimeno (10km-6m)
PASSIGNANO SUL TRASIMENO	▶	Tuoro sul Trasimeno (7km-4½m)
TUORO SUL TRASIMENO	▶	Castiglione del Lago (17km-10½m)
CASTIGLIONE DEL LAGO	▶	Paciano (13km-8m)
PACIANO	▶	Panicale (6km-4m)
PANICALE	▶	San Savino (11km-7m)
SAN SAVINO	▶	San Feliciano (2km-1m)
SAN FELICIANO	▶	Montecològnola (6km-4m)
MONTECOLÒGNOLA	▶	Perugia (27km-17m)

[i] Palazzo dei Priori, Piazza IV
Novembre 3, Perugia

▶ Take the **SS75 bis** to the turning signposted on the right for
Corciano.

1 Corciano

Within a turreted ring of 15th-
century walls, streets and alleyways follow the gradient of the
hill up to a typically Perugian
castle. The Palazzo Comunale
once belonged to the della
Corgna family, who assumed
control of Trasimeno in 1550.
Several residences used by
them include the 14th-century
castle of Pieve del Vescovo,
north of Corciano, which was
restored by Cardinal Fulvio in
1560–70, and is now abandoned.
Ancient recipes spruced up with
modern touches are offered by
the nearby Associazione
Enogastronomica (food and
wine association).

[i] Via della Corgna 6

▶ From Pieve del Vescovo return
to the **SS75 bis** and follow
this to the right to Magione.

2 Magione

At the entrance to the village
stands a 15th-century abbey, a
fortified mansion with corner

towers (not open to visitors),
originally a hostel erected by the
Knights Templar for pilgrims on
their way to Rome. In 1311–12,
after the Knights' possessions
had been seized by the State, the
building became a *mansio* (residence) of the Knights of Malta,
who still own it.

[i] Piazza della Repubblica
Italiana 3

▶ Take the provincial road
northbound, signposted for
Castel Rigone.

FOR HISTORY BUFFS

Pian di Càrpine – an area at
the foot of Magione – gave its
name to the adventurous Fra'
Giovanni del Pian di Càrpine,
who left Lyons in April 1245
and after a 14-month journey
reached Karakorum, capital of
Genghis Khan's Mongol
Empire. On his return home
in 1247, Giovanni wrote the
Historia Mongolorum, the first
description of the country
and people of Mongolia. Not
until 24 years later did an
adolescent Marco Polo sail
from Venice in the company
of his father Niccolò and
uncle Matteo.

Sails and aquatic birds, typical
scenes on Lake Trasimeno

3 Castel Rigone

A climb past olive groves leads
to the site of this magnificent
natural observatory. In the
village are remains of a castle
dating from 1297 and the
elegant sandstone sanctuary of
the Madonna dei Miracoli, built
in 1494 in the hope that it would
provide protection against the
plague. Its design was inspired
by the Renaissance forms of
the Madonna del Calcinaio
of Cortona.

▶ Descend westwards to the
SS75 bis, which leads to the
right to Passignano.

4 Passignano sul Trasimeno

The alleyways of the ancient
Passum Jani (Oasis of Janus)
climb from the shores of Lake
Trasimeno towards the fortifications at the top of the headland,

with its striking triangular Ponente tower (14th century). A seaplane factory was established at Passignano in 1923, later converted into a shipyard. Today, the town's main activities focus on lakeside tourism, encouraged by the boat service for Isola Maggiore, the second largest island on the lake (Isola Polvese is the biggest) and the only one still inhabited.

ⓘ *Via Trento e Trieste*

RECOMMENDED EXCURSION

The tranquillity of the olive, ilex and cypress trees of Isola Maggiore prompted St Francis to retreat here during Lent in 1211–13. The island's village, dominated by the Gothic parish church of San Michele Arcangelo, consists of a single paved street leading past 14th- to 15th-century houses to Romanesque San Salvatore. Lying in a state of abandon is neo-Gothic Guglielmi Castle (also known as Villa Isabella), where, in 1904, a lace workshop was set up to teach the women – already experts at net-weaving – 'Irish stitch', still a local speciality.

FOR HISTORY BUFFS

On a foggy day in 217 BC Hannibal's forces bore down from the hills above Tuoro on to the Roman legions. Trapped against the marshy lakeside, many Romans drowned trying to escape the Punic swords. A 7km (4-mile) route illustrates the crucial phases of this battle.

▶ *Continue west, turning right on to the SS416 for Tuoro.*

⑤ Tuoro sul Trasimeno

Tuoro was the scene of a bloody battle in which Rome suffered its worst defeat, at the hands of the Carthaginians (see above). The Renaissance Palazzo del Capra was built over the mausoleum of the consul Caius Flaminius, who died in the battle. Visit the Campo del Sole, on the lakeshore; 27 column-shaped sculptures executed by various artists between 1985 and 1989 form an enigmatic wood of stone around a solar symbol.

▶ *Return to the SS75 bis and follow it before turning left on to the SS71 for Castiglione del Lago.*

Olive trees at Castiglione del Lago

⑥ Castiglione del Lago

Overlooking Trasimeno from a high headland (in Etruscan and Roman times it was an island in the lake, which was then deeper and larger) are the beautiful Castiglione, the castle and cathedral, surrounded by walls. The fortunes of the della Corgna family, dukes of the town from 1550 to 1643, are reflected in their mansion, Palazzo della Corgna. Frescoes on the first floor celebrate family glories; the ground floor was reserved for social activities and conversation. A covered passageway links the mansion to the castle that Federico II of Swabia erected in the mid-13th century. Events are now held within its pentagonal walls, guarded by four towers and a high, triangular keep (contact the tourist office for details).

FOR CHILDREN

Every two years in spring, Castiglione del Lago hosts an international kite-flyers' meeting and the clear Umbrian sky is turned into an unforgettable, multicoloured palette.

ⓘ *Piazza Mazzini 10*

▶ *Continue south along the SS71 to the turning on the left for Paciano.*

⑦ Paciano

Six towers and perfectly preserved 14th-century walls enclose the streets of Paciano, perched on a spur where a temple to two-faced Janus is said to have stood. The oak and chestnut trees of Monte Pausillo occupy 300 hectares (741 acres), along with deer, fallow deer, mouflons and a rich undergrowth of mushrooms – a superb area for hiking.

▶ *Follow the signs for Panicale, bearing right at the two forks you come to.*

⑧ Panicale

In this scenic medieval village residents practice the rare craft of *ars panicalensis* – hand embroidery on tulle. Places of interest here include the collegiate church of San Michele, with its Renaissance doorways and frescoes by Perugino (*Martyrdom of St*

A traditional fishing net used on Lake Trasimeno

Sebastian, 1505), in the church of San Sebastiano.

ⓘ *Piazza Umberto I 9*

▶ *Descend via Lemura and Casalini to the coastal SS599 and follow this to the right to the turning on the left for San Savino.*

⑨ San Savino

Dominated by a 14th-century castle, San Savino sits near the mouth of an outlet dug by Romans to halt the frequent lake floods. Numerous species of fish, protected by a ban on fishing, come to reproduce in the canebrakes of the arm of the lake known as 'la Valle'.

▶ *Skirt the lake northwards to San Feliciano.*

⑩ San Feliciano

This is a pretty little fishing village on Lake Trasimeno, with a Museum of Fishing featuring aquariums, aviaries and everything about the lake, its people and animals. A ferry to Isola Polvese, opposite, operates from April to September. From the 13th century onwards the island was colonised by various religious organisations who built

their churches on it. Today, it is a protected nature reserve.

▶ *Continue to Monte del Lago, where you turn right towards Magione to come to Montecològnola.*

⑪ Montecològnola

The origin of this scenic village, defended by walls and towers, is revealed in the regular layout of its streets: it was founded and designed as a new town in 1293 by the inhabitants of Magione, who obtained Perugia's permission to create their new settlement.

▶ *Take the SS75 bis which leads back via Magione to Perugia.*

SPECIAL TO...

Trasimeno has always been Perugia's favourite lake. When Bonamico Buffalmacco was commissioned by the Perugians in the 14th century to paint their patron saint, Ercolano, he crowned him not with gold or gems but with 'a garland of dace (carp-like fish), the largest ever to come out of the lake'.

The Umbrian
Valley

Like balconies overlooking the historic route of the Via Flaminia, the towns in the Umbrian Valley face each other across two sides of the plain that stretches between Assisi and Spoleto. Rich with medieval and religious associations, particularly related to episodes in the life of St Francis, they also contain splendid works of art.

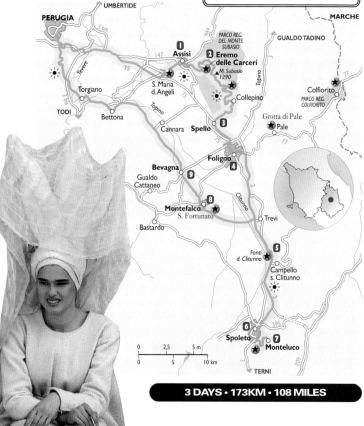

3 DAYS · 173KM · 108 MILES

ⓘ *Palazzo dei Priori, Piazza IV Novembre 3, Perugia*

▶ *After reaching the **SS75** dual carriageway, proceed towards Foligno to the signs for Santa Maria degli Angeli and Assisi.*

❶ Assisi

Lying on terraces on the slopes of Monte Subasio, Assisi is inextricably bound to its most famous son, St Francis. His life and ideology have transformed this medieval town into a monumental shrine, which draws hosts of pilgrims and visitors. Below town is the towering basilica of Santa Maria degli Angeli, begun in 1569 to incorporate the humble locations where Francis chose to live and die. Its vast dome is in startling contrast to the little chapel of the Porziuncola below, where the Franciscan Order was founded in 1206; and to the simple cell (known as the Transito Chapel) in which the saint died on 3 October, 1226.

At one end of the town you can climb on foot to the Basilica di San Francesco, made up of a crypt and two churches, one built over the other. The style combines Umbrian Romanesque with French-inspired Gothic. It took more than a century to build the whole complex, begun in 1228 under the direction of Friar Elia, and to fresco the interior. In the lower church, works by Giotto and his assistants alternate with paintings by Cimabue, Pietro Lorenzetti and Simone Martini.

SPECIAL TO...

The ruins of the house of Francis' father, rich merchant Pietro di Bernardone, are concealed among the pillars of the Chiesa Nuova, erected in 1615 at the expense of Philip III King of Spain. According to legend, in 1182 a mysterious pilgrim told the mother of the future saint to take refuge in a nearby stable to give birth, and this is where the oratory of San Francesco Piccolino now stands.

Rising from the massive basilica of San Francesco is the great bell tower of 1239

As well as Cimabue and Giotto, the anonymous 'Master of Isaaco' worked in the other church. Together they produced a prodigious decorative display, which has been described by some as representing the beginning of the history of western European painting.

The main street climbs from San Francesco past medieval Piazza del Comune, on which stands the Temple of Minerva (1st century BC, one of the best-preserved monuments of the classical world), to reach the secluded cathedral of San Rufino, a 13th-century Romanesque masterpiece. Lower down, a tangle of narrow streets leads to the Gothic basilica of Santa Chiara, where the remains of this saint have rested since 1260.

ⓘ *Piazza del Comune 22*

▶ *Follow the signs eastwards for the Eremo delle Carceri.*

2 Eremo delle Carceri

The rural convent was built in the 14th and 15th centuries on the spots where Francis and his companions incarcerated themselves in prayer. If you arrive early in the morning, you will still find silence and solitude, as well as a view of the thick ilex wood around it and the town. Go down steps and through narrow passages to visit the cave where the saint rested, the stone he sat on to meditate, the ilex tree where the birds are said to have listened to his famous sermon (although some say this was at Bevagna), and a stream that dried up so that the noise of its waters would not disturb the friars. In the park, lovely numbered paths lead to shelters used over the centuries by religious devotees.

Composition with flower petals for the flower festival at Spello

▶ *Cross Monte Subasio to Collepino; turn right for Spello.*

3 Spello

More than in any other centre in Umbria, the old town hall of *Hispellum* has retained important evidence of Roman presence. The 1st-century BC southern Consolare three-arched gate was integrated into the 14th-century ring of walls; a square tower near by is crowned, as it was in the 16th century, with an olive tree. The scenic Venere gate, to the west, is now enclosed by two majestic Romanesque towers. Between the two is the arch of the Urbica gate, flanked by walls of the Augustan era in Subasio stone. Not far away, along the old Via Flaminia, you can see the grassy remains of the amphitheatre. Spello's rare Renaissance masterpiece was funded by the Baglioni family, who, in 1501, commissioned Pinturicchio from Perugia to decorate a chapel in the church of Santa Maria Maggiore with frescoes.

ℹ️ *Piazza Matteotti 3*

▶ *Proceed southeast, following the signs for Foligno.*

View of the hilltown of Spello

4 Foligno

Lying in the valley of the Topino river, Foligno has one of the few old centres on flat ground in Umbria. Its excellent position and a manufacturing tradition dating from the 14th century have made it a busy town of commercial and industrial activity. Economic development, bombing and earthquakes (the last in 1997) have erased many traces of the past, although the Duomo (cathedral), with its bands of red and white stone, and the nearby Palazzo Trinci remain intact. The former has a fine side entrance (1201); its interior was transformed into neo-classical style by Giuseppe Piermarini of Foligno, royal imperial architect in Milan between 1779 and 1796. The Palazzo Trinci is one of the most interesting late-Gothic residences in central Italy; its fresco cycles constitute an encyclopaedia of the early 15th-century humanistic culture.

ⓘ *Corso Cavour 126*

▶ *Take the **SS3** south to the sign for the Fonti del Clitunno.*

FOR HISTORY BUFFS

Goldsmithery, silver-work, woodcarving, ceramics, yarns and hemp, wool and silk fabrics, paper-making, organ-making, metal-casting … the list of Foligno's output during its golden age (1310–1439) goes on and on. Its greatest pride dates, however, from the period of papal rule. In 1472 Emanuele Orfini of Foligno and the German printer Johann Numeister produced 300 copies of Dante's *Divine Comedy*, the first book printed in Italy in the Italian language. Fourteen complete copies are known to exist; the press believed to have been used for that edition can be seen at the printing documentation centre in the oratory of the Nunziatella.

---

5 Fonti del Clitunno

This little river flows into the Teverone, but before it reaches its destination its springs form a magical sheet of water dotted with green, grassy islets and weeping willows. This spot is said to have been an early

---

The Clitunno springs

tourist attraction, at the time of Roman writer and orator Pliny the Younger (1st century BC), who refers to villas, inns and public baths built in the vicinity. The site was sacred to the god Clitunno; the pagan *sacellum* mentioned by Pliny inspired the early Christian temple (thought to date some time between the 4th and 9th centuries), encountered on the right just before reaching the springs.

ⓘ *Viale Europa Unita 1*

▶ *Continue along the **SS3** to Spoleto.*

6 Spoleto

Spoleto has a long history, evident everywhere, from the massive polygonal walls, raised by the Umbrians in the 4th

---

SPECIAL TO…

Between 10 and 17 September, ten horsemen representing the ten districts of Foligno race each other in the Giostra della Quintana.

RECOMMENDED WALK

In Spoleto you can visit the 'Torri' bridge-aqueduct (crossed on foot; actually there are no towers, but the two main pylons have rooms for sentinels). Pass beside the stronghold to reach the 230m (754 feet) structure, which crosses the Tessino chasm on ten pointed arches, resting on pillars up to 76m (249 feet) tall. Continuing to the right, descend to admire the Romanesque reliefs (12th–13th century) of the façade of San Pietro, before returning to the old centre. This splendid walk, with views of the town and Monteluco, can be prolonged to visit the church of San Paolo inter Vineas, which has a fine cycle of 13th-century frescoes in the transept.

century BC, to the 'inner thoroughfare' that, in the middle of the 19th century, tore into the steep winding streets of the lower town from north to south, to allow the passage of carts and carriages. The Roman colony founded in 274 BC survives near the Tessino river in traces of the amphitheatre and three arches of the Sanguinario, or 'bloody bridge', so called perhaps because Christians were martyred there. Slightly further north stands the basilica of San Salvatore, a remarkable early Christian construction with a nave and two aisles dating from the 4th to the 5th century. Along the Via Flaminia, place-names tell of a yet more eventful history. Via di Porta Fuga ('street of the escape gate') and the 13th-century Olio (oil) tower are thought to be references to the tale that Hannibal was seen off with boiling oil by the inhabitants of Spoleto, when they were besieged in 217 BC. Higher up are the steps and orchestra of the theatre, the Druso arch, the remains of a temple and a

The spectacular bridge of Torri di Spoleto which crosses the Tessino

luxurious residence said to have belonged to Emperor Vespasian's mother. Nothing remains, though, of the thriving early Middle Ages. In 576 Spoleto became the capital of a powerful duchy, but Barbarossa destroyed all traces of this period in 1155, when he razed 'the well-fortified town defended by a hundred towers' to the ground. That's when the present Duomo (cathedral, consecrated in 1198) was built, a splendid Romanesque backdrop to the funnel-shaped square reached down Via dell'Arringo. The frescoes in the apse (1467–9) are said to be by Filippo Lippi; 30 years after their execution, Pinturicchio decorated the Eroli Chapel. In the meantime, Cardinal Albornoz had consolidated papal power over Spoleto (the Duchy formally ceased to

A detail of the façade of Spoleto's Duomo, its rich rose window adorned with tracery and mosaics

BACK TO NATURE

Heading east from Foligno along the SS77, after 24km (15 miles) you will come to the undulating Colfiorito plateaux, what remains of ancient lakes, now dried up. The most significant of the seven karst depressions is the Colfiorito marsh, an ecosystem of extraordinary importance for rare species of flowers and marsh vegetation, as well as migratory and aquatic birds, gastropods and amphibians. Remains of fortified Iron-Age structures are also found in the area, which forms part of a regional park.

Above: the Umbrian landscape towards Montefalco
Right: frescoes in the church of Sant'Agostino, Montefalco

exist in 1231). He ordered Gattapone to construct the intimidating stronghold on the hill (1359–70) and to link it with the road by means of the

RECOMMENDED EXCURSION

Pale is a small village to the east of Foligno on the SS77 to Colfiorito. Tucked into the harsh, calcareous stone of the sheer Sasso di Pale rock is the Eremo di Santa Maria Giacobbe, built in the late 13th century and inhabited until 1963. Clearly visible from below – it is reached up a steep path across a scree – are the hermits' caves scattered around a little church (ask for the keys in the village), partially hewn into the rock and rich in votive frescoes of the 14th to 16th centuries.

breathtaking Torri bridge. The theatres, Nuovo and Caio Melisso, date from the late 19th century and are famous for hosting the Festival dei Due Mondi (now the Spoleto Festival), first held by the composer Giancarlo Menotti in 1958.

i *Piazza della Libertà 7*

▷ *Follow the signs for Monteluco.*

7 Monteluco

Behind the Rocca, you can climb to the 773m (2,536 feet) sanctuary of Monteluco. The little chapel where Francis prayed, some cells and a well of cool water brought forth by the saint are all still there. Lovely scenic spots and small caves are scattered throughout the woods below. Monteluco wood was sacred to the Roman god Jupiter; as early as the 3rd century BC a special *lex spoletina* (Spoleto Law) prohibited tree-felling. Towards the end of the 5th century, it was inhabited by Syrian hermits, and later by Benedictines and Franciscans. A community of artists, painters and architects from Spoleto formed here in the early 16th century, forming a religious community in 1547 which was dissolved two and a half centuries later, at the time of French occupation.

▷ *Descend to Spoleto and take the SS3 northbound as far as Trevi, where you turn left for Montefalco.*

8 Montefalco

Just before reaching Montefalco you come to a church dedicated to San Fortunato, who died in 390. It has frescoes by Benozzo Gozzoli, and Franciscan stories and pictures painted by Tiberio d'Assisi in 1512 adorn the chapel that overlooks the court-yard. In the village, perched above the picturesque Topino and Clitunno plains, follow Via della Ringhiera Umbra, which descends from the main square to an opening in the walls commanding an outstanding view.

Halfway down, you can visit the former church of San Francesco, now the Civic Museum. This important church was used for public functions and assemblies; it was almost entirely covered in frescoes from the 14th century on. The artists who worked here include Perugino (*c*1450–1523), but its fame is due mainly to

the fascinating cycle of the life of St Francis painted by Florentine Benozzo Gozzoli in 1452, on the walls of the central apse. This illustrious work influenced Umbrian painting for half a century.

i *Via Ringhiera Umbra*

▷ *Follow the signs for Bevagna.*

9 Bevagna

Bevagna's charming asymmetrical main square, Piazza Silvestri, has hardly changed since its construction between 1195 and 1270. On one side, the Romanesque façade of San Michele has a doorway that reuses marble from classic times. The church of San Silvestro, opposite, crowned by a three-light window, is connected by a large arch to Palazzo dei Consoli, erected on the transepts of a loggia (the modern steps flanking it give access to a 19th-century theatre). Wander through the quiet streets of the town – already prosperous in Roman times – to discover the remains of a temple dating from the 2nd century BC, incorporated

A figure carved on the doorway of San Michele in Bevagna

into a deconsecrated church. These include a large mosaic, featuring the marine creatures of Porta Guelfa.

i *Via I° Maggio 1*

▷ *Return to Perugia via Bettona and Torgiano.*

THE LEGEND OF
ST FRANCIS OF ASSISI

'Destroy all that has been written about Francis.' This was the order given in 1266 by Bonaventura da Bagnoregio, general minister of the Franciscan Order and author of the founding saint's 'official' biography (*Legenda maior*, 1263). His order was duly executed, although several Cistercian archives escaped the Franciscan friars' attention. A clash between 'rich' conventuals and 'poor' spiritual fathers was tearing the Order apart, and the message of evangelical poverty was in danger of being lost altogether. So da Bagnoregio considered it vital to eliminate all details of Francis' life that might open the Order to charges of subversion. As a result, the texts that trace Francis' steps through life are more intent on emphasising the stages of his sanctity than on describing the man's life.

Peter's house

It all started in Assisi (see Tour 22), in the home of Francis' father, a wealthy cloth merchant called Pietro di Bernardone. While Pietro was away on business, his wife Monna Pica, from Provence, gave birth in a nearby stable to a baby boy she called Giovanni (1182). On his return from France, Pietro had the baby baptised as Francesco. Young Francis attended the school annexed to the church-hospital of San Giorgio. He grew to be a wealthy and ambitious but dissatisfied young man; despite being shut into the house, he persisted in visiting the poor and sick, and had an encounter with lepers outside the Moiano gate. The 12th-century painted crucifix (now in Santa Chiara) of a country church in poor repair (San Damiano) spoke to Francis, saying: 'Go and repair my house, which, as you see, is all in ruin'. Francis obeyed. After publicly renouncing his wealth and possessions in the Vescovado at Assisi, in 1206 he took up a nomadic life, travelling to Spain and, in 1219, to Egypt, where he encountered crusaders laying siege to Damietta, and was greeted respectfully by the Muslim Sultan Malik-al Kamil.

First steps

Francis made countless visits to Umbria and Tuscany. On the first, having left his father's home in Assisi, he sought shelter in the abbey of Vallingegno (see Tour 20). From here he went on to Gubbio (see Tour 20), where he later tamed a ferocious wolf near the Vittorina Church. In San Francesco della Pace you can see the stone on which he stood to preach. Francis' first steps towards his destiny are retraced by the Assisi-Gubbio Sentiero Francescano della Pace, a splendid country excursion with an extension planned that will take visitors as far as Verna (contact tourist offices for details).

Stage in a life

At Cannara, south of Assisi, Francis founded the Third Order, for laypeople of both

The Eremo delle Carceri, Assisi

sexes (Buona Morte Church). At Bevagna (see Tour 22) he preached to the birds on the Pian d'Arca (his stone podium is in San Francesco). At Vecciano, near Montefalco (see Tour 22) he made a spring gush forth. At Bovara, near Trevi, he prayed before a crucifix (now in San Pietro di Bovara). At Narni (see Tour 24) he cured a paralysed man. At Lugnano in Teverina (see Tour 24) he performed a miracle, depicted in a fresco in San Francesco Church. The oldest and perhaps truest likeness of the saint is a 1235 panel by Bonaventura Berlinghieri in San Francesco at Pescia (see Tour 5). Francis visited Siena (see Tour 15) and stayed at the Camàldoli hermitage (see Tour 13), in the convent of Monte Casale overlooking Sansepolcro (see Tour 14), in the Belverde caves above Cètona (see Tour 18), on Isola Maggiore on Lake Trasimeno (see Tour 21) and at Monteluco (see Tour 22). In 1220 he met Pope Honorius III in Orvieto (see Tour 23). The Duomo of Spoleto (see Tour 22) displays a letter he wrote to his friend Leo, who lived with him at the Verna hermitage (see Tour 13). This was a crucial phase in his life; in 1224 Francis

was here when he received the stigmata, the first of many in the history of Christianity. The previous year, the Pope had officially sanctioned his rule.

Two churches for Francis

But by this time Francis was exhausted. In 1226, after a stay at the Celle hermitage of Cortona (see Tour 14), he died on the outskirts of Assisi in a small room (Transito Chapel); it's now incorporated, together with the Porziuncola, into the basilica of Santa Maria degli Angeli. Immediately after his death, Friar Elia – minister-general of the Order between

Francis receiving the oral confirmation of the Rule from Pope Innocent III, by Giotto, in the upper basilica, Assisi
Below: *The Stigmata* (Chapel of the Antico Tribunal, Anghiari)

1232 and 1239 – ordered the construction of an immense, T-shaped church in his honour. In fact, he built two – one above the other. In 1230 the lower church of the basilica of San Francesco became Francis' tomb: an incongruous resting-place for a man who had chosen to live in the hovel of the Porziuncola and on the remote crag of the Eremo delle Carceri.

From Orvieto to
the Tevere Valley

Tempting food and wine, medieval surroundings, Renaissance highlights – as often happens in Umbria, past and present are inextricably entwined on this highly enjoyable tour.

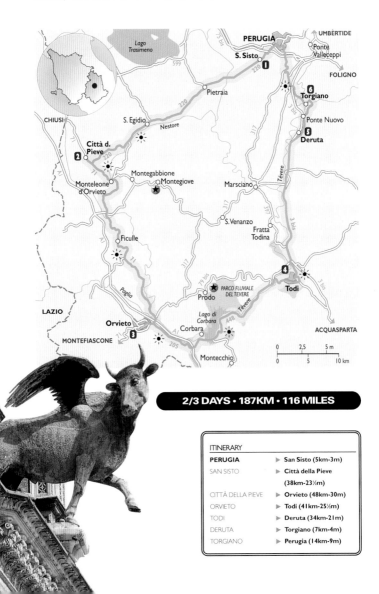

2/3 DAYS · 187KM · 116 MILES

ITINERARY	
PERUGIA	▶ **San Sisto (5km-3m)**
SAN SISTO	▶ **Città della Pieve**
	(38km-23½m)
CITTÀ DELLA PIEVE	▶ **Orvieto (48km-30m)**
ORVIETO	▶ **Todi (41km-25½m)**
TODI	▶ **Deruta (34km-21m)**
DERUTA	▶ **Torgiano (7km-4m)**
TORGIANO	▶ **Perugia (14km-9m)**

ℹ️ *Palazzo dei Priori, Piazza IV Novembre 3, Perugia*

▶ *Take the SS220 to San Sisto.*

🔟 San Sisto

Just outside Perugia on the SS220 (Via Pievaiola), the Nestlé-Perugina chocolate factory has an annexe housing the Perugina History Museum. Here, the company's products and advertising campaigns, going back to its foundation in 1907, reflect 100 years of Italian life and habits. Intriguing gimmicks include love letters inserted into Baci Perugina wrappings (1922) and a collection of figurines, which sparked off a collecting craze in the 1930s.

▶ *Continue along the SS220 and turn right on to the SS71 for Città della Pieve.*

🔢 Città della Pieve

A turreted 1326 Rocca, or stronghold, recalls the turbulent days when this city's Perugian and Guelph rulers had to subdue the pro-Ghibelline *comune*. Città della Pieve is striking for the colour of its bricks, of which it was a renowned producer in the Middle Ages. Around it, the soft shades of the hills fade into the distant blue of the mountain contours, from the Cimini to Pratomagno. The same shades appear in the background of the *Adoration of the*

SPECIAL TO...

From Christmas to Epiphany, the basements of Palazzo della Corgna in Città della Pieve are filled with life-size wooden animals and figures set amid straw and humble furnishings. This is the monumental Crib, which local artists and craftsmen, inspired by Perugino's fascinating *Adoration of the Magi*, dedicate every year to a particular theme. A Palio is held on the second to last Sunday in August.

Historic procession against the backdrop of Orvieto's Duomo

Magi, painted on the premises of the Compagnia dei Disciplinati, now the oratory of Santa Maria dei Bianchi, in 1504 by Pietro Vannucci. Although popularly known as Perugino, the artist was actually born in Città della Pieve, in about 1450. On the square, the fine Palazzo della Corgna faces the Pubblico tower (12th–14th century, in travertine stone and bricks, 38m/125 feet high) and the Duomo (cathedral), which houses a work signed by Perugino in 1514.

In the northern third of the town the Vescovo tower is a reminder of the town's harsh military past, with its large, pointed arches designed to accommodate war machines. There's a more romantic atmosphere in the picturesque alleyway known as 'Baciadonne' (kiss the ladies) because it's just half a metre (1.5 feet) wide (a person could lean out of the window and kiss someone in the opposite house).

ℹ️ *Via Roma 19*

▶ *Follow the SS71 southbound via Monteleone d'Orvieto and Ficulle to Orvieto.*

🔢 Orvieto

A small and orderly 'city of the dead' – the Etruscan necropolis of Crocifisso del Tufo – nestles at the foot of an enormous tufa rock; on its flat summit stands Orvieto. As you climb to the eastern edge of the town, you reach the signs of a complex historic stratification: a scenic clearing, with the ruins of the water, cross a bridge on the bottom and climb up again without obstructing each other.

In the centre, the three districts of the medieval town are situated around the civic tower and Palazzo dei Signori Sette (seven lords – the consuls representing the guilds). To the north is the square overlooked by the elegant windows of Palazzo del Popolo, erected between the 13th and 14th centuries along with the bell tower.

To the west is Piazza della Repubblica, with the 13th-century Palazzo del Comune, renewed in the 1500s, and the collegiate of Sant'Andrea, in the shadow of a great tower. To the southeast, enclosed between the terraced canons' houses and mansions housing major museums, stands the extraordinary Duomo (cathedral), begun in 1290, developed by the Sienese Lorenzo Maitani (1310–30) and given a rose window and doorway by Andrea Orcagna. The grandiose Gothic triptych on the façade, completed in the 16th century, shines with polychrome marble, sculptures and mosaics. Inside, in the chapel of San Brizio, frescoes were painted between 1477 and 1504 by Luca Signorelli on the theme of the end of the world; Fra' Angelico also had a hand in their creation. The cathedral's working hours were sounded from the Maurizio tower (a corruption of *ariologium de murriccio*, 'the

works clock') by the 'robot' cast in 1348.

In western Orvieto you pass through medieval districts to

Piazza del Popolo, Orvieto

Etruscan temple of Belvedere (late 5th century BC); the adjacent remains of the Rocca, erected for Cardinal Albornoz in 1364; and a low, circular building, below which the San Patrizio well plunges 62m (203 feet). This was built between 1527 and 1537 as part of a project by Antonio da Sangallo the Younger to give the town a water reserve in the event of a siege. Around the central duct of the well, 13m (43 feet) wide, a number of windows light two spiral staircases with 248 steps each. Using these, the beasts of burden could descend, draw

San Giovenale, built in 1004 on the edge of a precipice. The frescoes inside (13th–16th century) feature an unusual 'tree of life', symbolising Paradise and the renewal of eternal life. Walking south along delightful streets such as Via Malabranca, Via della Cava (in Etruscan times the only access

Piazza del Popolo in Todi, with Palazzo dei Priori behind

to the town) and Via Ripa Medici, you reach the attractive Piazzale della Porta Romana, which commands a sweeping view of the valley crossed by the medieval aqueduct.

i *Piazza del Duomo 24*

▶ *Continue along the SS448 eastwards to the turning signposted on the right for Todi.*

❹ Todi

Romans called this *Tuder*, a name derived from the Etruscan *Tular*, or 'border' – referring to the division between the Etruscan world, west of the Tiber, and the Umbrian-Sabellian territories to the east, towards the Nera basin and the Piceno area. Today, Todi is another evocative medieval town, culminating in the rectangular Piazza del Popolo. Built over large Roman reservoirs, this surprisingly flat space in a town of steep gradients is enclosed and, until the 16th century, was reached through four corner gates. Between the 13th and 14th centuries it was the seat of

Monument to Jacopone da Todi, Franciscan and poet, in Todi

civic power. At one end stand the three seats of the town judiciary – Palazzo del Popolo or Comune, Palazzo dei Capitani or Nuovo, built in 1293 with a

The dome of the church of Santa Maria della Consolazione in Todi

Gothic façade (picture gallery on the top floors of both buildings) and Palazzo dei Priori, of Gothic foundation, extended and completed in the 14th century, together with its trapezoid tower. On the opposite side, the Duomo (cathedral; 12th–14th century) has a carved wooden door beneath a magnificent 16th-century rose window.

Two of the three sculptures from the façade, kept in the crypt, are attributed to Giovanni Pisano (*c*1250–*c*1320). Set slightly apart is the Church of San Fortunato, at the top of a flight of steps. The incomplete façade has a fine Gothic doorway; inside are frescoes including one by Masolino da Panicale (*c*1383–1447).

The Renaissance seems to have found a place in Gothic Todi only outside the three rings of walls (Etruscan, Roman and comunal), in the church of Santa Maria della Consolazione. Isolated and compact, this Greek cruciform building has four apses, a luminous interior and a high dome begun in 1508 but not completed until 1607. Its exemplary central plan led experts to attribute the design to Bramante (1444–1514), but records mention other masters, including Baldassarre Peruzzi, Vignola and Ippolito Scalza.

RECOMMENDED EXCURSION

About 12km (7 miles) east of Monteleone, past Montegabbione, with its walls and towers, you come to the former Franciscan convent of the Scarzuola, where architect Tommaso Buzzi created his 'ideal city' between 1960 and 1981. Seven theatre spaces – the open-air Arnie theatre, the Torre, the water theatre, the round and the never-ending patios, the sports theatre and, lastly, on the summit, the theatre of the Acropolis – create a fantastic maze, enriched with quotations and references to masters of the past (visit by appointment).

Majolica shop in Deruta

ⓘ *Piazza Umberto I 6*

▶ *After reaching the **SS3 bis** dual carriageway, proceed towards Perugia to the exit for Deruta.*

5 Deruta

A row of ceramics factories and displays gives away Deruta's main trade. By the 14th century residents were already exploiting the excellent local clay; the

A room in the Wine Museum in Torgiano

ceramics industry produced its greatest results in the first half of the 16th century. Antique specimens of iridescent majolica are on display in the Regional Ceramics Museum, set up in the former convent of San Francesco. Nearly 600 pieces of votive majolica, dating from the 16th to the 18th century, line the interior of the 17th-century sanctuary of the Madonna dei Bagni. Modern production is displayed in the pottery workshops in the lower part of town.

ⓘ *Piazza dei Consoli 4*

▶ *Continue north via Ponte Nuovo following the signs for Torgiano.*

6 Torgiano

This village on an outcrop at the confluence of the Tiber and the Chiascio was fortified in the 13th century. Its coat-of-arms – a tower enveloped by a scroll with bunches of grapes – indicates its principal attraction: a wine museum. Set up in 20 fine rooms in the 17th-century Palazzo Graziani-Baglioni, it gives a thorough review of vine-growing and wine-production. Torgiano produces an excellent red wine.

ⓘ *Town Hall (Municipio)*

▶ *Continue north following the signs for Perugia.*

SPECIAL TO...

The theme of Torgiano's Wine Museum is illustrated with a selection of Cycladic jugs and Hittite ceramics, Attic amphorae, Etruscan bronzes and Bucchero pottery, Roman glass, della Robbia ceramics, farming tools, 'waffle' irons and great presses. There's also a library for wine experts, and the annexed Osteria (inn) serves typical Umbrian wines and food.

Southern
Umbria

Terni has been an industrial centre since 1875–81, when the state set up the royal arms factory here. But there's a surprise in store here for romantic visitors: a 17th-century basilica, south of town, is the final resting place of St Valentine, the bishop who was executed in 270, and was to become the patron saint of lovers.

2 DAYS • 172KM • 107 MILES

Orvieto • Lago di Corbara • TODI • PERUGIA • Naia • SPOLETO
PARCO FLUVIALE DEL TEVERE • UMBRIA • Acquasparta **2**
8 ○ **Baschi** • Dunarobba
Foresta fossile ★ • Monte-castrilli • **1** ★ **Càrsulae** • S. Gemini Fonte
★ Guardea • **3**
Lago di Alviano • S. Gèmini ○ • Cesi
LAZIO • **7** ○ **Alviano** • **6** • **Lugnano in Teverina** • Campitello
6 ○ **5** • **Amelia** • 204 • **TERNI**
• Nera
Attigliano • **4** • **Narni** • l'Àia
Bomarzo • Nera
VITERBO • Orte • 0 2,5 5 m
• ROMA • 0 5 10 km

ITINERARY	
TERNI	▶ **Càrsulae** (17km-10½m)
CÀRSULAE	▶ **Acquasparta** (5km-3m)
ACQUASPARTA	▶ **San Gèmini** (10km-6m)
SAN GÈMINI	▶ **Narni** (12km-7½m)
NARNI	▶ **Amelia** (13km-8m)
AMELIA	▶ **Lugnano in Teverina** (11km-7m)
LUGNANO IN TEVERINA	▶ **Alviano** (5km-3m)
ALVIANO	▶ **Baschi** (21km-13m)
BASCHI	▶ **Terni** (78km-49m)

ℹ️ *Viale C Battisti, Terni*

▶ *Take the **SS79** towards San Gemini and turn right after Campitello to proceed via Cesi and San Gemini Terme to the Càrsulae archaeological site.*

1 Càrsulae

Founded in the 3rd century BC along the western branch of the ancient Via Flaminia between *Narnia* and *Tuder*, the Roman town of Càrsulae flourished in Augustan times (27 BC–AD 14), but declined when the main thoroughfare was moved to the east. Having been abandoned, it was finally destroyed by

FOR CHILDREN

On the return journey on the motorway, a pleasant stop for young and old alike is a visit to the Mostri di Bomarzo Park, in Lazio, 6km (4 miles) east of the Attigliano exit on the A1. In 1558, Prince Pier Francesco Orsini, known as Vicino, created a trail amid the oak and chestnut trees and populated it with huge creatures sculpted in stone, half-hidden in the vegetation. While visiting this baroque fantasy, take time to test your sense of balance in the 'sloping house'.

RECOMMENDED EXCURSION

Dunarobba, 13km (8 miles) southwest of Acquasparta, has an extraordinary fossil forest, where sections of petrified sequoia trees, with diameters of up to 1.5m (5 feet) rise 5–10m (16–33 feet) from the ground. They stood more than a million years ago on the edge of Lake Tiberino, which extended over 120km (75 miles) between San Sepolcro and Spoleto, fed by a large river that periodically flooded the lands between Todi and the Terni depression.

barbarians and earthquakes. Among the remains scattered about the archaeological site are the forum with basilica, temples, tombs and a leisure complex with theatre and amphitheatre. Also found here is the church of San Damiano, erected in the 11th century reusing classical structures and materials.

▶ *Continue north to the **SS3 ter**, which leads to the right to Acquasparta.*

2 Acquasparta

For many centuries Acquasparta administered its own territories, under the name Terre Arnolfe:

The extraordinary fossilised sequoia trees in Dunarobba forest

lands assigned by the Emperor Otto I in 966 to a nobleman, Arnolfo. In 1606, under Church rule, a new statute was issued delineating the Terre Arnolfe, after Pier Luigi Farnese had sold the lands to the Cesi family. Three years later, Prince Ferdinando Cesi founded Acquasparta's version of the glorious Lincei Academy, created in Rome six years earlier. Galileo Galilei was a guest here in 1624. Cesi money was also responsible for Palazzo Cesi, in the centre of the town. Built between the 16th and 17th centuries, it has splendid carved wooden ceilings and frescoes exalting the virtues of the owners. Ruins of the medieval castle walls and round towers survive.

ℹ️ *Via Roma 1*

▶ *Take the **SS3 ter** southbound to San Gèmini.*

3 San Gèmini

The centre of this village is dominated by Palazzo Pubblico (13th century), with its truncated tower and external steps protected by an arch. As well as the 14th-century Duomo (cathedral) note the fine

The Sangemini mineral water springs, close to the town of the same name

doorway of Gothic San Francesco, and the Romanesque one with mosaics of the parish church of San Giovanni Battista, founded in 1191. The remains of a tomb known as the Grotta degli Zingari, and of a villa with mosaics, testify to the Roman origin of this settlement.

☐ *Via Garibaldi 1 (seasonal)*

FOR HISTORY BUFFS

Nicknamed Il Gattamelata (the honeydew cat) for his shrewd-ness and smooth manners, Erasmo da Narni was one of the most valiant *condottieri* (mercenary leaders) of his time. Born in Narni in 1370 (probably in Via Gattamelata), he fought under Braccio da Montone and Piccinino, and from 1437 served as captain general of Venice, leading his troops against the Viscontis. He died in Padua in 1443; Donatello immortalised his stern expression in a famous bronze equestrian monument.

▶ *Continue along the SS3 ter southbound then follow the signs for Narni.*

❹ Narni

Ancient Narni extends along a spur above the Nera gorge. From the northern district, with its regular streets dating from Roman times (299 BC), it climbs to two labyrinthine medieval districts and the spectacular Rocca, the papal stronghold,

erected in the late 14th century by Cardinal Egidio Albornoz. On the square, once called 'del Lago' after the reservoir below, stands the Duomo (cathedral), a grand Romanesque monument built in 1047. A further aisle was added to the original nave and two aisles in the 14th century, to incorporate the votive chapel of

The 14th-century Rocca (stronghold) of Narni

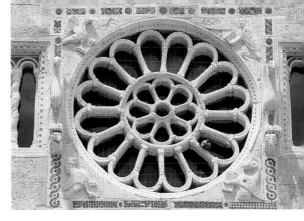

The rose window of the church of Santa Maria Assunta at Lugnano

the first bishops of Narni. The bell tower is built on Roman walls, with a Romanesque stone base and Renaissance upper section. Descend to the centre of medieval Narni, Piazza dei Priori, which features the arches of a 14th-century loggia attributed to Gattapone and the massive Palazzo del Podestà. Lower down, a church partially hewn from the rock beneath the complex of San Domenico provides access to the chamber where the Tribunal of the Holy Inquisition used to meet; the plaster of an adjacent cell still bears graffiti scratched by prisoners.

ⓘ *Piazza dei Priori 3*

▶ *After reaching the SS205, proceed northwest to Amelia.*

5 Amelia
Originally an Umbrian stronghold, Amelia later fell to the Romans and was taken over by the Church from 1307. Set on a hill on the ridge between the Tiber and Nera rivers, it has historic charm enhanced by beautiful countryside; the local willows, pears, figs and apples are much admired. Visible

beside the Roman gate, rebuilt in the 17th century and the only point of access permitted by the contours of the hill, are sections of pre-Roman polygonal walls (6th–4th century BC); a huge Roman reservoir (open to visitors), divided into ten vaulted chambers, extends beneath Piazza Matteotti. As well as fine 15th- and 16th-century mansions, you can visit the church of San Francesco (1287), with its red stone façade and Gothic doorway. A chapel houses six tombs of the Geraldini family; the tomb of Matteo and Elisabetta was made in 1477 by Agostino di Duccio. At the top end of the village, beside the Duomo (cathedral), stands a mighty 12-sided bell tower (1050).

ⓘ *Via Orvieto 1*

▶ *Follow the signs for Lugnano in Teverina, to the west.*

6 Lugnano in Teverina
High on its solitary hill, this village was fought over for many years by Todi, Orvieto and Amelia. Its pride is the 12th-century collegiate church of Santa Maria Assunta, one of the most significant Romanesque buildings in Umbria. A portico supported by spiral and smooth columns precedes the four-pitched façade and large rose window. The interior, with a nave and two aisles, has a finely enclosed *schola cantorum*, iconostasis and a presbytery raised above the crypt.

▶ *Proceed north on the SS205 and turn left for Alviano.*

7 Alviano
The medieval village of Alviano is set in a beautifully scenic position, overlooking the Tiber Valley and surrounded by hills. Its parish church has 15th-century frescoes; there's also a grandiose square-plan castle with corner towers and a Renaissance courtyard rebuilt by Bartolomeo d'Alviano (1455–1518), a captain in the service of the Venetian Republic. It now houses a fine Folk Museum.

▶ *Back on the SS205, continue left via Guardea, following the signs for Baschi.*

8 Baschi
A 16th-century parish church with a 15th-century polyptych dominates this little village scenically perched on a spur. If you're after refreshments before returning to Terni, call in at Cannitello, on the main road for Todi, where you'll find chef Vissani, a star of Italian cuisine.

▶ *From Baschi, go to the A1 motorway at Orvieto and follow this to Orte before taking the SS204 back to Terni.*

BACK TO NATURE

About 8km (5 miles) north of Alviano Scalo, on the road along the edge of an artificial basin (formed by damming the Tiber), is a marsh area with nature trails and huts for watching migratory birds.

Valnerina & the
Sibillini Mountains

Along the lush Nera river gorges, this tour enters the lesser-known heart of southern Umbria, and ventures to the mountain that separates it from the Marche region. These are lands of mystics and saints, of hermitages and abbeys, and of the myths and legends of an ancient civilisation.

3 DAYS · 243KM · 151 MILES

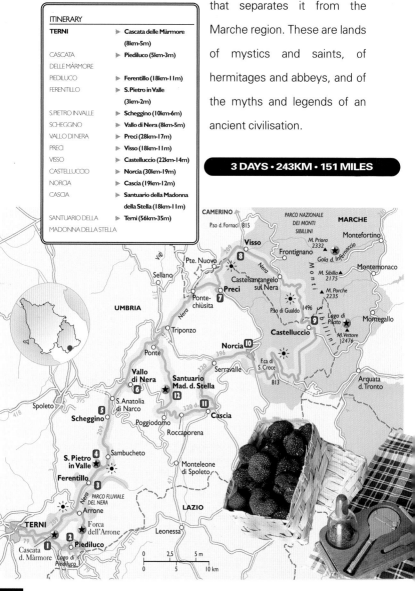

The spectacular drop of the
Màrmore waterfall

ⓘ *Viale C Battisti, Terni*

▶ *Take the **SS19** along the so-called Strada Inferiore (signposted, as is the Strada Superiore) to the Cascata delle Màrmore.*

❶ Cascata delle Màrmore

Only those arriving from below will be able to appreciate the roaring grandeur of the three falls of the Velino that plunge spectacularly 165m (541 feet) from the Màrmore plateau down to the Nera river. In midsummer much of the water disappears, absorbed by the hydroelectric stations which have radically altered the landscape. In fact, the falls are not even the work of nature. In 271 BC Roman consul Manlio Curio Dentato had a channel dug to reclaim the marshy Rieti plain. The source of constant discord between the people of Rieti, Terni and Valnerina, the falls underwent significant changes between the 16th and 18th centuries and were dammed up in the 1920s and 1930s.

RECOMMENDED WALK

A route at the Màrmore falls links the Strada Inferiore and the Strada Superiore to the Observatory, a small loggia built in 1781 so that visitors could admire the spectacle close up. Other impressive views can be enjoyed from the scenic points created along the paths that skirt the three falls; in certain weather conditions the spray creates amazing colour effects.

▶ *Continue along the **SS79** and turn right for Piediluco.*

❷ Piediluco

Approximately 20m (66 feet) deep, lovely Lago di Piediluco – from the Latin for 'at the foot of the woods' – is now exploited as

a reservoir for the area's hydroelectric plants (a 42km/26-mile channel carries the water of the Nera river). The lake's shores were already inhabited between the Bronze and Iron ages; boats and fishing equipment have

FOR CHILDREN

The famous echo that could repeat up to two 11-syllable sentences on the lakeshore opposite Piediluco no longer exists; it has been eliminated by newly built houses. What is left of it can be heard a few dozen metres off the shady shore, if you hire a boat.

been sculpted on the doorway of the Gothic parish church in the village of Piediluco, which is overlooked by the ruins of a 14th-century stronghold.

▶ *Proceed briefly along the **SS79** then turn left and drive via Forca dell'Arrone to the **SS209**, following this to the right to Ferentillo.*

❸ Ferentillo

The two villages that form Ferentillo straddle the Nera river near a wooded gorge defended by two strongholds (one reduced to ruins, the other with towers and a keep). Thrillseekers should visit the crypt (13th- to 14th-century) of San

Stefano Church. Resting on the walls and pillars are about 20 mummies, with hair, nails and body-hair intact, as well as traces of clothing. Their preservation is due to the sand, rich in nitrates and chloride, on which the corpses were laid, and constant ventilation from the windows.

☐ *Via della Vittoria 61*

▶ *Proceed along the SS209 to the turning on the left to Abbazia di San Pietro in Valle.*

❹ **Abbazia di San Pietro in Valle**

The abbey was founded around 720 by Faraoldo, the Lombard Duke of Spoleto, after he had been granted a vision of St Peter (the scene is depicted in the left arm of the transept). After falling into ruin following Saracen incursions, the abbey was restored at the command of emperors Otto III and Henry II in the 10th to 11th centuries. Here you can admire several

Above: St Paul sculpted on the jamb of a door
Below: the abbey of San Pietro in Valle

Roman sarcophagi, a rare Lombard main altar and 15th-century frescoes in the apse. Most important of all is the fresco cycle painted on the walls of the nave, showing stories from the Old (left) and New (right) Testaments. Dating from

SPECIAL TO...

The Ferentillo mummies tell some remarkable stories. The corpse of a man who died under the surgeon's knife shows signs of the fatal operation; another exhibits dagger blows; a painful grimace appears on the face of a man killed by an incurable disease that deformed his mouth and prevented him from eating. There's also a Chinese bride and groom who sought refuge here in vain, hoping to escape the cholera that had infected them in Rome.

the 12th to 13th centuries, it is a masterpiece of Romanesque painting in Italy.

▶ *Back on the SS209, continue right to Scheggino.*

❺ **Scheggino**

According to contemporary chronicles, the women of Scheggino covered themselves with glory when, in 1522, the castles of Valnerina rebelled against Spoleto, and the women's strenuous defence

The churches of Santa Maria and
Sant'Agostino at Visso

run by the Benedictine abbey of
Sant'Eutizio, the main political,
economic and cultural centre in
the area between the 10th and
12th centuries, and its surgeons
had access to a well-stocked
library. Inside the abbey
complex, 3km (2 miles) southeast of Preci, you can visit the
caves of hermits who, at the end
of the 6th century, formed a
community under the guidance
of hermits Spes and Eutizio.

*i Via Madonna della Peschiera,
Casa del Parco*

▶ *Go back and turn right off the
provincial road to travel via
Saccovescio to the SS209, and
take this to the right to Visso.*

8 Visso
An austere ancient village, Visso
lies in the Marche, where the
upper reaches of the Nera river
flow. For a long time, Visso chal-
lenged Norcia for control of the
high pastures on the Sibillini
mountains. Towering inside the
Romanesque-Gothic collegiate
church of Santa Maria, on a fine
square surrounded by 15th- and
16th-century houses and
mansions, is a 14th-century St
Christopher standing more than
10m (33 feet) high, among
several fine frescoes.

saved the triangular stronghold
from a memorable siege.

▶ *Continue on the SS209 to the
turning signposted on the
right for Vallo di Nera.*

6 Vallo di Nera
Vallo di Nera is particularly
noted for the integrity of its
13th-century spiral plan. Houses
are propped against each other
with the aid of arches, as a
protection against earthquakes.
Steep, narrow streets link the
streets on level ground that
adapt to the contours of the hill
and lead to the 16th-century
doorway of San Giovanni
Battista (13th to 14th century,
with an apse entirely covered in
16th-century frescoes). At the
bottom, where the turreted ring
of walls is interrupted, beautiful

votive frescoes of the 14th and
15th centuries by artists from
Umbria and Marche adorn the
interior of Santa Maria Church.

▶ *Back on the SS209, drive on
to Pontechiùsita, where the
provincial road to Preci
branches off to the right.*

7 Preci
Repeatedly devastated by wars
and earthquakes (the last in
1997), Preci has an unusual
history. Between the 16th and
18th centuries, it had a flourishing school of surgery which
specialised in the treatment of
eye complaints (including
cataract operations), hernias and
kidney stones, as well as castra-
tions performed on budding
castrato singers in the 17th and
18th centuries. The hospital was

FOR HISTORY BUFFS

Desolate Pian Perduto ('lost
plain') earned its name in 1522,
when the people of Norcia
fought in vain for it, hand to
hand against the people of Visso.
'Norcia, with more forces,
believes it will win,/But Visso,
with trust in the saints, knows it
will win' say the first lines of epic
poem *La Battaglia del Pian
Perduto*, composed before the
1800s by a shepherd-storyteller
from Visso. Poetic challenges
were a traditional way of passing
the nights while guarding the
flocks. Incidentally, Pian Perduto
still belongs to Visso.

Flower-lovers will enjoy the orchids (about 30 species) that grow in the grounds of Villa Franchetti, on the road to Forca dell'Arrone. Not to be missed in June is the spectacular carpet of flowers on the Castelluccio plain: violets, daffodils, tulips, gentian and gentianella, buttercups, red and yellow poppies, asphodel, peonies, saxifrage, lilies, crucifers, lily of the valley, nigritelle, dwarf juniper, alpine wall germanders, black whortleberry and bearberries are just some of the 1,800 species that brighten the meadows and slopes of the Sibillini mountains. Lake Pilato sits at 1,940m (6,365 feet), at the centre of Monte Vettore's amphitheatre. The *Chirocephalus marchesonii*, a tiny reddish crustacean that swims backwards with its abdomen upwards, lives in its waters – its only known habitat.

▶ *Follow the signs for Castelsantangelo sul Nera and then turn right for Castelluccio.*

9 Castelluccio

High on a hill that separates Pian Perduto from Pian Grande, at the foot of the Sibillini, this mountain village (1,452m/4,764 feet), built by the people of Norcia to defend their eastern border, seems to float on the smooth basin of a dried-up glacial lake. Until the mid-20th century, this ancient site could only be reached on foot or on horseback. On winter evenings, long tolls of the bell guided wayfarers through the fog and snow that blanked out the fields, famous now for their tasty lentils. Bawdy words, written in lime

Hang-gliders in the mountain meadows around Castelluccio

and often in verse by bored shepherds far from home, are now fading on the walls of the village houses, stables and shelters.

▶ *Follow the signs for Norcia, always bearing right at the four main forks in the road.*

10 Norcia

Enclosed within its unbroken ring of walls (more than 2km/1 mile long), this elegant town – *Vetusta Nursia* to the Romans, who took it from the Sabines in 290 BC – stands on the edge of a fertile plain, dominated by the Sibillini mountain range. Wide streets, two-storey houses and walls reinforced with projected footings were all built to guidelines issued by the papacy in 1730 after yet another devastating earthquake. The main square is dominated by the powerful Castellina, built by Vignola in 1554 for the papal governors. The 14th-century façade of San Benedetto Church is flanked by a 16th-century portico, beneath which are the old measures for cereals, adapted in the 19th century to the metric system. According to tradition, a Roman chamber in the crypt below, the site of an ancient house, is where Benedetto (*c*480–546), founder of Western monasticism, and his twin sister, Scolastica, were born. Their stories are told in the 15th-century frescoes that adorn the church of Santa Scolastica, at the cemetery. There are several *norcinerie* here – pork butchers: the word was coined here. They overflow with salami, cheeses and black truffles (festival in February).

[i] *Town Hall*

▶ Take the SS396 west, then the SS320 to the left to Cascia.

⓫ Cascia

Cascia's old centre was changed by 20th-century development, designed to make room for the influx of devotees of Santa Rita (1381–1457, canonised in 1900). An enormous basilica was erected between 1937 and 1947 beside the monastery where Rita Lotti lived her last 40 years

as an Augustinian. A crystal urn contains her mummified body. Forced to marry at a very young age, for 18 years she suffered at the hands of a brutal husband and was only able to embrace the religious life after his death. A number of prodigious events marked her simple peasant existence: a swarm of bees surrounding her in her cradle; a white rose flowering in winter; a wound caused by a thorn from Christ's crown. She prayed that God would grant her twin children innocent deaths before they were old enough to repeat their father's sins – and her prayer was answered.

[i] *Piazza Garibaldi 1*

▶ After reaching Roccaporena, to the east, take the unsurfaced road (difficult in rain) that leads to the Poggiodomo-Ponte, asphalted, then turn right to the

unsurfaced road signposted on the left for the sanctuary of the Madonna delle Stella.

⓬ Santuario della Madonna della Stella

From the bottom of a small, wooded valley, a path climbs steeply to a church partially hewn from the rock. The interior (ask for the keys in nearby Roccatamburo), with 14th-century frescoes, gives access to 20 or so monastic cells, also dug into the stone. Founded in 1308 by the Augustinians (although the cells date from Lombard times), the hermitage was abandoned in the 17th century and restored in 1833. No one has lived here since 1949.

▶ Back on the asphalt road, continue left to the SS209, which leads left to Terni.

A winter view of Lake Pilato, in the Sibillini mountains

RECOMMENDED EXCURSION

On the watershed between the Adriatic and the Tyrrhenian seas, Monti Sibillini National Park has, since 1993, protected a mountain range about 40km (25 miles) long, full of rock faces, gorges and ravines, karst phenomena and glacial cirques. A splendid excursion visits Monte Vettore (2,476m/8,123 feet) and the double lake of Pilato (or 'degli Occhiali'). According to tradition, the Roman procurator of Judaea responsible for Christ's Crucifixion committed suicide here and, for this reason, it is shrouded in dark legends. The east side gives access to the amazing Infernaccio gorges and the blocked but scenic Sibilla cave.

PRACTICAL INFORMATION

ACCOMMODATION & RESTAURANTS

Following is a selection of hotels (⌂), farm holiday centres (⌂≉) and camping sites (⚠) that can be found along the routes of each tour, along with suggestions for restaurants (🍴🍴) to take a break.

Accommodation prices

Accommodation is divided into three price categories based on the cost of a double room per night:
€ – up to €50
€€ – €50–€100
€€€ – over €100

Restaurant prices

Restaurants are divided into three price categories based on the cost of a three-course meal, excluding drink:
€ – up to €20
€€ – €20–€40
€€€ – over €40

TOUR I
MASSA

⌂ Excelsior €€€
Via C Battisti 1, Marina di Massa. Tel: 0585 8601, fax: 0585 869795.

⚠ International Partaccia I
Via delle Pinete 394. Tel: 0585 780133, fax: 0585 774511.
Open Apr–Sep.

🍴🍴 Da Riccà €€–€€€
Lungomare di Ponente.
Tel: 0585 241070.
Fish dishes. Closed Mon and period between Dec & Jan.

FORTE DEI MARMI

⌂ Raffaelli-Villa Angela €€€
Via Mazzini 64. Tel: 0584 787472, fax: 0584 787115.
Closed Dec & Jan.

🍴🍴 Lorenzo €€–€€€
Via Carducci 61. Tel: 0584 84030.
Creative fish cuisine. Closed Mon & period between Dec & Jan.

VIAREGGIO

⌂ Grand Hotel & Royal €€€

Via Carducci 44. Tel: 0584 45151, fax: 0584 31438.
Open Apr–Oct.

🍴🍴 Il Porto €€–€€€
Via M Coppino 319. Tel: 0584 383878.
Fresh fish and seafood. Closed Thu, Jul & period in Jan & Nov.

TOUR 2
LUCCA

⌂ Ilaria €€€
Via del Fosso 26. Tel: 0583 469200, fax: 0583 991961.

⌂ La Luna €€
Via Fillungo ang, Corte Compagni 12. Tel: 0583 493634, fax: 0583 490021.
Closed for period in Jan.

⌂ Piccolo Hotel Puccini €
Via di Poggio 9. Tel: 0583 55421, fax: 0583 53487.

🍴🍴 Giulio €
Via delle Conce 47. Tel: 0583 55948.
Closed Sun (except third in month), Mon, period in Aug & Christmas.

TOUR 3
BARGA

⌂ La Pergola €
Via San Antonio 1. Tel: 0583 711239, fax: 0583 710433.

🍴🍴 Alpino €€
Via Pascoli 41. Tel 0583 723336.
Typical local cuisine. Closed Nov & Mon in winter. Also hotel.

CASTELVECCHIO PASCOLI

⌂🍴🍴 Il Ciocco €€€
Near Il Ciocco. Tel: 0583 7191, fax: 0583 723197.

TORRE DEL LAGO PUCCINI

⚠ Del Lago
Via Puccini 273. Tel: 0584 359702, fax: 0584 359622.
Open all year round.

🍴🍴 Butterfly €€
Belvedere Puccini 24/26, Lago di Massaciuccoli. Tel: 0584 341024.
Regional cuisine. Closed Thu and period between Oct & Nov. Also hotel.

TOUR 4
PISA

⌂ D'Azeglio €€€
Piazza Vittorio Emanuele II 18/B. Tel: 050 500310, fax: 050 28017.

⌂ Verdi €€
Piazza Repubblica 5. Tel: 050 598947, fax: 050 598944.

⚠ Torre Pendente
Viale delle Cascine 86. Tel: 050 561704, fax: 050 561734.
Open Apr–mid-Oct.

🍴🍴 La Rota €€
Via Aurelia 276, Madonna dell'Acqua. Tel: 050 804443.
Tuscan cuisine. Closed Tue.

MARINA DI PISA

⚠ Internazionale
Via Litoranea 7. Tel: 050 35211, fax: 050 500470.
Open May–Sep.

🍴🍴 L'Arsella €€
Via Padre Agostino. Tel: 050 36615.
Fish dishes. Closed Tue evening & Wed, mid-Jan–Feb.

SAN GIULIANO TERME

⌂ Granduca €€
Via del Brennero 13. Tel: 050 814111, fax: 050 818811.
Restaurant.

🍴🍴 Sergio a Villa di Corliano €€
Near Rigoli. Tel: 050 818858.
Tuscan cuisine. Closed Wed & in Jan & Feb.

TOUR 5
PISTOIA

⌂ Leon Bianco €€
Via Panciatichi 2. Tel: 0573 26676, fax: 0573 26704.

🍴🍴 San Jacopo €–€€
Via Crispi 15. Tel: 0573 27786.
Traditional Tuscan cuisine. Closed Mon, Tue lunchtime & period in Aug.

ABETONE

⌂ Regina €€
Via Uccelliera 9. Tel: 0573 60007, fax: 0573 60257.
Open Christmas–mid-Apr & Jul–mid-Sep.

Visiting Sovana, in the Maremma near Grossetana

⚲ Bucaneve
Via La Secchia 102, near Le Regine. Tel: & fax: 0573 60202.
Open all year round.
¶¶ Da Pierone €–€€
Via Brennero 556. Tel: 0573 60068.
Traditional cuisine. Closed Thu & period in Jun & Oct.

MONTECATINI TERME
▦ Imperial Garden €€
Viale Puccini 20. Tel: 0572 910862, fax: 0572 910663.
Open mid-Mar–mid-Nov.
▦ Nuovo Excelsior €€
Via Felice Cavallotti 115. Tel: 0572 70212, fax: 0572 70138.
Open Apr–Oct.
¶¶ La Torre €€
Piazza Giusti 8, Montecatini Alto. Tel: 0572 70650.
Tuscan cuisine. Closed Tue.

PRATO
▦ Giardino €€
Via Magnolfi 4. Tel: 0574 606588, fax: 0574 606591.

TOUR 6
VOLTERRA
▦ ¶¶ Nazionale €€
Via dei Marchesi 11. Tel: 0588 886284, fax: 0588 84097.
▦ Villa Nencini €€
Borgo Santo Stefano 55. Tel: 0588 86386, fax: 0588 80601.
⌂⚘ Tenuta Orgiaglia
Near Ponsano. Tel: & fax: 0588 35029.
Open all year round.
⚲ Le Balze
Via di Mandaringa, near Borgo San Giusto. Tel: & fax: 0588 87880.
Open Mar–mid-Oct.
¶¶ Vecchia Osteria dei Poeti €–€€
Via Matteotti 55. Tel: 0588 86029.
Tuscan cuisine. Closed Thu & mid-Jan–mid-Feb.

PIOMBINO
▦ ¶¶ Centrale €€€
Piazza Verdi 2. Tel: 0565 220188, fax: 0565 220220.
⚲ Pappasole
Near Riotorto. Tel: 0565 20414, fax: 0565 20346.
Open mid-Apr–mid-Oct.

CASTAGNETO CARDUCCI
▦ ¶¶ I Ginepri €€
Viale Italia 13, Marina di Castagneto Carducci. Tel: 0565 744027, fax: 0565 744344.
Open Mar–Oct.
¶¶ Da Ugo €€
Via Pari 3A. Tel: 0565 763746.
Traditional cuisine. Closed Mon (except Jul & Aug) & in Nov.

TOUR 7
PORTOFERRAIO
▦ Viticcio €€
Near Viticcio. Tel: 0565 939058, fax: 0565 939032.
Open Apr–Oct.
⌂⚘ Casa Marisa
Near Schiopparello 12. Tel: & fax: 0565 933074.
Open all year round.
¶¶ Da Vittorio €€
Via dell'Amore 54. Tel: 0565 917446.

Local fish dishes. Closed Tue, Epiphany–Feb.

CAPOLÌVERI
▦ Capo Sud €€
Via Capo del Marinaro 311. Tel: 0565 964021, fax: 0565 964263.
Open May–Sep.
⚲ Croce del Sud
Near Morcone. Tel: & fax: 0565 968640. *Open Apr–Oct.*

RIO MARINA
▦ ¶¶ Rio €€
Via Palestro 31. Tel: 0565 924225, fax: 0565 924162.
Open mid-Mar–mid-Nov.

TOUR 8
CASTIGLIONE DELLA PESCAIA
▦ L'approdo €€€
Via Ponte Giorgini 29. Tel: 0564 933466, fax: 0564 933086.
▦ Corallo €€
Via Sauro 1. Tel: 0564 933668, fax: 0564 936268.
Closed Nov–Jan.

¶¶ **Romolo €€–€€€**
Corso Libertà 10. Tel: 0564
933533.
*Maremma cuisine. Closed Tue, &
early Nov–mid-Dec.*

MASSA MARITTIMA
🏨 **Duca del Mare €**
Piazza Alighieri 1. Tel: 0566
902284, fax: 0566 901905.
*Closed mid-Nov–mid-Dec & mid-
Jan–mid-Feb.*

TOUR 9
SCANSANO
🏨¶¶ **Antico Casale di
Scansano €€**
Near Castagneta. Tel: 0564
507219.
Closed mid-Jan–Feb.

SATURNIA
🏨 **Villa Clodia €€**
Via Italia 43. Tel: 0564 601212,
fax: 0564 601305.
Closed period in Dec.
¶¶ **Due Cippi–Da Michele €€**
Piazza Vittorio Veneto 26A.
Tel: 0564 601074.
*Regional cuisine. Closed Mon &
Sun evening in low season, mid-
Feb–mid-Mar. Also hotel.*

ORBETELLO
🏨 **Vecchia Maremma €€**
Near Quattrostrade. Tel: 0564
862147, fax: 0564 862347.
🏕 **Voltoncino**
Near Albinia. Tel: 0564 870158,
fax: 0564 70415.
Open mid-May–mid-Sep.

TOUR 10
FIRENZE
🏨 **Villa Le Rondini €€€**
Via Bolognese Vecchia 224. Tel:
0554 00081, fax: 0552 68212.
🏨 **Morandi alla
Crocetta €€€**
Via Laura 50. Tel: 0552 344747,
fax: 0552 480954.
🏨 **Cimabue €€**
Via B Lupi 7. Tel: 0554 71989,
fax: 0554 75601.
Closed period in Dec.
🏨¶ **Le Macine**
Viuzzo del Pozzetto 1, near
Bagno a Ripoli. Tel: & fax: 0556
531089. *Open year round.*
¶¶ **Pane e Vino €€**
Via San Niccolò 70a/r. Tel: 0552
476956.

*Tuscan cuisine. Open evenings,
closed Sun & period in Aug.*
¶¶ **Sagrestia €€**
Via Guicciardina 27/R. tel: 0552
10003.
*Traditional cuisine. Closed
Mon.*

TOUR 11
SAN GIMIGNANO
🏨 **Leon Bianco €€**
Piazza della Cisterna 13. Tel:
0577 941294, fax: 0577 942123.
*Closed mid-Jan–mid-Feb & period
in Nov–Dec.*
🏨¶ **Fattoria Poggio Alloro**
Near Sant'Andrea 23. Tel: 0577
950276, fax: 0577 950290.
Open all year round.
¶¶ **La Mangiatoia €€**
Via Mainardi 5. Tel: 0577
941528.
*Tuscan specialities. Closed 4–25
Nov and Tue.*

TOUR 12
SESTO FIORENTINO
🏨 **Villa Villoresi €€€**
Via Ciampi 2. Tel: 0554 43212,
fax: 0554 42063.

FIESOLE
🏨 **La Fattoria Maiano €€**
Via Benedetto da Maiano 11,
near Maiano. Tel: 0555 99600,
fax: 0555 99640.
🏕 **Panoramico**
Via Peramonda 1, near Prato ai
Pini. Tel: 0555 99069, fax: 0555
9186.
Open all year round.
¶¶ **Cave di Maiano €€–€€€**
Via delle Cave 16, near Maiano.
Tel: 0555 9133.
*Tuscan cuisine & barbecues.
Closed Thu and period in Aug.*

TOUR 13
AREZZO
🏨 **Continentale €€**
Piazza Guido Monaco 7. Tel:
0575 20251, fax: 0575 350485.
🏨¶ **Magnanini Massimo**
Via Fontebranda 47. Tel: & fax:
0575 27627.
Open all year round.
¶¶ **Cantuccio €–€€**
Via Madonna del Prato 76.
Tel: 0575 26830.
*Tuscan cuisine & barbecues. Closed
Wed and period in Jul.*

CAMÀLDOLI
🏨 **Il Rustichello €€**
Via Corniolo 14. Tel: 0575
556020, fax: 0575 556046.
¶¶ **Cedro €–€€**
Via Camaldoli 20, near
Moggiona. Tel: 0575 556080.
*Casentino cuisine. Closed Mon in
winter.*

TOUR 14
CITTÀ DI CASTELLO
🏨 **Tiferno €€**
Piazza R Sanzio 13. Tel: 0758
550331, fax: 0758 521196.
🏨¶ **Villa Bice**
Villa Zampini 43/45, near
Cerbara. Tel: & fax: 0758
511430.
Open all year round.
🏕 **Montesca**
Near Montesca. Tel: 0758
558566, fax: 0758 520786.
Open mid-Apr–Sep.
¶¶ **Il Postale di Marco e
Barbara €€**
Via Raffaele de Cesare 8. Tel:
0758 521356.
Closed Mon and Sat lunchtimes.

CORTONA
🏨 **San Luca €€**
Piazza Garibaldi 2. Tel: 0575
630400, fax: 0575 630150.
🏨¶ **I Pagliai**
Near Montalla 23. Tel: 0575
605220, fax: 0575 603676.
Open all year round.
¶¶ **Osteria del Teatro €–€€**
Via Maffei 5. Tel: 0575 630556.
*Tuscan cuisine. Closed Wed in
winter & period in Nov.*

CASTIGLION
FIORENTINO
🏨 **Relais San Pietro in
Polvano €€€**
Near Polvano 3. Tel: 0575
650100, fax: 0575 650255.
¶¶ **Da Muzzicone €€**
Piazza San Francisco 7.
Tel: 0575 680346.
Local cuisine. Closed Tue.

TOUR 15
SIENA
🏨 **Garden €€€**
Via Custoza 2. Tel: 0577 47056,
fax: 0577 46050.
🏨 **Santa Caterina €€**
Via Piccolomini 7. Tel: 0577
221105, fax: 0577 271087.

Piccolo Hotel Il Palio €
Piazza del Sale 19. Tel: 0577 281131, fax: 0577 281142.

Siena Colleverde
Strada Scacciapensieri 47. Tel: 0577 280044, fax: 0577 333298.
Open mid-Mar–mid-Nov.

Marsili €€
Via del Castoro 3. Tel: 0577 47154.
Tuscan cuisine. Closed Mon.

Osteria Le Logge €€
Via del Porrione 33. Tel: 0577 48013.
Closed Sun & period between Nov & Dec.

**TOUR 16
CASTELNUOVO
BERARDENGA**
Posta del Chianti €€
Near Colonna del Grillo. Tel: 0577 353000, fax: 0577 353050.

Castell'in Villa Myths €€
Near Castell'in Villa. Tel: 0577 359356.
Tuscan cuisine. Closed Mon & mid-Jan–mid-Feb.

CASTELLINA IN CHIANTI
Salivolpi €€
Via Fiorentina 89. Tel: 0577 740484, fax: 0577 740998.

Luxor
Near Trasqua. Tel: & fax: 0577 743047.
Open mid-May–mid-Sep.

**Antica Trattoria La Torre
€–€€**
Piazza del Comune. Tel: 0577 740236.
Chianti cuisine. Closed Fri & period in Sep.

**TOUR 17
MONTALCINO**
La Crociona
Near La Croce. Tel: & fax: 0577 848007.

Taverna dei Barbi €€
Near Podernovi. Tel: 0577 841200.
Regional cuisine. Closed Tue evening, Wed (except Aug) & period in Jan.

PIENZA
Relais il Chiostro di Pienza €€€
Corso Rosellino 26. Tel: 0578 748400, fax: 0578 748440.
Closed Jan–mid-Mar.

MONTEPULCIANO
Il Marzocco €€
Piazza Savonarola 18. Tel: 0578 757262, fax: 0578 757530.
Closed for period Nov–Dec.

SERRE DI RAPOLANO
Due Mari €€
Via Giotto 1. Tel: 0577 724070, fax: 0577 725414.
Closed Jan.

**TOUR 18
RADICÒFANI**
La Palazzina
Near Le Vigne. Tel: & fax: 0578 55771.
Open all year round.

CHIUSI
Le Querce €€
Near Querce al Pino. Tel: 0578 274308, fax: 0578 274449.
Closed mid-Jan–mid-Feb.

La Sfinge €€
Via Marconi 2. Tel: 0578 20157, fax: 0578 22153.
Closed Feb–early Mar.

La Fattoria
Lago di Chiusi. Tel: 0578 21407, fax: 0578 20644.
Open May–Oct.

Il Zaira €€
Via Arunte 12. Tel: 0578 20260.
Regional cuisine. Closed Mon (except holidays) in winter & period in Nov.

**TOUR 19
PERUGIA**
Relais San Clemente €€€
Near Bosco. Tel: 0755 915100, fax: 0755 915001.

Il Covone €€
Strada Fratticiola 2, near Ponte Pattoli. Tel: 0756 94140.

Paradis d'Été
Strada Fontana 29/G, near Colle della Trinità. Tel: 0755 173121, fax: 0755 176056.
Open all year round.

Enoteca Gio €–€€
Via R D'Andreotto 19. Tel: 0755 731100.
Umbrian cuisine. Closed Sun evening & Mon lunchtime.

Ricciotto €€
Piazza Dante 19. Tel: 0755 721956.
Umbrian cuisine. Closed Sun.

**TOUR 20
GUBBIO**
Gattapone €€
Via Ansidei 6. Tel: 0759 272489, fax: 0759 272417.
Closed mid-Jan–mid-Feb.

San Marco €€
Via Perugina 5. Tel: & fax: 0759 221222.

Sant'Erasmo
Vocabolo Sant'Erasmo 37, near Padule. Tel: 0759 271024, fax: 0759 291017.
Open all year round.

Villa Orto Guidone
Near Orto Guidone. Tel: 0759 272037, fax: 0759 276620.

Taverna del Lupo €€–€€€
Via Ansidei 6. Tel: 0759 274368.
Umbrian cuisine. Closed Mon.

NOCERA UMBRA
La Lupa
Near Colpertana. Tel: 0742 813539, fax: 0742 813679.
Open all year round.

**TOUR 21
PASSIGNANO
SUL TRASIMENO**
Lido €€
Via Roma 1. Tel: 0758 27219, fax: 0758 27251.
Open Apr–Oct.

Florida €
Via II Giugno 2. Tel: 0758 27228.
Closed mid-Nov–mid-Feb.

La Corte €–€€
Via Rigone 1, Castel Rigone. Tel: 0758 453224.
Regional cuisine. Closed period between Jan & Feb.

CASTIGLIONE DEL LAGO
Fazzuoli €
Piazza Marconi 11. Tel: 0759 51119, fax: 0759 51112.
Closed mid-Dec–Feb.

Poggio del Sole
Near Ceraso, Sanfatucchio. Tel: & fax: 0759 680221.
Open all year round.

Cantina €–€€
Via Vittorio Emanuele 89. Tel: 0759 652463.
Umbrian & lake cuisine. Closed Mon except in summer.

PANICALE
🏠 🍴 **Le Grotte di Boldrino** €€
Via V Ceppari 43. Tel: 0758 37161, fax: 0758 37166.

🏠⚜ **La Rosa Canina**
Via dei Mandorli 23, Casalini. Tel: & fax: 0758 350660.
Open late Mar–early Nov & Christmas.

TOUR 22
ASSISI
🏠 **San Francesco** €€€
Via San Francesco 48. Tel: 0758 12284, fax: 075 812567.

🏠 **Minerva** €
Piazzetta Bonghi 7. Tel: 0758 12416, fax: 0758 13770.
Closed period in Dec & Jan.

🏠⚜ **La Castellana**
Near Costa di Trex 4. Tel: & fax: 0758 019046.
Open all year round.

🍴 **Frantoio** €€
Via Fontebella 25. Tel: 0758 12977.
Reginal cuisine. Closed Mon from Nov–Feb.

SPOLETO
🏠 🍴 **Aurora** €€
Via Apollinare 3. Tel: 0743 220315, fax: 0743 221885.

⛺ **Monteluco**
Near San Pietro. Tel: & fax: 0743 220358.
Open Apr–Sep.

🍴 **Tartufo** €€
Piazza Garibaldi 24. Tel: 0743 40236.
Regional cuisine revisited. Closed Sun evening, Mon & period in Jul.

Handmade pottery

TOUR 23
ORVIETO
🏠 **Palazzo Piccolomini** €€
Piazza Ranieri 36. Tel: 0763 341743, fax: 0763 391046.
Closed mid-Jan–Feb.

🍴 **Osteria dell'Angelo** €€–€€€
Piazza XXIX Marzo 8/A. Tel: 0763 341805.
Experimental cuisine. Closed Mon & period in Jul.

TODI
🏠 **Villa Luisa** €€
Via Cortesi 147. Tel: 0758 948571, fax: 0758 948472.

🍴 **Cavour** €–€€
Corso Cavour 21–23. Tel: 075 8943730.
Closed Wed in winter, Christmas– New Year & period between Jan and Feb.

TOUR 24
TERNI
🏠⚜ **La Prima Mela**
Strada di Collestacio 18, Cesi. Tel: 0744 241255.
Open all year round.

🍴 **Alfio** €–€€
Via Galilei 4. Tel: 0744 420120.
Umbrian cuisine. Closed Sun & period in Aug.

ACQUASPARTA
🏠 **Castello di Casigliano** €€
Piazza Corsini 1. Tel: 0744 943428, fax: 0744 944056.

NARNI
🏠 **Dei Priori** €€
Vicolo del Comune 4. Tel: 0744 726843, fax: 0744 726844.

AMELIA
🏠 **Scoglio dell'Aquilone** €€
Via Orvieto 23. Tel: 0744 982445, fax: 0744 983025.

🏠⚜ **San Cristoforo**
Strada San Cristoforo 16. Tel: 0744 988249, fax: 0744 988459.
Open all year round.

🍴 **Il Carleni** €–€€€
Via Pellegrino Carleni 21. Tel: 0744 983925.
Country cuisine. Closed Tue & period between Jan & Feb.

TOUR 25
CASCATA DELLE MÀRMORE
⛺ **Cascata delle Màrmore**
Near I Campacci a Màrmore. Tel: & fax: 0744 67198.
Open Apr–Sep.

NORCIA
🏠 🍴 **Grotta Azzurra** ££
Via Alfieri 12. Tel: 0743 816513, fax: 0743 817342.

🍴 **Trattoria del Francese** €–€€
Via Riguardati 16. Tel: 0743 816290.
Umbrian cuisine, with game. Closed Fri in winter & period in Nov.

CASCIA
🏠 🍴 **Cursula** €€
Viale Cavour 3. Tel: 0743 76206, fax: 0743 76262.
Closed Jan–Feb.

🏠⚜ **Casale Sant'Antonio**
Near Casali Sant'Antonio. Tel: 0743 76819.
Open Mar–Sep.

i Tourist Information Office
12 Number on tour

**TOUR
INFORMATION**

The addresses,
telephone numbers
and opening times
of the attractions
mentioned in the
tours, including the
telephone numbers
of the Tourist
Information
Centres are listed
below, tour by tour.

TOUR 1

i Lungomare Vespucci
24, Marina di Massa.
Tel: 0585 240046.

i Via del Plebiscito,
Carrara.
Tel: 0585 641422.

i Via A Franceschi 8,
Forte dei Marmi.
Tel: 0584 80091.

i Via Donizetti 14,
Marina di Pietrasanta.
Tel: 0584 20331.

i Viale Carducci 10,
Viareggio.
Tel: 0584 962233.

1 Carrara
Academy of Fine Arts
Palazzo Cybo Malaspina,
Via Roma 1.
Tel: 0585 71685.
Visits by request.

Marble Museum
Viale XX Settembre 85.
Tel: 0585 845746.
*Open Jun–Sep, 10–8;
May, 10–5; Oct–Apr,
8.30–1.30.
Closed Sun.*

3 Fantiscritti
Open-air museum
Tel: 0585 70981.
Visits by request.

5 Fosdinovo
Castle
*Guided tours: Mon &
Wed–Sat 9, 10, 11, 4 &*
5, Sun 9, 10, 11, 3, 4,
5 & 6.
Closed Tue.

6 Sarzana
**Museum of Stelae-
Statues**
Castello del Piagnaro,
Pontrèmoli.
Tel: 0187 831439.
*Open Apr–Sep, 9–noon,
3–6; Oct–Mar, 9–noon,
2–5.
Closed Mon.*

7 Luni
Luni Museum
Tel: 0187 66811.
*Open 9–6.
Closed Mon.*

For Children
Pitagora New Park
Lido di Camaiore.
Tel: 0584 611008.
*Open Jun–Aug,
9am–midnight; Oct–May,
9–8.*

10 Viareggio
Galleria del Libro
Via Margherita 33.
Tel: 0584 962734.
Open daily 9–1, 3.30–7.

TOUR 2

i Piazza Guidiccioni 2,
Lucca.
Tel: 0583 91991.

7 Case dei Guinigi
Guinigi Tower
Via Sant'Andrea.
*Open summer, 9–7.30;
winter, 10–4.30. Closed
Mon.*

**8 Duomo di San
Martino**
Tomb of Ilaria del
Carretto
Sagrestia del Duomo.
*Open Apr–Oct, daily
10–6; Nov–Mar,
Mon–Fri 10–3, Sat–Sun
10–6.*

Special to...
National Picture Gallery
Palazzo Mansi, Via Galli
Tassi 43.
Tel: 0583 55570
*Open 8.30–7, Sun 8.30–1.
Closed Mon.*

TOUR 3

i Piazza Guidiccioni 2,
Lucca.
Tel: 0583 91991.

i Via Umberto I, Bagni
di Lucca.
Tel: 0583 805745.

i Piazza Angelio 3,
Barga.
Tel: 0583 724745.

i Piazza delle Erbe 10,
Castelnuovo di
Garfagnana.
Tel: 0583 65159.

i Alpi Apuane Nature
Visitor Centre, Piazza
delle Erbe 1,
Castelnuovo Pascoli.
Tel: 0583 644242.

i Piazza Duomo 11,
Pietrasanta.
Tel: 0584 795260.

1 Villa di Camigliano
Near Camigliano.
Tel: 0583 928041.
*Open daily 10–1, 2.30–6.
Closed Tue in Mar.*

2 Villa Mansi
Segromigno in Monte.
Tel: 0583 920234.
*Open Feb–Oct,
9.30–12.30, 3–sunset;
Nov–Jan, 10–12.30,
3–5.*

3 Villa Reale
Marlia.
Tel: 0583 30108.
Visits on request.

4 Bagni di Lucca
Spa establishment
Piazza San Martino II.
Tel: 0583 87221.
Open Apr–late Nov.

**Recommended
Excursion**
Civic Museum
Via del Mangano 17,
Coreglia Antelminelli.
Tel: 0583 78082.
*Open Jun–Sep, Mon–Sat
9.30–12.30, Sun 10–1,
3–6; Oct–May, Mon–Sat
9.30–12.30.*

**Recommended
Excursions**
Grotta del Vento
*Open Apr–Sep, daily
10–6; Oct–Mar, holidays
only.*

**6 Castelvecchio
Pàscoli**
**House of Giovanni
Pascoli**
Colle di Caprona.
Tel: 0583 766147.
*Open Apr–Sep, Tue
3.30–6.45, Wed–Sun
10.30–1, 3–6.45;
Oct–Mar, Tue 2–5.15,
Wed–Sun 9–1,
2.30–5.*

**7 Castelnuovo di
Garfagnana**
**Exhibition on Ancient
Ligurian Civilisation**
Rocca di Castelnuovo,
Piazza Ariosto 1.
Tel: 0583 644414.
Visits by request.

TOUR 4

i Via Pietro Nenni 24,
Pisa.
Tel: 0509 29777.

i Piazza Stazione 13.
Pisa.
Tel: 050 42291.

i Airport.
Tel: 050 503700.

i Via del Pretorio 1,
Vicopisano.
Tel: 050 796511.

i Piazza Garibaldi 1,
Calci.
Tel: 050 939523.

i Largo Shelley, San
Giuliano Terme.
Tel: 050 815064.

Practical Information

ℹ️ Tourist Information Office
⓬ Number on tour

❶ Tenuta di San Rossore
Visitor Centre
Tel: 050 530101.
Open all year round, Sun & holidays all day, Tue & Thu afternoon only.

❸ Marina di Pisa
Migliarino San Rossore Massaciùccoli Natural Park
Consorzio del Parco, Via Aurelia Nord 4.
Tel: 050 525501.
Tours by appointment 8–2.

For Children
Fantasilandia
Viale del Tirreno 42, Tirrenia.
Tel: 050 30326.
Open Jun–Aug, daily 8am–midnight; Oct–May, Sat–Sun 8am–midnight.

❻ Certosa di Pisa
Via Roma, Calci.
Tel: 050 938430.
Open Tue–Sat 8.30–6.30, Sun 8.30–12.30.

Museum of Natural and Territorial History
Certosa.
Open mid-Jun–mid-Sep, Tue–Fri 10–7, Sat–Sun & holidays 4pm–midnight; mid-Sep–mid-Jun, Tue–Sat 9–6, Sun 10–7. Closed Mon, Christmas & New Year.

❼ San Giuliano Terme
San Giuliano Hot Springs
Largo Shelley 18.
Tel: 050 818047.

TOUR 5

ℹ️ Piazza Duomo 4, Pistoia.
Tel: 0573 21622.

ℹ️ Via Marconi 28, San Marcello Pistoiese.
Tel: 0573 630145 or 622300.

ℹ️ Via Nazionale 42, Cutigliano.
Tel: 0575 630352
(seasonal).

ℹ️ Via Brennero, Abetone.
Tel: 0573 60231.

ℹ️ Piazza Castello 118, Pietrabuona.
Tel: 0572 408292.

ℹ️ Viale Verdi 66, Montecatini Terme.
Tel: 0572 772244.

ℹ️ Piazza Medici 1, Poggio a Caiano.
Tel: 0558 798779.

ℹ️ Piazza Santa Maria delle Carceri 15, Prato.
Tel: 0574 24112.

❷ Gavinana
Ferrucciano Museum
Piazza Francesco Ferrucci.
Tel: 0573 61289.
Open summer, 10–noon, 5–7, holidays 9.30–12.30, 4–7; Oct–May, Sat 3–5, Sun 10–noon.

Back to Nature
Abetone botanical forest garden
Fontana Vaccaia.
Tel: 0573 60363.
Open 9–1, 3.30–7. For bookings contact Comando Forestale.

❺ Popiglio
Museum of Holy Art and Popular Devotion
Church of Santa Maria Assunta.
Tel: 0573 374247.
Open Jul–Aug, Tue–Sun 4–7; Sep–Oct, Apr–Jun, Sat–Sun 4–7; Nov & Mar visits by request. Closed Mon.

❽ Collodi
Villa Garzoni and Gardens
Tel: 0572 429116.
Open daily 8–1 hour before sunset.

Pinocchio Park
Tel: 0572 429342.
Open daily 8.30–1 hour before sunset.

❾ Montecatini Terme
Hot Springs
(Tettuccio, Excelsior, Redi, Torretta, Leopoldine, Tamerici, La Salute spas).
Tel: 0572 7781.
Open Apr–Oct. Excelsior all year.

❿ Poggio a Caiano
Medici villa
Piazza dei Medici 14.
Tel: 0558 77012.
Open Jun–Aug, 8.15–7.30; Sep–Oct, Apr–May, 8.15–5.30; Nov–Feb, 8.15–3.30; Mar, 8.15–4.30.

⓫ Prato
Palazzo Datini
Via Ser Lapo Mazzei 13.
Tel: 0574 21391.
Open Mon–Sat 9–noon, 4–7.

TOUR 6

ℹ️ Piazza Cavour 6, Livorno.
Tel: 0586 898111.

ℹ️ Piazza del Municipio. Livorno,
Tel: 0586 204611.

ℹ️ Calata Carrara, Livorno.
Tel: 0586 210331.

ℹ️ Via Aurelia 632, Castiglioncello.
Tel: 0586 754890.

ℹ️ Via G Turazza 2, Volterra.
Tel: 0588 86150.

ℹ️ Via Roma, Campiglia Marittima.
Tel: 0565 838958
(seasonal).

ℹ️ Via Ferruccio 4, Piombino.

Tel: 0565 220852
(seasonal).

ℹ️ Via della Marina 8, Marina di Castagneto-Donoràtico.
Tel: 0565 744276
(seasonal).

❷ Castiglioncello
National Archaeological Museum
Rosignano Marittimo, Palazzo Bombardieri, Via del Castello.
Tel: 0586 724288 for information.

❹ Volterra
Mario Guarnacci Etruscan Museum
Via Don Minzoni 15.
Tel: 0588 86347.
Open mid-Mar–late Oct, 9–7; Nov–mid-Mar, 9–2. Closed Christmas & New Year.

Civic Art Gallery
Palazzo Minucci Solaini, Via Sarti 1.
Tel: 0588 87580.
Open mid-Mar–late Oct, 9–7; Nov–mid-Mar, 9–2. Closed Christmas & New Year.

❻ Larderello
Museum of Geothermal Energy
Piazza Leopolda.
Tel: 0588 67724.
Open daily 9–6. Closed Christmas & New Year.

❼ Venturina
Terme di Caldana
Tel: 0565 851066.
Open 1 May–31 Oct.

❿ Rocca di San Silvestro
Mining park and museum
Tel: 0565 838680.
Open Sat, Sun & holidays 9–6, Tue & Fri by appointment only.

⓫ Castagneto Carducci
Archive Museum

Via Carducci 1.
Tel: 0565 765032.
Open Mon–Fri 10–1, Sun 3–6.

Carducci Centre
Via Carducci.
Tel: 0565 795032.
Open daily by request 10–noon, 4–6.

🔢 Santuario di Montenero
Tel: 0586 57771.

TOUR 7

i Calata Italia 26, Portoferraio.
Tel: 0565 914671.

🔢 Portoferraio
Civic Archaeological Museum
Forte Linguella.
Tel: 0565 937330.
Open winter 3–6. Closed in summer.

Palazzina dei Mulini
Via Mulini 1.
Tel: 0565 915846.
Open Mon–Sat 9–7, Sun & holidays 9–1.

For Children
Elbaland
Near San Giovanni.
Tel: 0335 8194680.
Open Apr–Oct, 9–midnight.

🔢 Villa di San Martino
Villa Napoleonica
Tel: 0565 914688.
Open Mon–Sat 9–7, holidays 9–1.

🔢 Rio Marina
Elba Mineral Museum
Piazza Salvo D'Acquisto 1.Tel: 0565 962747.
Open Apr–mid-Oct, Mon–Sat 9–noon, 3–6, holidays 9–noon.

TOUR 8

i Via Monterosa 206, Grosseto.
Tel: 0564 462611.

i Piazza Garibaldi, Castiglione della Pescaia.
Tel: 0564 933678.

i Via Giacomelli 11, Follònica.
Tel: 0566 263332.

i Via N Parenti 22, Massa Marittima,
Tel: 0566 902756.

🔢 Parco dell'Uccellina
Via Aurelia Antica, near Pianacce, Alberese.
Tel: 0564 407111.
Visitor Centre: Via del Fante.Tel: 0464 407098.
Tel for opening times.

🔢 Centro Carapax
Vanelle.
Tel: 0566 940083.

🔢 Massa Marittima
Archaeological Museum
Palazzo Pretorio, Piazza Garibaldi.
Tel: 0566 902289.
Open Apr–Sep, 10–12.30, 3.30–7; Oct–Mar, 10–12.30, 3.30–5.

Mining Museum
Via Corridoni.
Tel: 0566 902289.
Visits by request.

🔢 Roselle
Archaeological excavations
Tel: 0564 402403.
Open May–Aug, 9–7.30; Sep–Apr, 9–6.30.

TOUR 9

i Monterosa 206, Grosseto.
Tel: 0564 462611.

i Palazzetto dell'Archivio, Sovana.
Tel: 0564 614074.

i Piazza Busati, Sorano.
Tel: 0564 633099.

i Piazza Garibaldi, Pitigliano.
Tel: 0564 616322.

i Piazza della Repubblica, Orbetello.
Tel: 0564 861226.

i Via Caravaggio 78, Porto Ercole.
Tel: 0564 831019.

i Archetta de Palio 1, Porto Santo Stefano.
Tel: 0564 814208.

i Via Cala di Forno 7, Talamone.
Tel: 0564 8604447.

🔢 Saturnia
Terme di Saturnia
Via della Follonata.
Tel: 0564 601061.

🔢 Sorano
Orsini Fortress and Museum of Medieval Art
Tel: 0564 633767.
Open Apr–Sep, 10–7; Oct–Mar, 10–4.

🔢 Pitigliano
Diocesan Museum of Holy Art
Palazzo Orsini.
Tel: 0564 615568.
Open Apr–Sep, 10–1, 3–8; Oct–Dec, 10–1, 3–7.

Museum of Civic Archaeology
Palazzo Orsini.
Tel: 0564 617019.
Open Apr–Sep, 10–7; Oct–Mar, 10–4.

For Children
Giardino dei Tarocchi
Near Pescia Fiorentina.
Tel: 0564 895122.
Open May–Oct. By appointment rest of year.

🔢 Ponte dell'Abbadia
Vulci National Museum
Tel: 0761 437787.
Open May–Sep, 9–1.30, 2.30–7 (or 6). Opening times may be reduced in winter. Closed Mon.

🔢 Ansedonia
Cosa ruins archaeological museum
Tel: 0564 881421.
Open Apr–Sep, 9–7; Oct–Mar, 9–2.

🔢 Orbetello
Talamone pediment
Piazza della Repubblica.
Tel: 0564 860447.
Open summer, 10–12.30, 4–8; winter, 10–noon, 4–8.

Laguna di Orbetello Natural Reserve
Tel: 0564 820297.

TOUR 10

i Via Cavour 1r, Florence.
Tel: 055 290832.

i Piazza della Stazione 4a, Florence.
Tel: 055 212245.

🔢 Piazza della Signoria
Palazzo Vecchio
Piazza della Signoria.
Tel: 055 2768325.
*Open 9–7 (Thu & holidays 9–2).
Closed New Year, Easter, 1 May, 15 Aug & Christmas.*

🔢 Galleria degli Uffizi
Piazzale degli Uffizi 6.
Tel: 055 23885.
*Open Tue–Sun 8.30–7.
For bookings tel: 055 294883 Mon–Fri 8.30–6.30, Sat 8.30–12.30.
Closed Mon & Christmas.*

🔢 Palazzo Pitti
Royal Apartments
Piazza de' Pitti.
Tel: 055 2388611.
Guided tours 8.15–6.50. Closed Mon.

Costume Gallery
Tel: 055 2388713.

Silver Museum
Tel: 055 2388710.

Practical Information

ℹ️ Tourist Information Office
🔢 Number on tour

*Open summer, 9–4.30;
winter, 9–3.30.
Closed first & third Mon
and second & fourth Sun
in the month.*

Palatina Gallery
Tel: 055 2388614.
*Open 8.15–6.30.
Closed Mon & holidays.*

Recommended Walk
Bòboli Gardens
Tel: 055 23885.
*Open summer 9–4.30;
winter 9–3.30.
Closed first & third Mon
and second & fourth Sun
in the month.*

🔢 **Cappella Brancacci**
Piazza del Carmine.
Tel: 055 2382195.
*Open 10–5, Sun &
holidays 1–4.30.
Closed Tue.*

Museum of the Old Florentine House
Palazzo Davanzati, Via
Porta Rossa 13.
Tel: 055 2388610.
*Open Tue–Sat 8.15–2.
Closed first & third Mon
and second & fourth Sun
in the month.*

🔢 **Orsanmichele**
Via dell'Arte della Lana.
Tel: 055 265171.
Visits by request.

🔢 **Piazza del Duomo**
Baptistery of San
Giovanni
Tel: 055 2302885.
*Open Mon–Sat noon–7,
Sun & holidays 8.30–2.
Closed New Year, Easter,
8 Sep & Christmas.*

Baptistery of Santa Maria del Fiore
Tel: 055 2302885.
*Open Mon–Sat noon–7,
Sun & holidays 8.30–2.
Closed New Year, Easter,
8 Sep & Christmas.*

Basilica of Santa Maria del Fiore

Tel: 055 2302885.
*Open Mon–Fri 10–5, first
Sat in month 10–3.30,
second, third & fourth Sat
in month 10–4.45, Sun &
holidays 1.30–4.45.
Closed 8 Sep.*

Museum of Works
Piazza del Duomo 9.
Tel: 055 294514.
*Open 9.30–7.30, Sun
9–1.40.
Closed 8 Sep & holidays.*

Special to…
Brunelleschi's dome
Tel: 055 2302885.
*Open 8.30–6.30.
Closed holidays.*

Giotto's bell tower
Tel: 055 2302885.
Open 8.30–7.30.

🔢 **Palazzo Medici-Riccardi**
Via Cavour 1.
Tel: 055 2760340.

Chapel of the Magi
*Open 9–7. Booking
recommended.
Closed Wed.*

🔢 **Basilica di San Lorenzo**
Piazza San Lorenzo.
Tel: 055 2166634,
*Open 10–5.
Closed holidays.*

Medicea Laurenziana Library
Piazza San Lorenzo 9.
Tel: 055 214443.
*Entry allowed for study only
Mon, Fri & Sat 8–1.45,
Tue–Thu 8–5.
Closed Sun.*

Chapel of the Principi (Cappelle Medicee)
Piazza Madonna degli
Aldobrandini 6.
Tel: 055 23885.
*Open 8.15–5.
Closed second & fourth
Sun and first, third & fifth
Mon in the month, &
holidays.*

Opificio delle Pietre Dure workshop
Via degli Alfani 78.
Tel: 055 265111.
*Open Mon–Sat 8.15–2,
Thu also 2–7.
Closed Sun & holidays.*

Special to...
Santa Maria Novella
Piazza Santa Maria
Novella.
Tel: 055 215918.
*Open 9.30–5, Fri, Sun &
holidays 1–5.*

Museum of Santa Maria Novella
Tel: 055 282187.
*Open 9–5, Fri & holidays
9–2.*

🔢 **Chiesa e Museo di San Marco**
Museum of San
Marco
Tel: 055 2388608.
*Open 8.30–1.50, Sat &
Sun 8.30–7.
Closed first, third & fifth Sun
and second & fourth Mon
in the month.*

🔢 **Galleria dell'Accademia**
Via Ricasoli 60.
Tel: 055 2388690.
*Open Tue–Sun 8.15–6.50.
Closed Mon.*

🔢 **Piazza della SS Annunziata**
Ospedale degli
Innocenti, picture gallery
Tel: 055 2491708.
*Open 8.30–2.
Closed Wed.*

Basilica of SS Annunziata
Tel: 055 2398034.
*Open 7–12.30, 4–6.30.
Sun & holidays 7–1.30,
4–7.*

Archaeological Museum
Via della Colonna 38.
Tel: 055 23575.
*Open Mon 2–9, Tue & Thu
8.30–7, Wed & Fri–Sat
8.30–2.
Closed holidays except
Sun.*

🔢 **Museo del Bargello**
Via del Proconsolo.
Tel: 055 23885606.
*Open 8.15–1.50. Closed
first, third & fifth Sun and
second & fourth Mon in
the month, & holidays.*

🔢 **Chiesa di Santa Croce**
Piazza di Santa Croce.
Tel: 055 244619.
*Open Mon–Sat
9.30–5.30, Sun & holidays
1–5.30.*

Pazzi Chapel, Museum of Works of Santa Croce and cloisters
Piazza di Santa Croce 16.
Tel: 055 2466105.
*Open Mon–Sat
9.30–5.30, Sun & holidays
1–5.30.*

Excursion
San Miniato al Monte
Via Monte Croci 34.
Tel: 055 215918
*Open Mon–Thu 9.30–5,
Fri–Sun & holidays 1–5.*

■ **TOUR 11**

ℹ️ Via Cavour 1r,
Florence.
Tel: 055 290832.

ℹ️ Piazza della Stazione
4a, Florence.
Tel: 055 212245.

ℹ️ Via Diaz 116, Lastra
a Signa.
Tel: 055 8722628.

ℹ️ Via Baccio 74,
Montelupo Fiorentino.
Tel: 0571 518993.

ℹ️ Piazza del Popolo,
San Miniato.
Tel: 0571 42745.

ℹ️ C/o railway station,
Castelfiorentino.
Tel: 0571 629049.

ℹ️ Via Cavour 32,
Certaldo.
Tel: 0571 664935.

[i] Piazza Duomo 1,
San Gimignano.
Tel: 0577 940008.

[i] Via Campana 43,
Colle di Val d'Elsa.
Tel: 0577 922791.

[i] Largo Fontebranda
3, Monteriggioni.
Tel: 0577 304810.

2 Artimino
Medici Villa,
Archaeological Museum
Viale Giovanni XXIII 5.
Tel: 055 8718124.
*Open Mon–Tue 9–12.30,
Thu–Sun on request.
Closed Wed.*

**3 Montelupo
Fiorentino**
Archaeological and
Pottery Museum
Palazzo del Podestà,
Via Sinibaldi 45.
Tel: 0571 51352.
*Open Tue–Sun 10–6.
Closed Mon, New Year,
Easter & Christmas.*

**Recommended
excursion**
Leonardo Museum
Vinci, Castello dei Conti
Guidi.
Tel: 0571 56055.
*Open Mar–Oct, 9.30–7;
Nov–Feb, 9.30–6.*

5 Castelfiorentino
Church of Santa
Verdiana, picture gallery
Tel: 0571 64096.
*Open Sat 10–7, Sun
10–noon, 4–7. Also by
request.*

Cultural Centre
Via Tieli 41.
Tel: 0571 64019.
*Open Tue, Thu, Sat 4–7,
Sun & holidays 10–noon,
4–7.*

6 San Vivaldo
*Open by request – contact
the tourist office, Piazza
del Popolo 11, tel: 0572
954412.*

7 Certaldo
Palazzo Pretorio
Piazzetta del Vicariato.
Tel: 0571 661219.
*Open summer, 10–12.30,
4.30–7.30; winter, 10–
12.30, 3–6. Closed Mon.*

**Boccaccio House,
Library and Study
Centre**
Via Boccaccio.
Tel: 0571 661252
*Open summer, Mon, Wed
& Fri 9–1, 3–7, Tue & Thu
9–1. Closed Sat; winter,
Mon–Fri 9–7, Sat 9–1.
Closed Sun.*

Special to…
Palazzo del Popolo,
Civic Museum, Torre
Grossa
Piazza Duomo.
Tel: 0577 940340.
*Open Mar–Oct,
9.30–7.20; Nov–Feb,
10.30–4.20.
Closed Fri in winter.*

**11 Certosa del
Galluzzo**
Tel: 055 2049226.
*Open 9–noon, 3–5.
Closed Mon.*

TOUR 12

[i] Via Cavour 1r,
Florence.
Tel: 055 290832.

[i] Piazza della Stazione
4a, Florence.
Tel: 055 212245.

[i] Palazzo dei Vicari,
Scarperìa.
Tel: 055 846509.

[i] Palazzo dei Vicari,
Via Togliatti 45, Borgo
San Lorenzo.
Tel: 055 8456230.

[i] Corso del Popolo
89, Vicchio.
Tel: 055 8448720.

[i] Via Portigiani 3/5,
Fièsole.
Tel: 055 598720.

1 Villa di Careggi
Viale Gaetano Pieraccini
21.
Tel: 055 4279755.
*Open Mon–Fri 8–6, Sat
8–1.
Closed Sun & holidays.*

2 Villa della Petraia
Via della Petraia 40.
Tel: 055 451208.
*Open summer, 8.30–6;
winter, 8.15–5.
Closed second & third
Mon in the month.*

3 Villa di Castello
Via di Castello 47.
Tel: 055 454791.
Gardens open 8.15–6.30.

Accademia della Crusca
Tel: 055 454277.
Open on request.

4 Sesto Fiorentino
'Montagnola' Etruscan
tomb
Via Fratelli Rosselli 95.
Tel: 055 44891.
Closed at present.

'Mula' Etruscan tomb
Via della Mula 2.
Tel: 055 44961.
Closed at present.

Special to…
Museum of Doccia
Porcelain
Via Pratese 31. Tel: 055
420491.
*Open Mon–Thu 10–1,
2–6.
Closed Fri–Sun.*

5 Parco Demidoff
Villa Medici-Demidoff
Pratolino, via Fiorentina 6.
Tel: 055 409155.
*Open Apr and Aug–Sep,
Thu–Sun & holidays 10–8;
May–Jul, Thu–Sun &
holidays 10–8.30; Mar,
10–6; Oct, Sun 10–7.
Closed Nov–Feb.*

7 Villa di Cafaggiolo
Tel: 055 8458793.
*Guided tours for groups
only.*

8 Bosco ai Frati
Museum of the Convent
of Bosco ai Frati
Tel: 055 848111.
Open 9–11.30, 3–6.

9 Sant'Àgata
Church of Sant'Àgata,
collection of sacred
art
Tel: 055 8430671.
Visits by request.

For Children
Craft and folk exhibition
Tel: 055 8406750.
*Open summer, Sun &
holidays 3.30–6.30;
winter, Sun & holidays
3–6. Rest of week by
request.*

10 Scarperìa
Knife Museum
Palazzo Vicari, Via
Solferino.
Tel: 055 8430671.
*Open Sat, Sun & holidays
10–1, 3.30–7.30.*

Mugello racing track
Senni. Tel: 055 8499111.

12 Vespignano
Giotto's House
Tel: 055 8497023.
*Open mid-Jun–mid-Sep,
Thu, Sat–Sun & holidays
10–noon, 4–7; mid-
Sep–mid-Jun, Sat–Sun
& holidays 10–noon,
4–7.*

13 Vicchio
Museo dell'Angelico
Tel: 055 43921.
*Open summer, 10–noon,
4–7, Thu–Sun; winter,
Sat–Sun only.*

15 Fièsole
Archaeological site
Via Portigiani 1.
Tel: 055 59477.
*Open summer, 9–7; winter
9–6. Closed Tue in winter.*

TOUR 13

[i] Piazza della
Repubblica 28, Arezzo.
Tel: 0575 20839.

ⓘ Via Cavour 11,
Poppi.
Tel: 0575 5021
(seasonal).

ⓘ Piazzale Roma 7,
Saltino.
Tel: 055 862003
(seasonal).

ⓘ Piazza Cavour 3, San
Giovanni Valdarno.
Tel: 055 9126321
(seasonal).

❶ Eremo della Verna
Tel: 0575 5341.
Open 6.30am–7.30pm.

❷ Poppi
Castle of the Guidi
Counts
Tel: 0575 520516.
*Open mid-Mar–end Jun,
10–6 (Sat 10–7); Jul–end
Aug, 10–7 (Sat 10–8);
Sep–end Oct, 10–6;
Nov–mid-Mar, 10–5.*

Foreste Casentinesi,
Monte Falterona and
Campigna National Park
Visitor centre, Badia
Prataglia.
Tel: 0575 559002.

**❹ Eremo di
Camàldoli**
Tel: 0575 556021.
Open 9–noon, 3–6.

**❺ Castello di
Romena**
Near Pratovecchio.
Tel: 057 558633.
Visits by appointment only.

❻ Pieve di Romena
Tel: 0575 581353.
Open 9–noon, 3–6.

❼ Vallombrosa
Abbey of Vallombrosa
Tel: 055 862251.
*Open summer, 6–noon, 3–
7; winter, 9–noon, 3–5.30.*

**❾ San Giovanni
Valdarno**
Museum of the Basilica
of Santa Maria delle
Grazie

Piazza Masaccio.
Tel: 055 9122445.
*Open Tue–Fri 11–1, 3–5,
Sat 11–1, 3–6, Sun 3–6.
Closed Mon.*

TOUR 14

ⓘ Piazza della
Repubblica 28, Arezzo.
Tel: 0575 20839.

ⓘ Piazza Umberto I,
Monterchi.
Tel: 0575 70092
(seasonal).

ⓘ Corso Matteotti
103, Anghiari.
Tel: 0575 749279
(seasonal).

ⓘ Piazza Garibaldi,
Sansepolcro.
Tel: 0575 740536.

ⓘ Piazza Matteotti,
Logge Bufalini, Città di
Castello.
Tel: 075 8554922.

ⓘ Via San Francesco 4,
Montone.
Tel: 075 930219.

ⓘ Via Nazionale 42,
Cortona.
Tel: 0575 630352.

ⓘ Piazza del Municipio
12, Castiglion Fiorentino.
Tel: 0575 658042
(seasonal).

❶ Monterchi
Madonna del Parto
Via della Reglia.
Tel: 0575 70713.
*Open Apr–Oct 9–1, 2–7
(Jul–Aug also 9pm–
midnight); Nov–Mar 9–1,
2–6.*

❷ Anghiari
State Museum
Palazzo Taglieschi, Piazza
Mameli 16.
Tel: 0575 788001.
*Open Mon–Fri 8.30–7,
Sat, Sun & holidays 11–6.*

❸ Sansepolcro
Civic Museum
Via Aggiunti 65.
*Open Jun–Sep, 9–1.30,
2.30–7.30; Oct–May,
9.30–1, 2.30–6.*

❹ San Giustino
Bufalini castle
*For details of opening
times contact the town
hall, tel: 075 8560321.*

❺ Città di Castello
Civic Tower
Piazza Gabriotti.
*Open 10–12.30,
3.30–6.30.
Closed Mon.*

Picture Gallery
Palazzo Vitelli alla
Cannoniera, Via della
Cannoniera 22/a.
Tel: 075 8520656.
*Open Apr–Oct, 10–1,
2.30–6.30; Nov–Mar,
10–12.30, 3–5.30.
Closed Mon.*

Burri Collection
Palazzo Albizzini,
Via Albizzini 1.
Tel: 075 8554649.
*Open Tue–Sat 9–noon,
2.30–6, Sun 10.30–12.30,
3–6.
Closed Mon.*

Burri Collection
Seccatoi Tabacchi, Via
Pierucci.
Tel: 075 8559848.
*Open Apr–Dec, Tue–Sat
9–noon, 2.30–6, Sun
10.30–12.30, 3–6. From
Jan–Mar visits by
appointment only.
Closed Mon.*

❻ Montone
Town Museum
Former Convent of San
Francesco, Via San
Francesco.
Tel: 075 99306139.
*Open summer, Fri, Sat &
Sun 10.30–1, 3.30–6;
winter, Sat & Sun
10.30–1, 3.30–5.30.*

❼ Umbèrtide
Rocca
Piazza Fortebraccio.
Tel: 075 9413691.
*Open summer,
10.30–12.30, 4.30–7.30;
winter, 10.30–12.30, 4–7.
Closed Mon.*

❿ Cortona
Museum of the Etruscan
Academy
Piazza Signorelli 9.
Tel: 0575 630415.
*Open 10–1, 3–5.
Closed Mon.*

Diocesan Museum
Piazza Duomo 1.
Tel: 0575 62830.
*Open Apr–Sep, 10–7;
Oct–Mar, 10–5.*

Recommended Walk
Girifalco fortress
*Contact tourist office in
Cortona for details.*

TOUR 15

ⓘ Piazza del Campo
56, Siena.
Tel: 0577 280551.

❸ Palazzo Pubblico
Civic Museum
Piazza del Campo 1.
Tel: 0577 292226.
*Open mid-Mar–Oct,
10–7; Nov–mid-Mar,
10–6.30.*

❺ Torre del Mangia
Piazza del Campo 1.
Tel: 0577 292232.
*Open mid-Mar–Oct,
10–7; Nov–mid-Mar,
10–4.*

**❼ Pinacoteca
Nazionale**
Palazzo Buonsignori,
Via San Pietro 29.
Tel: 0577 286143.
*Open Mon 8.30–1.30,
Tue–Sat 9–7, Sun &
holidays 8.15–1.15.*

**❽ Spedale di Santa
Maria della Scala**
Piazza del Duomo.
Tel: 0577 224811.

The façade of Orvieto's Duomo, a masterpiece of Italian Gothic style

Tel: 055 2011700.
Open Wed–Fri 10–1, Sat 10–1, 3–6.30, Sun 3–6.30.

8 Castellina in Chianti
Exhibition of Etruscan remains
Piazza del Comune.
Tel: 0577 742311.
Open 9–1.
Closed Sun.

TOUR 17

i Piazza del Campo 56, Siena.
Tel: 0577 280551.

i Corso Matteotti 18, Asciano.
Tel: 0577 719510.

i Costa Municipio 8, Montalcino.
Tel: 0577 849331.

i Via Marconi 13, Castiglione d'Orcia.
Tel: 0577 887363.

i Via Dante Alighieri 33, San Quìrico d'Orcia.
Tel: 0577 897211.

i Piazza Pio II, Pienza.
Tel: 0578 749071.

i Via Gracciano nel Corso 26, Montepulciano.
Tel: 0578 757341.

1 Asciano
Museum of Holy Art and Collegiate of Sant'Agata
Piazza Fratelli Bandiera.
Open by request – contact municipal tourist office tel: 0577 719510.

2 Abbazia di Monte Oliveto Maggiore
Tel: 0577 707061.
Open (excluding the enclosed complex)

Open summer, 10–6; winter, 10.30–4.30.

9 Duomo dell'Assunta
Piazza del Duomo.
Tel: 0577 283048.
Open summer, 9–7.30; winter, 7.30–5.30. Sun & holidays from 1.30 only.

10 Museo dell'Opera del Duomo
Piazza del Duomo 8.
Tel: 0577 283048.
Open mid-Mar–Oct, 9–7.30; Nov–mid-Mar, 9–1.30.

11 Battistero
Piazza San Giovanni.
Tel: 0577 283048.
Open mid-Mar–Oct, 9–7.30; Nov–mid-Mar, 9–5.

12 Casa di Santa Caterina
Costa di San Antonio, Vicolo Turatoio 8.
Tel: 0577 28011.
Open summer, 9–12.30, 2.30–6; winter, 9–12.30, 3.30–6.

14 Palazzo Piccolomini
State Archives and Museo
Via Banchi di Sotto 52.
Tel: 0577 247145.
The museum is closed at present for restoration.

TOUR 16

i Piazza del Campo 56, Siena.
Tel: 0577 280551.

i Via del Chianti 61, Castelnuovo Berardenga.
Tel: 0577 355500.

i Via A Casabianca, Gaiole in Chianti.
Tel: 0577 749411.

i Piazza Ferrucci 1, Radda in Chianti.
Tel: 0577 738494.

i Via G da Verrazzano 59, Greve in Chianti.
Tel: 055 8546287.

i Piazza Buendelmonti 30, Impruneta.
Tel: 055 2313729.

i Piazza del Comune 1, Castellina in Chianti.
Tel: 0577 742311.

2 Castello di Brolio
Tel: 0577 7301.
Open summer, 9–noon, 2–6; winter, 10–noon, 3–5.

Barone Ricasoli cellars
Tel: 0577 7301.
Visits by appointment.

3 Gaiole in Chianti
Castle of Spaltenna and monastery
Tel: 0577 749483. (Now a seasonal hotel.)

4 Badia a Coltibuono
Wine estate and restaurant
Tel: 0577 749424.

5 Radda in Chianti
Volpaia Castle
Tel: 0577 738066.

7 Impruneta
Museum of the Treasures of Santa Maria all'Impruneta
Piazza Buondelmonti.

i Tourist Information Office
12 Number on tour

summer, 9.15–noon,
3.15–6; winter, 9.15–noon,
3.15–5.

3 Montalcino
Fortress
Piazzale della Fortezza.
Tel: 0577 849211.
Open Apr–Oct, daily 9–8;
Nov–Mar, 9–6.
Closed Mon.

4 Sant'Àntimo
Abbazia di Sant'Àntimo
Tel: 0577 835659.
Open 10.30–12.30,
3–6.30, Sun & holidays
9.15–10.45, 3–6.

5 Rocca d'Orcia
Rocca di Tentennano
Tel: 0577 887363.
Open Easter–late May &
Oct, 10–12.30, 3–6;
Jun–Sep, 9.30–1, 3–7;
Nov–Easter, Sat, Sun &
holidays only 10–12.30,
3–6.

6 Bagno Vignoni
Bagno Vignoni Hot
Springs
Piazza del Moretto.
Tel: 0577 887365.
Open Jun–mid-Oct,
9.30–12.45, 4–7; mid-
Oct–May, 9.30–12.45,
Sun & holidays 3–6 only.

For Children
Val di Sole swimming
pool
c/o hotel Posta Marcucci,
Via Ara Urcea 43.
Tel: 0577 887112.

7 San Quìrico
d'Orcia
Horti Leonini gardens
Open 8–sunset.

8 Pienza
Cathedral
Piazza Pio II.
Tel: 0578 749071.
Open 7.30–1, 2.30–7.

Palazzo Piccolomini,
Museum
Piazza Pio II.
Tel: 0578 748503.
Open summer, 10–12.30,

4–7; winter, 10–12.30,
3–6.

9 Montepulciano
Palazzo Comunale
Visits: tower only
9.30–12.30.

Duomo (cathedral)
Open 9–12.30, 3–6.

Church of San Biagio
Open 9–12.30, 3–6.

Back to Nature
San Giovanni Battista
Spa Pool
Tel: 0577 724030.

i Piazza del Campo
56, Siena.
Tel: 0577 280551.

i Via Umberto 2,
Chiusdino.
Tel: 0577 751055.

i Piazza Garibaldi 17,
Santa Fiora.
Tel: 0564 977124.

i Via Adua 25,
Abbadia San Salvatore.
Tel: 0577 775811.

i Via R Magi 31,
Radicòfani.
Tel: 0578 55905.

i Via San Cassiano
11, San Casciano dei
Bagni.
Tel: 0578 58141.

i Piazza Garibaldi 63,
Cetona.
Tel: 0571 652730.

i Piazza Duomo 1,
Chiusi.
Tel: 0578 227667.

1 Abbazia di San
Galgano
Tel: 0577 756738.
Always open.

Church of Montesiepi
Open 9–sunset.

2 Bagni di Petriolo
Bagni di Petriolo Spa
Tel: 0577 757104.
Open Jun–Nov.

Back to Nature
Monte Amiata Fauna
Park
Arcidosso, Podere dei
Nobili.
Tel: 0564 966867.
Open 7.15am–sunset.
Closed Mon.

6 Abbadia San
Salvatore
Mineral Museum
Viale Hamman.
Tel: 0577 770324.

Church of the Abbey
of San Salvatore
Tel: 0577 778083.
Open 10–7.30.

7 Radicòfani
Rocca
Open summer, 10–7;
winter, 10–1, 3–5.

8 San Casciano dei
Bagni
San Casciano dei Bagni
Spa
Via del Giardino.
Tel: 0578 58023.
Open May–Oct.

9 Cetona
Hermitage of Santa
Maria a Belverde
Tel: 0578 238015.
Open 9–noon, 3–sunset.

Civic Museum
Via Roma 37.
Tel: 0578 238004.
Open Jun–Sep, 9–1, 5–7;
Oct–May, Sat 4–6, Sun
9.30–12.30, other days
by request.

10 Chiusi
Cathadral museum,
catacombs, labyrinth of
Lars Porsena
Piazza del Duomo.
Tel: 0578 8226490.
Open 9.30–12.45, Sun
& holidays also 3–6;
Easter–mid-Oct,
9.30–12.45, 4–7.

Guided tours of the
catacombs: summer, 11
& 5; winter, 11 (Sun &
holidays also 4).

National Archaeological
Museum
Via Porsenna 17.
Tel: 0578 20177.
Open Mon–Sat 9–2,
Sun & holidays 9–1.

i Via Mazzini 21,
Perugia.
Tel: 0755 75951.

i Via Mazzini 6,
Perugia.
Tel: 0755 728937.

i Sala San Severo,
Palazzo dei Priori,
Piazza IV Novembre 3,
Perugia.
Tel: 0755 736458.

1 Via Bagliona
Rocca Paolina
Access from Via Marzia,
Piazza Italia, Via Masi.
Open 8–7.

2 Fontana
Maggiore
Etruscan well
Palazzo Bourbon-
Sorbello, Piazza
Piccinino 1.
Tel: 0755 733669.
Open Apr–Oct, 10–1.30,
2.30–6.30; Nov–Mar,
weekdays 10.30–1.30,
2.30–5.

5 Collegio della
Mercanzia
Palazzo dei Priori, Corso
Vannucci 15.
Tel: 0755 730366.
Open Mar–Oct & 20
Dec–6 Jan, Mon–Sat 9–1,
2.30–5.30, Sun & holidays
9–1; Nov, Dec & Jan–Feb,
Tue, Thu & Fri 8–2, Wed
& Sat 8–5, Sun & holidays
9–1.
Closed Mon, Christmas
& 1 May.

6 Collegio del Cambio
Palazzo dei Priori, Corso Vannucci 25.
Tel: 0755 728599.
Open Tue–Sat 9–12.30, 2.30–5.30, Sun & holidays 9–1.
Closed Mon, Christmas & 1 May.

7 Sala dei Notari
Palazzo dei Priori, Piazza IV Novembre.
Open 9–1, 3–7.
Closed Mon except Jun & Aug.

8 Galleria Nazionale dell'Umbria
Palazzo dei Priori, Corso Vannucci 19.
Tel: 0755 721009.
Open Mon–Sat 8.30–7.30.
Closed New Year, 1 May & Christmas.

Excursion 1
Volumni Hypogeum
Via Assisana 53, Ponte San Giovanni.
Tel: 0753 93329.
Open Sep–Jun, 9–1, 3–6.30; Jul & Aug, 9.30–1, 4.30–6.30.

Excursion 2
Città della Domenica
Tel: 0755 054941.
Open mid-Mar–mid-Sep, 9–7; mid-Sep–mid-Nov, Sat, Sun & holidays only.

TOUR 20

|i| Via Mazzini 21, Perugia.
Tel: 0755 75951.

|i| Via Mazzini 6, Perugia.
Tel: 0755 728937.

|i| Sala San Severo, Palazzo dei Priori, Piazza IV Novembre 3, Perugia.
Tel: 0755 736458.

|i| Piazza Oderisi 6, Gubbio.
Tel: 0759 12172.

|i| Via Calai 39, Gualdo Tadino.
Tel: 0742 350493.

|i| IAT del Folignate, Norcera Umbra.
Tel: 0742 350493.

3 Gubbio
Civic Museum and Picture Gallery
Palazzo dei Consoli. Piazza Grande.
Tel: 075 9274298.
Open Apr–Oct, 10–1.30, 3–6; Nov–Mar 2–7.

Roman Theatre
Via del Teatro Romano
Tel: 0759 220992.
Open Apr–Sep, 8.30–7.30; Oct–Mar, 8–1.30.

Palazzo Ducale and Museum
Via Federico da Montefeltro.
Tel: 075 9275872.
Open Tue–Fri 8.30–7, Sat–Sun 8.30am–11pm.

4 Monte Catria
Monte Cucco Regional Park
Sigillo.
Tel: 075 9177326.

7 Gualdo Tadino
Rocca Flea, Picture Gallery
Tel: 075 9150248.
Closed for restoration.

TOUR 21

|i| Via Mazzini 21, Perugia.
Tel: 0755 75951.

|i| Via Mazzini 6, Perugia.
Tel: 0755 728937.

|i| Sala San Severo, Palazzo dei Priori, Piazza IV Novembre 3, Perugia.
Tel: 0755 736458.

|i| Via della Corgna 6, Corciano.
Tel: 075 6979109.

|i| Piazza della Repubblica Italiana 3, Magione.
Tel: 075 843859.

|i| Via Trento e Trieste, Passignano sul Trasimeno.
Tel: 075 827635.

|i| Piazza Mazzini 10, Castiglione del Lago.
Tel: 075 9652484;

|i| Piazza Umberto 19, Panicale.
Tel: 075 837581.

2 Magione
Castle of the Knights of Malta
Tel: 075 5009681.
Visits by request.

4 Passignano sul Trasimeno
Lake Trasimeno Regional Park
Tel: 0758 28059.
Always open. (Including the comunes of Castiglione del Lago, Magione, Panicale & Tuoro sul Trasimeno.)

5 Tuoro sul Trasimeno
Outdoor Museum of Campo del Sole
Near Punta Navaccia-Lido di Tuoro.
Tel: & fax: 075 82520.
Always open.

Centre of Documentation for Hannibal and the Battle of Trasimeno
Via Ritorta 1. Tel: & fax: 075 82520.
Open 3–6.

6 Castiglione del Lago
Palazzo della Corgna
Piazza Gramsci 1.
Tel: 075 9658210.
Open May–end Jun, 10–1.30, 4–7.30; Jul–end Aug, 10–1.30, 4.30–8; Nov–Apr, Sat–Sun 9.30–4.30.

8 Panicale
Church of San Sebastiano
For information on opening times contact the tourist office, tel: 0758 37183.

9 San Savino
'La Valle'
Tel: 075 8476007.
Guided tours by appointment.

10 San Feliciano
Lake Trasimeno Museum of Fishing
Via Lungolago della Pace e del Lavoro 20.
Tel: & fax: 075 8479261.
Open 8.30–7.30

TOUR 22

|i| Via Mazzini 21, Perugia.
Tel: 0755 75951.

|i| Via Mazzini 6, Perugia.
Tel: 0755 728937.

|i| Sala San Severo, Palazzo dei Priori, Piazza IV Novembre 3, Perugia.
Tel: 0755 736458.

|i| Piazza del Comune 22, Assisi.
Tel: 075 812534.

|i| Piazza Matteotti 3, Spello.
Tel: 0742 301009.

|i| Corso Cavour 126, Foligno.
Tel: 0742 354459.

|i| Viale Europa Unita 1, Campello sul Clitunno.
Tel: 0743 521030.

|i| Piazza della Libertà 7, Spoleto.
Tel: 0743 238921.

|i| Via Ringhiera Umbra, Montefalco.
Tel: 0742 378673.

Practical Information

[i] Via 1° Maggio 1,
Bevagna.
Tel: 0742 360123.

1 Assisi
Basilica of Santa Maria
degli Angeli
Tel: 075 80511.
Open 6.30–8.

Museum of Porziuncola
Tel: 075 80511.
*Open Apr–Sep, 9–12.30,
3–6; Oct–Mar, 9–noon,
3–6.*

Basilica of San
Francesco
*Open summer,
6am–6.45pm (lower
basilica), 8.30–6.45
(upper basilica); winter,
6–6 (lower basilica),
8.30–6 (upper basilica).*

Temple of Minerva
Open 7–noon, 2–sunset.

Cathedral of San Rufino
Open 7–noon, 2–sunset.

Basilica of Santa Chiara
Tel: 0758 12282.
Open 7–noon, 2–sunset.

**2 Eremo delle
Carceri**
Colle San Rufino.
Tel: 075 812450.
Open 6.30am–8pm.

3 Foligno
Palazzo Trinci and
Picture Gallery
Piazza della Repubblica.
Tel: 0742 357697.
*Open 10–7.
Closed Mon, except
Easter, Christmas, 1 May.*

4 Fonti del Clitunno
Tel: 0743 521141.
*Open Jan–Feb, 10–4.30;
1 Mar–15 Mar, 9–6;
16 Mar–31 Mar, 9–6.30;
1 Apr–15 Apr, 9–7.30;
16 Apr–30 Apr, 9–8;
May–Aug, 8.30–8;
1 Sep–15 Sep, 8.30–6.30;
16 Sep–30 Sep, 9–7; Oct,
9–6; Nov–end Dec,
10–4.30.*

Temple of Clitunno
Tel: 0743 275085.
*Open Apr–Oct, 9–7;
Nov–Mar, 9–2.
Closed Mon.*

Back to Nature
Colfiorito Regional
Park
Tel: 0742 2681011.

6 Spoleto
Roman theatre and
archaeological museum
Via Sant'Agata.
Tel: 0743 223277.
*Open 8.30–7.30.
Closed Easter, Assumption
& Christmas.*

Casa Romana
Via Visiale.
Tel: 0743 224656.
*Open mid-Mar–mid-Oct,
10–8; mid-Oct–mid-Nov,
10–6.*

Duomo (Santa Maria
Assunta)
Piazza del Duomo.
Tel: 0743 44307.
*Open Mar–Oct, 8–1, 3–7;
Nov–Feb, 8–1, 3–5.30.*

Festival dei Due
Mondi/Spoleto Festival
General direction of
Via del Teatro. Tel: 0743
44325,
Public relations, Piazza
del Duomo 8. Tel: 0743
220321.

8 Montefalco
Civic Museum of San
Francesco
Via Ringhiera Umbra.
Tel: 0742 379598.
*Open Jun–Jul, 10.30–1,
3–7; Aug, 10.30–1,
3.30–7.30; Mar–May &
Sep–Oct, 10.30–1, 2–6;
Nov–Feb, 10.30–1,
2.30–5.
Closed Mon Nov–Feb.*

9 Bevagna
Roman mosaics
Near Town Hall
(Municipio).
Tel: 0742 360306.
Visits by request.

TOUR 23

[i] Via Mazzini 21,
Perugia.
Tel: 0755 75951.

[i] Via Mazzini 6,
Perugia.
Tel: 0755 728937.

[i] Sala San Severo,
Palazzo dei Priori, Piazza
IV Novembre 3, Perugia.
Tel: 0755 736458.

[i] Via Roma 19, Città
della Pieve.
Tel: 0578 298031.

[i] Piazza del Duomo
24, Orvieto.
Tel: 0763 341911.

[i] Piazza Umberto I 6,
Todi.
Tel: 075 8943395.

[i] Piazza dei Consoli 4,
Deruta. Tel: 075
9711559.

[i] Town Hall
(Municipio), Torgiano.
Tel: 075 988601.

1 San Sisto
Historical Museum of
Perugia Perugina
Nestlè Italiano
Establishment.
Tel: 075 52761.
*Open 9–12.30, 2.30–5,
Sat, Sun mornings by
appointment – tel: 075
5276796.*

2 Città della Pieve
Oratory of Santa Maria
dei Bianchi, Palazzo della
Corgna, Church of
Sant'Agostino
Tel: 0578 299375.
*Open May–Sep, 9.30–1,
4–7; Oct–Apr, 10–12.30,
3.30–6.30.*

**Recommended
Excursion**
Buzzi's 'ideal city'
Exconvent of Scarzuola.
Tel: 0763 837463.
Visits by appointment only.

3 Orvieto
Necropolis of
Crocifisso del Tufo
Tel: 0763 343611.
*Open Apr–Sep, 8.30–7;
Oct–Mar, 8.30–5.*

San Patrizio well
Viale Sangallo.
Tel: 0763 343768.
*Open Apr–Sep, 10–7;
Oct–Mar, 10–6.*

Civic tower
Corso Cavour.
Tel: 0763 344567.
*Open May–Aug, 10–8;
Mar–Apr & Sep–Oct,
10–7; Nov–Feb, 10.30–1,
2.30–5.*

Duomo (Cathedral)
Piazza del Duomo.
Tel: 0763 341167.
*Open Apr–Sep,
7.30–12.45, 2.30–7.15;
Mar & Oct, 7.30–12.45,
2.30–6.15; Nov–Feb,
7.30–12.45, 2.30–5.15.*

Chapel of San Brizio
Duomo, Piazza del
Duomo 26.
Tel: 0763 342477.
*Open Mon–Sat: Apr–Sep,
10–12.45, 2.30–7.15;
Mar & Oct, 10–12.45,
2.30–6.15; Nov–Feb,
10–12.45, 2.30–5.15.
Sun & holidays
2.30–5.45; Jul–Sep,
2.30–6.45.*

Special to...
National Archaeological
Museum
Papal Palaces, Piazza del
Duomo.
Tel: & fax: 0763 341039.
*Open 9–1.30, 2.30–7, Sun
& holidays 9–2.*

Museum of Works
Piazza del Duomo.
Tel: 0763 340336.
Closed for restoration.

Emilio Greco Museum
Palazzo Soliano, Piazza
del Duomo.
Tel: 0763 344605.
Open Apr–Sep, 10.30–1,

3–7; Oct–Mar, 10.30–1,
2–6.
Closed Mon.

Museum of Civic
Archaeology
Palazzo Faina, Piazza del
Duomo 29.
Tel: 0763 341511.
Open Apr–Sep, 10–6;
Oct–Mar, 10–5.
Closed Mon.

Special to…
Underground complex
of Santa Chiara mill
Tel: 0763 344891.
Visits by request.

4 Todi
Picture Gallery
Palazzo del Popolo,
Piazza del Popolo.
Tel: 075 8944148.
Open Apr–Aug, 10.30–1,
2.30–6; Mar & Sep,
10.30–1, 2–5; Oct–Feb,
10.30–1, 2.30–4.30.
Closed Mon, except Apr.

Duomo (Cathedral)
Open Apr–Oct,
8.30–12.30, 2.30–6.30;
Nov–Mar, 8.30–12.30,
2–4.30.

Church of San
Fortunato
Open Apr–mid-Oct,
9–12.30, 3–7; mid-
Oct–late Mar,
9.30–12.30, 3–5.
Closed Mon.

Church of Santa Maria
della Consolazione
Open Apr–Sep, 9–1,
2.30–6; Oct–Mar, Sun &
holidays only 10–12.30,
2.30–6.

5 Deruta
Regional Ceramics
Museum
Largo San Francesco.
Tel: 075 9711000.
Open Apr–Jun, 10.30–1,
3–6; Jul–Sep, 10–1,
3.30–7; Oct–Mar,
10.30–1, 2.30–5.
Closed Tue.

Sanctuary of the
Madonna dei Bagni
Tel: 075 973455.
Visits by direct request.

6 Torgiano
Wine Museum
Palazzo Graziani-Baglioni,
Corso Vittorio Emanuele
II.
Tel: & fax: 075 9880200.
Open summer 9–1, 3–7;
winter, 9–1, 3–6.

TOUR 24

| i | Viale C Battisti 5,
Terni.
Tel: 07444 23047.

| i | Via Roma 1,
Acquasparta.
Tel: 0744 930644.

| i | Via Garibaldi 1, San
Gèmini.
Tel: 0744 630130
(seasonal).

| i | Piazza dei Priori 3,
Narni.
Tel: 0744 715362.

| i | Via Orvieto 1,
Amelia.
Tel: 0744 981453.

1 Càrsulae
Archaeological site
Open Apr–Sep, 9–7;
Oct–Mar, 9–5. For
information, tel: 0755
727141.

For Children
Mostri di Bomarzo
Park
Bomarzo, Villa Orsini
Tel: 0761 924029.
Open 8.30–sunset.

2 Acquasparta
Fossil Forest of
Dunarobba
Viale Matteotti 9,
Avigliano Umbro.
Tel: 0744 940348.
Open Apr–Oct, Sun &
holidays 9.30–11.30, 3–5;
Jul–Sep, also Sat 5–7.

4 Narni
Complex of San
Domenico
Tel: 0744 722292.
Open Jun–Oct, Sun &
holidays 10–1, 3–6;
Nov–May, 11–1, 3–5.
Always by appointment.

5 Amelia
Roman reservoir
Piazza Matteotti.
Open Sat 3–6, Sun
10.30–12.30, 3–6.

7 Alviano
Folk Museum
Castello di Alviano.
Tel: 0744 904421.
Open 10–1, 3–7.

Back to Nature
Alviano marsh area
Orvieto World Wildlife
Fun, Centre of
Documentation, Castello
di Alviano.
Tel: 0744 904421.
Open 9–1, or by
appointment.

8 Baschi
Vissani
SS448 Civitella del Lago.
Tel: 0744 950396.
Closed Sun, Wed & Thu at
midday.

TOUR 25

| i | Viale C Battisti 5,
Terni.
Tel: 07444 23047.

| i | Via della Vittoria 61,
Ferentillo.
Tel: 0744 780990.

| i | Via Madonna della
Peschiera, Casa del
Parco, Preci.
Tel: 0743 937000.

| i | Town Hall
(Municipio), Norcia. Tel:
0743 828044.

| i | Piazza Garibaldi 1,
Cascia.
Tel: 0743 71401.

1 Cascata delle
Màrmore
Piazza G Byron.
Tel: 0744 62982.
Open Jan, Sat–Sun &
holidays noon–1, 3–4; Feb,
Sat–Sun & holidays 11–1,
4–5; Mar–Apr, Mon–Fri
noon–1, 4–5, Sat–Sun &
holidays 11–1, 4–9; May,
Mon–Fri noon–1, 4–5,
Sat–Sun & holidays 10–1,
3–10; Jun–Aug, Mon–Fri
noon–1, 4–6, 9–10,
Sat–Sun & holidays 10–1,
3–10; Sep, Mon–Fri
noon–1, 4–5, 8–9,
Sat–Sun & holidays 10–1,
3–9; Oct, Fri 3–5, Sat–Sun
& holidays 11–1, 3–7;
Nov–Dec, Sat–Sun &
holidays noon–1, 3–4.

3 Ferentillo
Museum of Mummies
Via della Rocca, Precetto.
Tel: & fax: 0743 54395.
Open summer,
9.30–12.30, 2.30–7.30;
winter 9.30–12.30,
2.30–6.

4 Abbazia di San
Pietro in Valle
Tel: 0744 780316.
Open 9.30–1, 2.30–5.

7 Preci
Abbey of Sant'Eutizio
Piedivalle.
Tel: 0743 99659.
Open 10–noon, 3–6.

Recommended
Excursion
Monti Sibillini National
Park
Tel: 0743 71401.

10 Norcia
Civic Diocesan Museum
Church of San
Benedetto, Piazza San
Benedetto, Castellina.
Tel: 0743 817030.
Reservation required.

12 Santuario della
Madonna della Stella
Always open.

INDEX

Index and acknowledgements

Picture acknowledgements

AA PHOTO LIBRARY 17, 18–19, 45b, 54, 69, 121, 122a, 140, 144–5, 147a; G ANDREINI 8, 34, 96, 99, 128, 131, 141a, 162;
ARCHIVI ALINARI 85; F BINI 26b; S CELLAI 9, 10, 13, 16, 19a, 23, 33a, 36, 37, 66, 67, 68, 70–71, 72b, 74, 75, 76, 77, 78, 79, 81, 84, 89a,
100, 101, 102a, 107b, 110, 115a, 147b; C CIABOCHI 73b, 97b; R CONTI 118, 119a, 120, 123; CORTE/CARDONE 112;
P DEL DUCA 107a, 108; G FIESOLI 97a; M FRASCHETTI 115b, 145, 149, 150a; S GALEOTTI 73a, 94, 113a; M MARCHETTI 109;
T MIYAOKA 64–5; M. MORETTI 72a; L PESSINA 24, 28, 29; M PEZZOTTA 46; REALY EASY STAR 12a, 26a, 59a, 70, 125, 136, 154b;
REALY EASY STAR/M ANDREINI 53b, 139; REALY EASY STAR/P BENINI 124; REALY EASY STAR/E CARLI 14a, 57b, 65, 80, 92, 102b;
REALY EASY STAR/C CONCINA 5, 60, 62, 83a, 93, 137, 144; REALY EASY STAR/G CORTE 111a;
REALY EASY STAR/DI PAOLO 51, 55, 114; REALY EASY STAR/F FERRARIS 35b; REALY EASY STAR/D FRACCHIA 63b;
REALY EASY STAR/G FURGHIERI 156a; REALY EASY STAR/S GALEOTTI 95b, 132, 143, 155, 156b;
REALY EASY STAR/GLAMOUR INTERNATIONAL 40; REALY EASY STAR/F IORIO 146; REALY EASY STAR/M MARCHETTI 6;
REALY EASY STAR/T MIYAOKA 52, 63a, 105b, 106, 159; REALY EASY STAR/L PESSINA 10–11, 14b, 25, 127b, 151, 152, 153, 154a;
REALY EASY STAR/A PICONE 7a; REALY EASY STAR/G RODANTE 45a, 105a, 117, 134a, 157;
REALY EASY STAR/M RUBINO 133; REALY EASY STAR/L A SCATOLA 41, 43; REALY EASY STAR/T SPAGONE 7b, 12b, 15, 21, 33b, 35a,
38, 39, 47, 48, 49, 56, 58, 59b, 61, 86, 87, 88–9, 90, 91, 95a, 98, 103, 104, 116, 119b, 122b, 126–7, 129a, 130, 134b, 135, 138, 141b, 142, 148,
150–1, 169; REALY EASY STAR/R VALTERZA 20, 22, 30, 57a, 82, 111b, 129b; REALY EASY STAR/C A ZABERT 53a, 83b;
LA SCATOLA 31, 42; G P SENZANONNA 27; F SPANO 113b.